Victorian Christmas in Print

Nineteenth-Century Major Lives and Letters

Series Editor: Marilyn Gaull

The nineteenth century invented major figures: gifted, productive, and influential writers and artists in English, European, and American public life who captured and expressed what Hazlitt called "The Spirit of the Age." Their achievements summarize, reflect, and shape the cultural traditions they inherited and influence the quality of life that followed. Before radio, film, and journalism deflected the energies of authors and audiences alike, literary forms such as popular verse, song lyrics, biographies, memoirs, letters, novels, reviews, essays, children's books, and drama generated a golden age of letters incomparable in Western history. *Nineteenth-Century Major Lives and Letters* presents a series of original biographical, critical, and scholarly studies of major figures evoking their energies, achievements, and their impact on the character of this age. Projects to be included range from works on Blake to Hardy, Erasmus Darwin to Charles Darwin, Wordsworth to Yeats, Coleridge and J. S. Mill, Joanna Baillie, Jane Austen, Sir Walter Scott, Byron, Shelley, Keats to Dickens, Tennyson, George Eliot, Browning, Hopkins, Lewis Carroll, Rudyard Kipling, and their contemporaries. The series editor is Marilyn Gaull, PhD from Indiana University. She has served on the faculty at Temple University, New York University, and is now Research Professor at the Editorial Institute at Boston University. She brings to the series decades of experience as editor of books on nineteenth century literature and culture. She is the founder and editor of *The Wordsworth Circle*, author of *English Romanticism: The Human Context*, publishes editions, essays, and reviews in numerous journals and lectures internationally on British Romanticism, folklore, and narrative theory.

PUBLISHED BY PALGRAVE:
Shelley's German Afterlives, by Susanne Schmid
Romantic Literature, Race, and Colonial Encounter, by Peter J. Kitson
Coleridge, the Bible, and Religion, by Jeffrey W. Barbeau
Byron: Heritage and Legacy, edited by Cheryl A. Wilson
The Long and Winding Road from Blake to the Beatles, by Matthew Schneider
British Periodicals and Romantic Identity, by Mark Schoenfield
Women Writers and Nineteenth-Century Medievalism, by Clare Broome Saunders
British Victorian Women's Periodicals, by Kathryn Ledbetter
Romantic Literary Families, by Scott Krawczyk
Victorian Christmas in Print, by Tara Moore

FORTHCOMING TITLES:
Reading Popular Culture in Victorian Periodicals, by Alberto Gabriele
From Song to Print, by Terence Hoagwood
Gothic Romanticism, by Tom Duggett
Royal Romances, by Kristin Samuelian

Victorian Christmas in Print

Tara Moore

palgrave
macmillan

First published in 2009 by
PALGRAVE MACMILLAN®
in the United States—a division of St. Martin's Press LLC,
175 Fifth Avenue, New York, NY 10010.

Where this book is distributed in the UK, Europe and the rest of the world, this is by Palgrave Macmillan, a division of Macmillan Publishers Limited, registered in England, company number 785998, of Houndmills, Basingstoke, Hampshire RG21 6XS.

Palgrave Macmillan is the global academic imprint of the above companies and has companies and representatives throughout the world.

ISBN: 978–0–230–61654–7

Library of Congress Cataloging-in-Publication Data

Moore, Tara (Tara Stern)
Victorian Christmas in print / Tara Moore.
p. cm.—(Nineteenth-century major lives & letters)
ISBN 978–0–230–61654–7 (alk. paper)
1. Christmas in literature. 2. Christmas stories, English—History and criticism. 3. English literature—19th century—History and criticism. 4. National characteristics, English, in literature. 5. Books and reading—Great Britain—History—19th century. 6. Authors and readers—Great Britain—History—19th century. 7. Christmas—Economic aspects—Great Britain—History—19th century. 8. Literature publishing—Economic aspects—Great Britain—History—19th century. 9. Publishers and publishing—Great Britain—History—19th century. 10. Literature and society—Great Britain—History—19th century. I. Title.

PR878.C52M66 2009
820'.9334—dc22 2008051017

A catalogue record of the book is available from the British Library.

Design by Newgen Imaging Systems (P) Ltd., Chennai, India.

First edition: August 2009

10 9 8 7 6 5 4 3 2 1

Printed in the United States of America.

For my family, for all the regular calendar days
that tie us together

Contents

Figures

Acknowledgments

I wish to thank The Friends of Rockwood for their generous grant, as well as the University of Delaware for a yearlong fellowship that allowed me to devote myself to this subject. While I researched and wrote about the Victorians' reading communities, I found myself blessed with communities of my own. I would like to express my gratitude to the interlibrary loan departments at the University of Delaware and the Pennsylvania State University for the constant gift of books. Among the mentors and friends who have given indispensable advice, I wish to thank Kevin Kerrane, Heidi Kaufman, Barbara Gates, Sally Mitchell, Carl Dawson, Charles Robinson, and Maria Frawley. Cheryl Wilson has provided camaraderie and guidance along the way. I would also like to thank the scholars and organizers of the Research Society for Victorian Periodicals for their gracious comments and contagious enthusiasm.

Finally, I wish to thank my parents, who embrace their role as loving grandparents and give me the time and the space to write, and my husband, Daniel Moore, who not only helps with my ongoing goal to design our family Christmas, but also joyfully engages in discussions of Victorian literacy and modern syntax. Thank you.

Introduction

In 1846 *Punch* wryly noted, "The Literature of England promises, or rather threatens, to be inundated this year with a flood of Christmas Books. Every little author is preparing a five-shilling volume in imitation of the *Christmas Carol*."[1] That "[e]very little author" saw the possibility of profiting from the burgeoning Victorian Christmas print market can be seen in the growing number of Christmas books reviewed each December for an eager reading audience. Altogether these authors, both the recognizable ones and those long forgotten, shaped a Christmas print market that would last into the twentieth century.

The press has long been a site of identity formation, and Christmas print matter cultivated a particular in-group. For example, the December 1848 Christmas supplement of the *Illustrated London News* initiated a widespread popularity for the Christmas tree in England. While scattered families had decorated their homes with Christmas trees before 1848, the mass-produced illustration helped codify the tradition into English custom. In the illustration, a table-top Christmas tree beams candlelight on three generations of the royal family. The artist surrounds the engraving in a frame composed of game and produce. "The Royal Christmas Tree" appeared just five years after Charles Dickens's first and most famous Christmas book, *A Christmas Carol* (1843), restarted a trend in Christmas publishing. As print material, the royal image instructed Victorians in one small aspect of the growing commercial craze of Christmas. On a much larger scale, the outpouring of Christmas print materials gave further instruction on how to celebrate this new symbol of Englishness, the Victorian Christmas.

The importance Christmas historians allocate to the trend-setting Christmas tree illustration and Charles Dickens's *A Christmas Carol* attests to the interconnectedness of the Christmas genres and the evolution of the cultural Christmas. This study considers the interplay of identity formation between the genres that inhabited the Christmas print market by contextualizing seasonal publishing trends and the depictions of Christmas-keeping within seasonal output. The Christmas novel, with its seasonal narrative marketed in a distinctive book form, was intended to stand out materially from the mainstream novel and warrants its own unique inquiry into consumer receptions. Christmas novellas, numbers, and annuals jostled for attention in the reviews from the 1840s on, and readers could also find Christmas-related articles interspersed with nonseasonal copy in the regular December and January numbers of weeklies and monthlies. The genres commented on each other through reviews and through adaptations of narrative forms. Christmas books opened the market for annual Christmas numbers, which often functioned as less expensive formats for telling novella-sized stories. Found in the more common, anthology-like Christmas numbers, short stories, ghost tales, and poems continued to develop ideals of Christmas and Christmas reading found in the early, successful Christmas books.

Like the word "England," "English" is a "highly emotive word,"[2] and the phrase "English Christmas" contains echoes of the Anglo-Saxon baronial hall, but it has also been corrupted for modern readers by the iconic *A Christmas Carol* and its adaptations. When I use the term "English Christmas" I take into account that the nineteenth-century Christmas was never a universal practice. Many in Presbyterian Scotland rejected Christmas for decades, but, even south of Hadrian's Wall, a citizen from one county might not recognize the Christmas rites of another county. The Christmas that came to inform Christmas rituals repeated in print was not the Scottish Christmas, nor was it the Welsh Christmas, but neither was it a universal English Christmas. In Hereford, for instance, celebrants impaled a plum cake on a cow's horn, then dashed cider in the cow's face and watched where the plum cake fell as a way of forecasting the next harvest.[3] This pseudo-sacrificial ritual did not catch on in the rest of England or in the rest of Great Britain. An antiquarian audience no doubt found and relished articles on regional Christmas practices, but, for the most part, books and periodicals only heralded certain Christmas rituals as unifying ones. Robert Chambers's edited miscellany, *The Book of Days* (1873), attests that Christmas is "still the holiday in which of all others throughout the year, all classes of English society most generally participate" with family reunions, church rituals, and food.[4] The Christmas that most often appears in print might more accurately be attributed to the London Christmas or the abridged version of it that authors saw fit to worship in print. At the start of the century antiquarians bemoaned the supposed death of Christmas, then Dickens and his ilk began proliferating a certain version of urban Christmas—plum pudding, mourning the lost, holly, and hearth-love—and by the latter part of the century consumption of seasonal print entered into the performance of the holiday. At this point magazines took an interest in how "Britons" celebrated Christmas in India or Egypt, and they compared those hot Christmases to the ideal version of English Christmas rather than the traditional Scottish New Year or more regional rites. Christmas rarely served to connect England with other locations that also celebrated the holiday. For example, an 1861 *Punch* article quipped about French cultural tourists accessing the true Christmas via a substitute for the English hearth: "the French have but a vague idea of Christmas, and we ought clearly not to laugh at them for coming over here to get a proper knowledge of it. Nor is the Crystal Palace a bad place for the purpose; supposing that the foreigner have no fireside to go to where he can learn the meaning of the words 'an English home.'"[5] That "proper knowledge" is the dominant English narrative of Christmas. I will use the phrase "English Christmas" under caution that it is a vexed term; nonetheless, as the educational campaign spread, Scots and the non-English began to adopt Christmas customs that were not previously found in their regions. Furthermore, I follow the lead of nineteenth-century writers who repeatedly use the term "England" and "Englishmen" when they imagine the Christmas festival taking place beyond the borders of the British Isles. Authors who very occasionally refer to celebrants as "Britons" consistently narrate these Britons meditating on "Old England," the "English" weather, and "English" church bells.

Authors and publishers set this identity-building feast for an audience eager to spend their money for the reading materials that were to become as iconic as the Christmas feast. Christmas publishing allowed authors to wear a multitude of hats as they maximized the selling power of Christmas. Juliana Ewing, Mary Elizabeth Braddon, Charles Dickens, William Thackeray, and others put their talents toward earning themselves a slice of the Christmas pudding. This increasingly meant producing gift-appropriate materials. Gifts were not always part of the English Christmas equation, but as the century progressed, books became a standard element on Christmas shopping lists. Initially it looks like gifts were most often of food stuffs, but the annual market began including print material in that category. Giftbooks were reviewed in articles with titles like "Christmas Presents" in January 1828.[6] By the early 1840s many nonliterary and inedible objects were also being marketed for the new Christmas trend. The idea of presents at Christmas was taking hold by 1843. Even before the late December publication of *A Christmas Carol*, a poetical draper was fashioning his wares within a new Christmas ritual:

> The old Christmas customs are all very pleasant,
> But the *best* is the custom of making a present.
> 'Tis pleasing to see, at the close of the year,
> The neat Christmas tokens that timely appear.
> The gaily-wrought desk and the choicely-bound book,
> Are beautiful "presents" which temptingly look.
> Yet a "suit of new clothes" would excel even these,
> And in truth, would have double the power to please.[7]

The "choicely-bound book" for Christmas would go through several festive transformations and leave a bigger footprint in nineteenth-century records of Christmas than commercially produced clothing. These texts began as gift commodities during the literary annuals fad, evolved briefly into units of middle-class ideology separated from the giving phenomenon, and then developed back into gift merchandise.

Recent Christmas scholarship consistently presents Dickens's *A Christmas Carol* as the reinvigorator of Christmas or, more incredibly, the inventor of the modern Christmas. For example, a recent study of films and Christmas, *Christmas at the Movies*, includes Kim Newman's "You Better Watch Out: Christmas in Horror Film," a chapter on a surprisingly large number of horror films that enjoy shredding the illusion of the happy family Christmas. Newman finds the literary heritage of these supernatural Christmas narratives in Charles Dickens's *A Christmas Carol*, "followed up with a series of [his] less-remembered Christmas stories."[8] The next supernatural Christmas narratives she finds are M.R. James's ghost stories of the 1890s. Granted, Newman's chapter is not about the history of Christmas fiction, but her generalization represents a very common scholarly misconception: that Charles Dickens's *A Christmas Carol* jump-started Christmas out of scratch all by itself. In the introduction to *Charles Dickens' Christmas Ghost Stories*, Peter Haining claims that Dickens's holiday publications "inaugurated a tradition of ghost story telling" at Christmas time, an inaccurate assertion that ignores the eighteenth-century oral tradition.[9] Meanwhile, David Parker's and Mark Connelly's recent Christmas scholarship undermines the popular belief in Charles Dickens's invention of Christmas, and goes so far to say that the Victorians in general and Dickens specifically did not invent Christmas at all, but only shaped and amplified the celebration.[10] Such is indeed the case. Nonetheless, Dickens's texts cast an enormous shadow over the nineteenth century's literature of Christmas. Authors and reviewers looked to him as a Christmas print trendsetter, and he made an impact on every genre available in the Christmas print market, from periodical frameworks to novel bindings, and even the element of poetry modeled in his periodicals. The character of nineteenth-century Britain helped to spread the type of Christmas Dickens and his fellow authors depicted in literature. New and cheaper print advancements intersected with the increased materialism at Christmas, which grew out of middle-class leisure and wealth, to produce a boom in Victorian Christmas publishing. Shrewd publishers and authors adapted older oral and print traditions of Christmas to suit the reading needs and spending habits of a wide range of consumers.

Creators of Christmas print transcended genres to maximize consumer spending during December. For example, Thackeray wrote influential reviews of Christmas books before trying his hand at writing a series of novels himself. *Punch* creators mocked Christmas traditions, including reading customs, but away from the mahogany table many of the comic wits and illustrators joined Thackeray in filling bookstalls with Christmas volumes. Mary Elizabeth Braddon edited Christmas numbers of periodicals and wrote a late-century Christmas book about children and Christmas customs in Cornwall. The chronological evolution of the Christmas print market informs my ordering of chapters that chart the evolution of what made Christmas print marketable. Each chapter explains the evolution of a focal genre and introduces texts and consumer trends that exemplify that genre.

The largely secularized ideology of mid-century Christmas continued to change subtly after the mid-1840s, and Christmas books supplied a forum for the dissemination of what started out as an English Christmas ideology. Like the much-imitated print version of Prince Albert's royal Christmas tree, the Christmas books I discuss in chapter one ratified a host of actions and views that came to be associated with a certain time of year known for both leisure and commercial extravagance. The Christmas season also became a celebration of an ideology of the Victorian home despite the trauma an increasingly commercial society brought to that home. Christmas books with a Christmas narrative instructed their audience in a newly codified national ritual, and, before long, households across the British Empire had turned print narratives, such as those found in the royal Christmas tree illustration and in Christmas books, into their own seemingly traditional routines.

Chapter one dives into a detailed reading of the Christmas book market, giving attention to the evolution of mid-winter publishing through a collaborative 1830s text by Thomas Hervey and Robert Seymour. Along with a publishing history, this chapter contextualizes the identity-building attractions of narrating an English Christmas and shows how Gaskell achieved this end in her Christmas book *The Moorland Cottage.* Diaries, letters, and reviews reveal that Christmas readers wanted to be moved to tears, and they needed literature to help them reach the necessary elation expected of the season. Chapter two reconstructs the Christmas reading audience and depends heavily on primary documentation and scenes of reading in an exploration of first audience reception. Victorian Christmas books supplied a festive fantasy for an audience with concerns about the continuance of their traditional families and nation. Scenes of reading like those in Dickens's *The Battle of Life* teach Christmas readers the social expressiveness contained in the seasonal reading experience. Publishers ordered up "English" sensibilities. Readers were thus able to express home-love through the medium of the Christmas book. In fact, emotional reaction to the holiday literature became a requisite performance.

Because *Punch* offered such a long-running alternative Christmas narrative, chapter three reads the way that institution supplied images to convey English Christmas identity while simultaneously undermining the growing consumerism of the holiday marketplace. Other periodicals help to inform the climate of the Christmas copy that ran alongside nonseasonal materials in the normal December and January numbers. I give special attention to the development of the identity-charged Christmas profile, a frequent item in the pages of December periodicals. Chapters four and five consider two different oral traditions and how they became commodified by the Christmas print market. Chapter four charts the progress of the nineteenth-century Christmas ghost tale, giving special attention to Charlotte Riddell's work for Routledge's Christmas Annual. Chapter five follows the evolving Christmas book market after the mid-century, including increasingly visual Christmas booksellers' displays and the stressful schedule authors like Lewis Carroll and Juliana Ewing kept supplying them. By this point the holiday market had grown to support the sales of a variety of genres, including children's books, scripts for home entertainment, and table books.

Chapter six examines one final Christmas genre, the poetry of the season. Scattered throughout poetic volumes and collected works, holiday verses echo with the evangelical voices that were otherwise pushed aside in the celebration of the largely secular Christmas. While so many poets used the holiday to voice religious sentiments, others like Swinburne parodied the typical hymns and sentiments to attack Christianity. Christmas verse also supplied other needs of the spirit, including attention to the contemplative character of the Victorian performance of Christmas. Chapter seven jumps ahead to the late-twentieth- and early-twenty-first century adaptations of the Victorian Christmas and its corresponding book sales. The Victorian Christmas walks and talks in many British and American reincarnations, but for those not amenable to buying tickets to "A Dickens of a Christmas" festival and others like it, the deluge of books for sale each Christmastime offers another avenue for joining in one nineteenth-century tradition.

Victorian Christmas readers who were themselves inundated with poetry, periodicals, and books for the season enjoyed seasonal publishing trends that promoted the need for occasional reading matter. Christmas books coincided with rare leisure time and the desire to indulge oneself and one's oral reading circle, setting up Christmas as the perfect time to read. The cold drove families to collect by the fire in the early dark of mid-winter. Mid-century Christmas book readers (mainly of the middle class) flocked to the much-touted Christmas narratives by famous authors of their day. Some volumes enjoyed amazing first-day sales. The publishing event took place on an anticipated, yearly schedule, as a growing readership took up the cause of Christmas. Moreover, the commercialization of Christmas customs prepared the way for the commodification of midwinter oral traditions into print media.

Chapter 1

Books for Christmas, 1822–1860

During the 1820s and 1830s, literary annuals dominated the end of the year seasonal market, and it seemed like they always would. Before annuals came about, a limited number of poems and masterpieces formed the booksellers' limited Christmas supplies, including Scott's *Lady of the Lake*, Goldsmith's *The Vicar of Wakefield*, and a short list of books for children like *Gulliver's Travels, Don Quixote*, and *Mother Goose* volumes.[1] Then came the annual. From the romantic style of engravings to the material object of the annual and its Christmas-less prose, gift books exclaimed their disinterest in all of the customs of Christmas except gift-giving. Fewer gifts were given in the early-century Christmas, but for those who did exchange presents, books featured as a traditional choice. Annuals served as anthologies of verse and prose illustrated with sentimental engravings or reproductions of high art. The gilt-edged annual was seen as "fitting ornamentation" for middle-class homes, a "status gift rather than a book to read."[2]

The midwinter publication of annuals belies their feeble role in Christmas identity formation. Publishers typically postdated their annuals, so the 1840 *Keepsake* appeared at the end of November 1839, but it could sell and be presented throughout 1840.[3] Editors avoided dated material so that the volumes could be presented (mainly to women) throughout the year as birthday gifts and school prizes. Despite titles like *Blossoms of Christmas* (1825) and *Christmas Box* (1828–1829), literary annuals almost never made direct reference to the midwinter holiday between their covers. Even if their contribution to the iconic Christmas was sparse, annuals did set a pattern for December book sales: 90 percent of annuals were sold by the end of February.[4] In an 1828 letter to Robert Southey, Caroline Bowles short-sightedly predicted the death of the genre: "This Annual mania cannot last; the market must soon be glutted."[5] Perhaps to Caroline Bowles's chagrin, the annual mania would peak in the 1830s and die out by 1860, and the annuals would be replaced by another mid-winter publishing fad long before its complete demise. Annuals set the stage for anthology-like Christmas numbers of periodicals, and, after a brief period during the 1840s and early 1850s, the market eventually returned to largely Christmas-free content published for a December market.[6]

W.H. Harrison, the editor of *The Keepsake*, prefigures the impending Victorian publication fashion with his 1832 volume, *Christmas Tales, Historical and Domestic*. The volume is notably decorated with a medallion of Sir Walter Scott, a figure known at that time for his Anglo-Saxon Christmas references in *Marmion* and his popularizing of the historical fiction Harrison emulates. Harrison's volume also shows how the annuals had "established with the public a taste for books well produced and tastefully illustrated, which they looked for at the Christmas season."[7] In keeping with the poems and short stories in the Regency annuals, to which he was a frequent contributor, Harrison tells his four tales in a Romantic, almost Byronic style, and they certainly avoid all mention of Christmas merriment and setting. Harrison's text gives evidence of a single author stepping away from the literary annual juggernaut to exploit the Christmas consumer, but he does so without making any concessions for the holiday behind the buying season. Later Christmas books and Christmas numbers would take that next step to infusing fiction with holiday scenes and an evolved Christmas ideology. A brief case-study of an early Christmas-themed product bridging the gap between Regency publishing and the Victorian Christmas phenomenon reveals the evolution of Christmas from a riotous hierarchical holiday to a decorous family celebration.

The Book of Christmas (postdated 1836) appeared during a relative lull in Christmas-keeping. Devoid of a unified character, the holiday was splintered according to region, and Christmas-keeping was on the decline in some circles. Thomas Hervey and Robert Seymour employ their distinct crafts—prose and illustration—to draft potential versions of Englishness within the framework of Christmas. The ensuing dialogue between their respective genres showcases the conflict about who was sanctioned to participate in the revived English Christmas on the eve of the momentous Victorian Christmas.

The mid-1840s would see an explosion in Christmas publications and Christmas culture, but, during the 1830s, the promise of the

Victorian Christmas slept fitfully. It was not unheard of for English citizens to pass the day unobserved, and the holiday was practically outlawed in parts of Scotland. Regional and religious practices prevented the early standardization of Christmas. In fact, Mary Howitt, who would herself contribute numerous stories to Christmas periodicals of the 1840s and 1850s, remembered her first childhood encounter with the urban celebration of Christmas around 1810 by means of less strict Quaker classmates: "In our home-life Christmas had been of no account. It was neither a season of religious regard nor yet of festivity. How astonished were we, then, to hear the London girls anticipating a great deal of pleasure and social enjoyment, with much talk of Christmas good-cheer!"[8] Hervey presented his *Book of Christmas* as an antidote to English ignorance about Christmas when he introduced his topic, saying "The revels of merry England are fast subsiding into silence, and her many customs wearing gradually away."[9] Consumers like Mary Howitt could reach for this illustrated volume for a brief lesson in Christmas identity formation.

The Book of Christmas joins an early nineteenth-century swell in Christmas folklore. The wide-ranging 1813 edition of John Brand's *Observations on Popular Antiquities* not only listed numerous regional Christmas traditions, it "laid the foundation for a science of folklore."[10] William Hone, editor of the serialized *Every-Day Book*, involved his readership in Christmas folklore collection when he called on his audience to submit Christmas carols for the 1825 season. William Sandys's collection *Christmas Carols Ancient and Modern* (1822 and 1833) attests to the dialogue between the nineteenth-century Christmas and preceding centuries as well as the renewed interest in fading folkways. Washington Irving famously chronicles the rites of a country house Christmas in the final chapters of *The Sketchbook of Geoffrey Crayon* (1819–1820). In *Leigh Hunt's London Journal* of 1834, a correspondent echoes Irving's descriptions of holiday-keeping and pointedly refers to the disappearance of such customs. The correspondent remembers holiday rites "at a house in D—shire, where the door has not been barred upon good old customs, and where Old Christmas is still welcomed and supported by a remnant of sincere and affectionate retainers."[11] These two descriptions present Christmas customs as the privilege of the landed gentry; they also suggest that readers needed to be reminded of what an "English" Christmas looked like.

As David Parker adamantly argues in *Christmas and Charles Dickens*, claims about a "widespread indifference to Christmas" before Dickens, even those made by contemporaries, are "simply untrue." However, the evidence clearly points to a lapse in Christmas celebration among fashionable quarters, in part because of the changes social hierarchies and baronial architecture faced. Industrialization shortened the length of the Christmas holiday, and the eighteenth century saw leaders of fashion turning away from Christmas. By the late eighteenth century, a new attitude about the holiday guided the fashionable back to Christmas, causing nostalgic remarks like those by Hunt's correspondent, Irving, and others interested in seeing Christmas reborn out of its own ashes. Parker attributes the renewed interest in Christmas to surges in evangelicalism and Romanticism. However, despite Mary Howitt's experience noted above, Londoners and "followers of metropolitan fashion" continued to register "coolness toward Christmas festivities" until 1843 and the beginning of Dickens's Christmas in print.[12]

Nearly a decade before that event, Thomas K. Hervey and Robert Seymour added their particular historicizing of Christmas to what Hervey presents as a vacuum in holiday observance. *The Book of Christmas* appeared in 1835 as a pastiche of Christmas poetry by Herrick, Scott, and others; folkloric history of Saturnalia, mistletoe, mumming, and other rites; and descriptions of contemporary practices like Christmas commercialism, story telling, and foodways. Other periodicals of the 1830s like *The Mirror* and *Athenaeum* also included brief articles about old Christmas customs at home and abroad.[13] Hervey's prose is largely an expansion of profiles of Christmas articles supplemented with literature and poetic references, but it is unique in its status as a volume rather than an article surrounded by nonseasonal text. By collecting contemporary as well as recently forgotten codes of Christmas in one volume, Hervey institutes a national Christmas narrative. In his introduction, Hervey portrays the holiday rites as "a chain of connection between the present and former times of the same land" that "prevent the national individuality from being wholly destroyed."[14] The book argues that the national individuality of a land never changes, that, regardless of population swings and shifting values, national identity remains constant. Such faulty presumptions are at the base of much early nineteenth-century Christmas folklore. No one vision of national identity pervaded the nineteenth century; instead, Englishness, or national identity in general, was created as it appeared to be described: the process of describing national identity created national identity.[15] As Hervey and Seymour described and depicted their version of what it looked like to be an English person celebrating Christmas, they engendered expectations within their readership.

Hervey was not alone in crafting a national Christmas identity for his readership; in fact, the book consigned his text to a subservient position. Seymour's plates came from a time when illustrators could expect their publishers to find authors whose work would appear secondary to the ascendant woodcuts. This sequence was clearly in order for *The Book of Christmas*, and Hervey emphasizes the fact by frequently pointing to Seymour's work and instructing the audience in Hervey's reading of the image: "we think that Mr Seymour has succeeded very happily in catching and embodying the mock heroic of the character" of the Christmas Prince shown on the frontispiece to the second part. Later, mid-century Victorians would expect illustrations to follow the text and mirror the verbal actions.[16] Shortly after his work with Hervey, Seymour would enter into a frustrating debate about whose work should drive *The Pickwick Papers*, Seymour's illustrations or Dickens's text. The argument ended when Seymour took his own life in April of 1836 after completing the illustrations for the first two installments of the serial. During the preceding Christmas season, however, Seymour maintained control of *The Christmas Book* project since the author clearly makes his text subservient to the illustrations. Attesting to the appeal of the Christmas illustrations, William Spooner also published the thirty-five plates independent of the text and sold it as *Seymour's Christmas Box and New Year's Gift of Thirty-five Illustrations* (1836). David Bland ponders, "perhaps drawings which come first cannot be called illustrations at all—it is rather the text that is an illustration."[17] Seymour's illustrations repeatedly dictate the prose. In fact, the Christmas Seymour creates differs from the one his collaborating author fashions, and that difference represents the transition between Regency and Victorian Christmases.[18]

The Book of Christmas joined the 1830s burst in national identity formation. Texts like John Stuart Mill's essay "The English National Character" (1834) and Benjamin Disraeli's *Vindication of the English Constitution* (1835) were among a spate of writings about national identity, a wave of focused creative energy that had no equal until the 1870s and the climate that generated the next major Reform Act.[19] In *The Book of Christmas*, both author and illustrator package Christmas as a transference of ethnically English traditions. Hervey's Christmas history takes in the Roman Saturnalia and (in passing) the rites of the druids, but he reorganizes Christmas history to emphasize certain Saxon traditions. Independent of Seymour's illustrations, Hervey strings together a particular sequence of Christmas history. Peter Mandler calls this "selective amnesia," a common feature of historians' constructions of national identity.[20] Writers of history often construct a line of descent that makes the preferred list of characteristics seem like they were always present, showing that "national character can be used quite subtly to reflect its exponents' current beliefs, anxieties, self-understandings and prejudices, while seeming to stand for timelessness and genuine cohesion."[21] This is like Walter Benjamin's simile of the historicist who "grasps the constellations which his own era has formed with a definite earlier one."[22] Hervey's Christmas sequencing includes descriptive passages of feasting from Walter Scott's Danes, King Arthur, and extensive passages about Christmas under Queen Elizabeth.

Hervey privileges the written, often literary accounts of English Christmas history, an approach that silences the illiterate and the unpublished except in the rare moments when earlier antiquaries like Brand speak for them. He lovingly describes Christmases of specific eras, but he slights others because they are not "worthy of imitation by us who 'are wiser in our generation.'"[23] This style of antiquarianism differs sharply from the Christmas folklore survivals Thomas Hardy would later memorialize in *The Return of the Native* and *Under the Greenwood Tree*. Rather, London traditions receive the most deference, and descriptions of urban customs like the Christmas Eve market and London caroling educate the rural reader in what Hervey favors as the national narrative of Christmas. Elsewhere the baronial past receives special sanction: "But all men, in all places, who would keep Christmas Eve as Christmas Eve should be kept, must set the wassail bowl a-flowing for the occasion" and "In the halls of our ancestors, this bowl was introduced with the inspiring cry of 'wassail' three times repeated."[24] In these passages and others like them Hervey reduces his readership's ancestry to a preferred class, race, and ritual: baronial, Saxon wassailers. This national narrative of Christmas becomes even more vexed when we consider the book's frequent nineteenth-century American publication, but even in Britain Hervey could not guarantee his audience really belonged to his preferred version; rather, his narrative supercedes the audience's true ancestry and allows them to perform the star role in the favored Christmas script of the moment.

The dialogue between the two genres, text and image, pulls Christmas in two different directions: the past and the present. Seymour stands as an icon from a Regency illustration tradition; meanwhile, Hervey writes like a Victorian. Seymour's *Sketches* (1834–1836), which came out as five series of etched plates, comically depict foolish Cockneys involved in sports, the same idea that was the impetus for Seymour's *Pickwick Papers*. When Charles Dickens rejected the work of Seymour and Robert Buss, and ended up with Harblot Browne as his illustrator for *Pickwick*, Dickens "almost emblematically changes graphic codes from eighteenth-century ones (caricature, exaggeration, the grotesque, sporting jokes, etching and copper engravings) to more obviously Victorian modes dependent on narrative, naturalistic characterization, and more gently mocking humour."[25] John Buchanan-Brown would call George Cruikshank, Seymour's longer-lived contemporary "this survivor of the Regency, this old bohemian."[26] While Seymour did not survive the Regency, he did contribute a lusty element to the 1830s Christmas narrative. His bulbous, ragged Christmas characters contrast with later Victorian Christmas illustrations of middle-class women decorating churches or sitting delicately with their families around a festive fire. When Seymour does depict the fireside circle, he shows a "withered crone" terrifying the younger members of her family with a ghoulish story.[27] The youngsters peer into the shadows outside the circle with fear. Victorian fireside circles would eventually show families looking lovingly, confidently at their paterfamilias as he regales them with Christmas stories. Unlike Seymour's frightened children, later family images idealized hearth love and domestic superiority. Seymour's characters are often ugly and frequently driven by their baser desires. For example, the gluttonous constables, their buttons nearly bursting, await the parish election (and the subsequent feast) in the "St. Thomas Day" plate while a raucous rabble fights below.

Hervey builds a Christmas identity different from the version of Englishness portrayed in Seymour's illustrations. The author romanticizes the poor; he describes a Christmas that has the moral effect of uniting the English classes and briefly—very briefly—obliterating class divides. He presents the Elizabethan Christmas as an annual reunion between the feasting wealthy and the feasting poor since "[t]he squire sat in the midst of his tenants as a patriarch might amid his family."[28] Hervey's Christmas narrative only allows the beggar a fleeting appearance in the Christmas performance before a swift and total disappearance. Seymour's illustrations show stark, lasting class delineations. The woodcuts fail to capture both poverty and abundant enjoyment; instead, in the image titled "Gate of the 'Old English Gentleman,'" Seymour shows groups of hunched figures reaching toward a basket full of foodstuff while a potbellied, wigged gentleman stands beside the hamper. The recipients of charity do not seem to be enjoying any great abundance. Just on the other side of the gate two servants avert their gaze from the interaction, but they reinforce the distinction between those who live inside the gate and those who claim the house's Christmas bounty once a year.

Seymour may represent the role of the poor with less idealism, but he also pushes his depictions of the poor toward caricature. At times Seymour mocks the contemporary poor by depicting ugly representatives of that class—carolers, waits, and galantee show people—trying to milk Christmas celebrants for all they can. Seymour isolates the waits as symbols of Christmastime, but his depiction dares readers to idealize the custom. The plates depict the poor with agency within Christmas commercialism; meanwhile, Hervey's prose transforms them into puppets dancing for the baronial conscience. Seymour populates his Christmas narrative with more working-class celebrants than rich ones, but Hervey addresses his prose to readers who are privileged enough to be aware of rites that take place in what he calls "higher scenes."[29] When blended with Hervey's rhetoric, Seymour's harsh treatment in the engravings suggests that anyone wanting to capitalize on Christmas forfeits his right of inclusion in the "noble" identity.

Elsewhere Seymour illustrates the drunkenness of a contemporary Christmas, but Hervey's more refined prose shuns any pointed reference to the underlying energy in the scene. In figure 1, an illustration titled "Waits," three flushed men and a boy play instruments while angry onlookers, woken from their sleep, shout from their windows and threaten the group with a dousing of water. In the background a woman dances wildly in the street. A bottle peeks out of one of the instrumentalist's pockets, and a light over a shop advertises fine gin. Intoxication is the subject of the image, a fact Seymour emphasizes by casting his scene in Hogarth's "Gin Lane" (1751). Seymour's streetlamps replace Hogarth's hanging signboards, and the architecture in the 1836 plate replicates the street corner, window ledge, door, and backdrop of Hogarth's more chaotic scene. While Seymour avoids the clearly self-destructive element of gin that is Hogarth's theme, the Christmas scene is clearly a descendant of the well-known engraving. Hervey's accompanying text, meanwhile, skirts the alcohol and focuses on the untimely hour of the music. Seymour's illustrations, however, escape such puritanical filters and capture the evolution of eighteenth-century excesses in the 1830s celebrations.

The 1830s Christmas may have seen many examples of naughty excess, but one that belied suspicion was the increasing glut of print materials. The 1830s book market was familiar with increased December sales resulting from the Christmas and New Year annuals, but *The Book of Christmas* failed to make its intended splash that first Christmas season. Henry G. Bohn, one of Seymour's publishers, recalls, "[t]his well executed, and now rare volume, failed to meet

Figure 1 Robert Seymour, "Waits," in Thomas K. Hervey's *The Book of Christmas: Descriptive of the Customs, Ceremonies, Traditions, Superstitions, Fun, Feeling and Festivities of the Christmas Season*, 1836.

Source: Author's Collection.

with the success it deserved, in consequence of not being ready till the day after Christmas, instead of a full month before as is usual with such publications."[30] Although the volume failed to maximize its initial sales, subsequent editions attest to publishers' faith in consumers' desire for more Christmas education. Editions appeared on both sides of the Atlantic at regular intervals until 1852, with another spurt of new editions in the 1880s. Hervey's book self-consciously posits itself as an object for an occasional market, and it presents English Christmas narratives—some of them quite fictional—to an audience similar to the one that would be reading the Christmas novels of Charles Dickens, Catherine Gore, and William. Thackeray in the subsequent decade. If *The Book of Christmas* entered the scene before the first Christmas novels with festive themes, it certainly helped pave the way for them. The marketing strategies apparent within the text show the swing toward Christmas book consumption. Hervey's prose repeatedly references the text as a conveyor of the new Christmas spirit, and he recommends that readers make use of his text as they prepare for the Christmas at hand. Seymour's plates also promote the text as a Christmas book. The book itself is displayed among a pile of "Christmas Presents," clearly marking the nonfiction volume as a specifically seasonal gift.[31] In an illustration called "Enjoying Christmas" a Pickwick-like figure rocks with laughter as he holds the clearly titled *Book of Christmas* in his hands: "Our readers had better take a biscuit and a glass of sherry before they venture upon the glimpses into those regions of banqueting which we are tempted to lay before them."[32] The Pickwickian reader has taken just such a precaution.

Annuals and other presentation editions opened the Christmas marketplace to books before Dickens's first Christmas book hit the streets for the 1843 season. Advertisements for ornamental presentation volumes were printed in *Martin Chuzzlewit* in December 1843, while at the same time Charles Dickens was creating an early festive narrative Christmas book. Reviews and catalogues attest that illustrations would continue to be a major selling item throughout the first wave of Christmas books, and design always remained integral to various branches of the market. The Christmas market of the 1840s stands out because it evolved to incorporate specific Christmas and domestic ideologies that went beyond visual entertainment.

The Christmas book genre certainly swelled after Dickens's ingenious pairing of seasonal fiction and seasonal sales. Before *A Christmas Carol*, festive-themed print for midwinter reading consisted of a handful of nonfiction Christmas books from the 1830s, including *The Book of Christmas*; periodical profiles and antiquarian articles; and periodical Christmas numbers like the one *Punch* initiated in 1841. The Christmas book trend mushroomed after 1843 and the subsequent year-long success of Dickens's *A Christmas Carol.* There were more than two dozen Christmas books published in the 1840s, with the largest numbers turning out for the 1844, 1845, and 1846 festive markets. John Sutherland has written that "[a]wareness of Victorian fiction as an industry is uncommon, even at the level of parenthesis or historical backing to scholarly discussion of canonical texts."[33] A study of the industry of Christmas in print reveals a schedule that focused on end-of-year production and profit.

The Christmas book market developed other patterns as well, including yearly publishing cycles. In his excellent archival study of monthly publication patterns, Simon Eliot finds evidence of a rising trend of increased new titles during October through December beginning in the 1830s. The spring months had previously shown the most new title activity, but by the 1840s, floods of new, late in the year titles established Christmas as the ultimate publishing season. Publishers had to reorganize their labor to meet the Christmas season market, and, at first, high numbers of titles in January suggest publishers frequently overshot the Christmas market. For example, Moxon's illustrated edition of Tennyson's poems missed the fall deadline by several months and finally came out in May 1857, to Moxon's financial detriment.[34] Later century statistics show publishers readjusting labor so that the highest number of new titles appeared in October, in plenty of time for the Christmas rush. Thus, "[t]he three-month Christmas season, so long regarded as the bane of the late twentieth century, was in fact evident in the publishing industry of the late nineteenth century." This trend continued until the First World War's restrictions evened monthly publishing considerably.[35]

Although publishers quickly stretched the term "Christmas book" beyond its 1840s definition, that first wave category bears defining.[36] By 1847 Thackeray refers to the trend as "that new branch of English literature."[37] In 1848 *The British Monthly Review* defined the "true" Christmas book, which

> must leave its reader when he finishes it prodigiously and perfectly happy. Its last word should be a signal for us to involuntarily, irrepressibly, and as if we could hail without a speaking trumpet the whole human race, high and low, rich and poor, young and old,—to shout out "A Merry Christmas and a Happy New Year."[38]

By buying a Christmas book, then, the consumer purchased a ticket into the emotional performance of Christmas. Thackeray, an influential reviewer for the genre, also insisted upon upbeat Christmas books. He censured Catherine Gore for a solemn, funereal ending to her second Christmas novel, *New Year's Day*, in which a boy's death prevents the anticipated reunion with his grandfather. Instead, Thackeray expected books for the holiday to be conveyors of mirth and wonder, "cheerfully ticklesome to the senses—mildly festive, benevolent, and brisk."[39] Texts taking part in the early, lucrative Christmas market include Augustus and Henry Mayhew's *The Good Genius* (1846), Catherine Gore's *The Inundation* (1848), Elizabeth Gaskell's *The Moorland Cottage* (1850), John Ruskin's *The King of the Golden River* (1851), and William Thackeray's set of five Christmas books. They enshrined middle-class ideology within the cultural climax of Christmas. Later in the century Anthony Trollope's *Harry Heathcote of Gangoil* (1873), Benjamin Farjeon's *Golden Grain* (1874), and Mary Elizabeth Braddon's *The Christmas Hirelings* (1894) joined the ranks of specifically festive, especially domestic, book narratives.

The material object of the Christmas book form also set it apart and marked texts for Christmas reading. Dickens first chose to bind his Christmas books in crimson cloth with gold stamps and foolscap octavo size. His five Christmas books looked like they belong to a series, and imitators bound their own volumes similarly. Others used the mark of the Christmas book to sneak into the December market; for example, an 1847 review warns readers that one "little red volume in size like a Christmas-book" was actually a joke book.[40] Initially, authors who retained the Christmas narrative in their seasonal volumes also copied the cloth cover and the gold stamping that made December booksellers' shops so festive in contemporary descriptions. Visual markers of Christmas reading became familiar and expected, and many readers could say, like one reviewer, that "of the many attractions which Christmas possesses in our old eyes . . . there are few to be compared to a quiet hour in our easy chair by the fire-side, while, spread out upon the table before us lie, in all the gorgeous array of their crimson and gold binding, the Christmas Books."[41] *Faces in the Fire* (1849) may well have been among the crimson pile two years later. This red-cloth bound text by George Frederick Pardon, otherwise Redgap, bears its title in gold, Cruikshank-like letters by T.H. Nicholson. It is the precise size of the Dickens series, and a book catalogue entry notes that "[t]his pretty book is . . . well worthy of a place besides [Dickens's Christmas books] in any collection."[42] That it would blend well visually cannot be disputed, but Redgap's narrative style lurches along in Dickens's more proficient shadow.

According to contemporary reports, much of the appeal was in the material object of the books; the content itself was fairly short. Thackeray's *The Kickleburys on the Rhine* was "only meant to make people laugh for half-an-hour over the Christmas fireside."[43] Slim, emotionally charged novels met the needs of the Christmas evening read. As consumer reports, reviews tell potential buyers when Christmas books could not be completed in the span of a single evening's reading circle. Due to circulating library economics, the 1840s single volume was an unpopular format for new fiction since the single volume format signaled a "cheap reprint, usually appearing two or three years after first publication."[44] Christmas books, however, were occasional literature specifically consumed as single helpings of holiday fiction in the face of libraries' demands for triple-decker narratives. For 5s., publishers sold short pieces of fiction that equaled the length of two numbers of a serialized novel, which cost 1s. each in the 1840s.[45] Considering quantity of print, the Christmas book was expensive, but its decorative cover and inset illustrations (at least in Dickens's books) meant that the extra value was placed on the material object of the book. Readers also placed value on the sentiments the books contained. When Dickens's collected Christmas books were published, the author recalled that his purpose had been to use "a whimsical kind of masque which the good humour of the season justified, to awaken some loving and forbearing thoughts, never out of season in a Christian land."[46]

In his letters, Dickens frequently refers to the Christmas book at hand as "my little Christmas Book," at once attesting to its size and the endearing quality it held even for the author, not to mention its fans.[47] The dimensions he initiated with *A Christmas Carol* frustrated him later when he said of *The Battle of Life*, "[w]hat an affecting story I could have made of it in one octavo volume."[48] Dickens employed theatrical visual techniques to cover the narrative brevity of the books, and the shortness of the Christmas book form challenged him to depict characters' changes within a short, almost unbelievable span of time.[49] The reading moment offered some reprieve from nonseasonal expectations, according to Thackeray. In one of his reviews he found *Cricket on the Hearth* a "good Christmas book" but "out of the holiday hubbub, . . . Mr Dickens will hardly paint so coarsely."[50] Dickens's illustrators likewise discovered that the size and format of the Christmas book dictated a new relationship between text and image. Even small designs dominated the page as Christmas book illustrators varied the shape of the wood blocks from the typical rectangular blocks—a unique approach among the Dickens canon.[51] This allowed the image to wrap around and even encircle brief fragments of the text. Illustrations took on new responsibilities since the fairytale aspect of Dickens's Christmas books asked illustrators to depict both the fantasy and the reality simultaneously.

By now it should be apparent that Charles Dickens haunts the topic of Victorian Christmas like one of his most persistent spirits. Social historians cite Washington Irving and Dickens, and occasionally their predecessor Walter Scott, as opening the door to the nostalgic, backward-looking, but commercialized new Christmas. Irving's lively depictions of Christmas at Bracebridge Hall participated in the trend of the medievalized eighteenth-century Christmas fantasy that continued to appear in periodical stories and a few Christmas books throughout the later part of the century. Dickens, however, turned Christmas into a publishing event. He was a "skilful populariser who embedded the themes and associations of Christmas in settings accessible to his readership."[52] Dickens's desire to make a statement for reform during a seasonal moment of compassion paired with his financial intuition led to a series of Christmas books: *A Christmas Carol* (1843), *The Chimes* (1844), *The Cricket on the Hearth* (1845), *The Battle of Life* (1846), and *The Haunted Man and the Ghost's Bargain* (1848). Dickens's holiday volumes met contemporary success, even though *A Christmas Carol* failed to produce the financial gains for which it had been designed. Dickens faced enormous debts in the winter of 1843 that left him rethinking his household management, and he anticipated that the success of his new Christmas book format would earn him at least £1,000 and save him from his debt. He demanded the extravagant format that would come to mark the entire genre of early Christmas books. Unbeknownst to Dickens, the niceties of binding and illustration were far too expensive to retail the book for 5s., the price the author stipulated. The resulting commission of £137 4s. 4d. was an abysmal disappointment, especially since Dickens had to pay £700 in court fees for prosecuting plagiarized editions. The financial loss was all the more vexing because the unprofitable volume sold so well. Between 19 December and 24 December *A Christmas Carol* sold 6,000 copies, and sales continued to climb throughout the spring. The text saw seven editions by May 1844. A displeased Dickens switched publishers and looked ahead to the publication of a "new" *Carol* to help relieve him of his debts. *The Chimes* duly appeared in time for Christmas 1844. *The Cricket on the Hearth*'s sales doubled those of its predecessors, and the first edition of 16,500 sold out by 31 December 1845.[53] In addition, theatrical versions of *Cricket* appeared almost immediately on seventeen London stages in the 1845 Christmas season.[54] The next year *The Battle of Life* sold 23,000 on the first day alone while Thackeray's first Christmas book, *Mrs. Perkins' Ball*, sold only 1,500 copies before the end of the year.[55]

One reviewer found it necessary in 1849 to remind his audience that "Christmas was Christmas . . . many, many centuries before Charles Dickens began to celebrate him in *Carols* and *Chimes*. But, as it is, a Christmas book from him is as regular as a Christmas goose; and the one is not more certain of being devoured than the other is of being read, extensively and with strong relish."[56] Reactions to Dickens's series of Christmas books were mixed. *The Chimes* received many poor reviews for its approach to poverty and culpability, and Wilkie Collins remarked that *The Battle of Life* was "condemned by the critics, pooh-poohed by the public, hissed at by the Lyceum, and finally dead-and-buried by *The Times*," but this did not stop everybody from reading it.[57] In 1861 Dickens claimed to have "devised a new kind of book for Christmas years ago."[58] Elsewhere he was the self-proclaimed "inventor of this sort of story."[59] All of his Christmas books were adapted into dramas, often to be performed days or even hours after the book became available for sale. Dickens followed this success with seasonal editions of his periodicals, modeling traditional Christmas story-telling in the frame narratives of the Christmas numbers of *Household Words* and *All the Year Round*. Dickens's Christmas work could not have been so galvanizing if his audience had not been interested in Christmas literature's social messages. As William Dean Howells has noted, "the need of his time contributed" to Dickens's Christmas successes, and it certainly had a memorable impact.[60] Reviewers would continually reference Dickens in their reviews of festive literature throughout the rest of the century, occasionally devoting whole columns to excerpted passages from *The Cricket on the Hearth* or the Cratchits' Christmas dinner before introducing any new Christmas books for sale.

One of the needs Christmas fulfilled was mediating the fears of conspicuous wealth within a framework of benevolence. Nonseasonal novels routinely attempted to negotiate a "penetrating anxiety[,] . . . that their social and moral world was being reduced to a warehouse of goods and commodities."[61] Authors, who typically set themselves and their narratives against commodification, saw that "literary work itself was increasingly commodified."[62] Writing for the midwinter season and its subtext of benevolence, Christmas authors pointedly wrote narratives encouraging charity. They put price tags on ideals that many felt should be freely exchanged. The format of the ideals—books—necessitated a commercial market. Christmas book writers occasionally had cause to become defensive about comodifying Christmas good cheer. One *Times* reviewer accused Christmas book authors of hiding monetary motivations behind the writing of books for the holiday, saying Christmas books served as "a kind of literary *assignats*, representing to the emitter expunged debts, to the receiver an investment of enigmatical value." The reviewer then attacked Thackeray's *The Kickleburys on the Rhine* as a model for this emotional fraud.[63] Thackeray's preface to the second edition included his rebuttal to the reviewer, and he reproduced the review in full before going on to imagine the likely scene of his book's purchase—a railway station. From there Thackeray proceeded to fume about how writers did indeed write for money, as did the *Times* reviewer. By imagining the scene of consumption and equating his Christmas book to a newspaper article, Thackeray emphasized the commodity and exchange of his Christmas narrative.[64] The *Times* reviewer provoked Thackeray when he presumed to unmask the authorial intention behind the Christmas novel, but the presumption represented the conflation of the material book and the commodified sentiments many readers believed they were buying. The *Times* reviewer must have been shocked to see how tame the 1850s Christmas book market looked besides markets of the 1860s and 1870s.

Among the sentiments for sale at Christmas, hearth-love featured heavily. The sweet, domestic stories of the first wave of Christmas books like Gore's *The Snow Storm* and Dickens's *The Cricket on the Hearth* engaged the stresses on the fast-changing Victorian society. With their domestic, hearth-loving plots, Christmas books provided the perfect stage for narratives concerned with the quickly receding past and fears of a fracturing, emigrating population. The heavy demand for Christmas books suggests that the texts provided a cultural outlet during a specific reading experience. Much of the readership needed a Christmas utopia, and there was something special about the midwinter reading moment that created a chance to imagine a utopian plane. Victorian society had perceived national or dominant values, noble standards many participants liked to believe that they and their neighbors held. Of course, much of the population naturally deviated from ideal behaviors. The Christmas books challenged this very common deviation. They allowed the reader to temporarily imagine that the Scrooges, the greedy emigrants, and the Tackletons were redeemable, regardless of the reality of this supposition. A critic with unclouded vision might have seen the reality of the English "values" as being commercial or even utilitarian, but readers bought a specific brand of books so that they could purposely delude themselves that such was not the case. The *British Monthly Review* writer who expected Christmas books to cause readers to heartily hail "the whole human race" attested to the deluded hope of Christmas readers: they wanted to read Christmas books so that they could transform their view of society.[65]

The first wave of Christmas books established a fictionalized Christmas utopia of the English nation; notably, this utopia was set on a trajectory of constant social improvement. The typical narrative began with an unflattering description of English life, but over the course of the story, the everyday nation was exchanged for a superior version. The Christmas nation moved toward a standard of noblesse oblige spearheaded by the middle class. Insensitivity, commercial greed, selfishness, and cynicism were abandoned or weeded out. Fragmented families were reunited, and the home nation was reconstituted as a caring place preferable to opportunities abroad. Inherent in the narrative of a Christmas nation was the hope that the novels' conclusions represented only the first step in national betterment, and that, should everyone adopt the dream of this Christmas nation, the happy results would escalate beyond comprehension. Heavy expectations from such short volumes!

The earliest Christmas books grew out of the reform novel of the early Victorian period. Dickens constructs his Christmas books as social discourses on popular sentiments toward poverty and the working class. Dickens's visit to a Ragged School of the Fields in London in October 1843 set him thinking about the plight of the poor and education. After speaking on this topic for the Athenaeum in Manchester, the author realized "that the best way to win the hearts and minds of his audience must be through a deeply felt narrative, a Christmas story."[66] Others carried the message of *A Christmas Carol* into new narratives. *The Winds and the Waves: A Legend of Christmas* (1848) propounded its reform rhetoric in an advertisement: "to all who desire the spiritual and temporal welfare of their poorer neighbors this work is respectfully dedicated."[67] Nearly thirty years later, Benjamin Farjeon's Christmas books could easily have borne the same dedication. Not all Christmas book narratives maintained the same rhetoric of reform; however, their reenactment of Dickens's narrative form in effect commented on issues of societal improvement. While many Christmas books lacked the Dickensian rhetoric of reform, their plots allegorically situated national problems within a domestic stage. By probing those anxieties, texts by authors like Catherine Gore, William Thackeray, Henry and Augustus Mayhew, and others imagined solutions for the English nation.

Many authors easily associated with the domestic novel tried their hand at a Condition-of-England approach to the Christmas narrative. By writing Christmas novels, authors used what Mary Poovey has called a "feminized genre that individualized and aroused sympathy."[68] Politics and economy resonated within the fictional worlds of Christmas books, especially because Christmas negotiated a relationship between the exterior marketplace and the idealized domestic space. Social historians agree that the Victorians turned Christmas into a "preeminently family festival."[69] J.M. Golby and A.W. Purdue argue that the "refurbishment" of the Victorian Christmas resulted from new middle-class "preoccupations" that included more wealth and leisure time than ever before as well as "the growing belief in the importance of the family unit."[70] Their collaborative study does not include the pull of empire or emigration in the preoccupations of the Victorians, but the authors do recognize that the Victorians used Christmas to try to fix social problems. The question of security loomed as the largest fantasy of the Christmas book, which served as the "vehicle" for conveying the values that motivated society.[71] The home became and remained the central focus for Christmas nostalgia. Home in the Christmas narrative often functioned as an allegory for the national predicament: the loss of citizens to enticement abroad and the financial decay of a society in desperate need of reform.

Not all of the stories were set at Christmas, and sometimes theme rather than setting won the book its place on publisher's Christmas lists. The holiday investment in the home paired with that ultimate Christmas plot point—the reunion scene—led to migration narratives, or, more precisely, narratives that pointed to the dangers of migration. In keeping with the home focus, the colonial outpost was seen as a danger that pulled men from the domestic space of family and Christmas. Midwinter reading practices required a sudden and complete restoration of the family, symbolizing a unified English nation. In *The Moorland Cottage*, Gaskell's Christmas book for the 1850 season, the protagonist and her lover debate the evils of their nation and the modern option of emigration. Here the heroine's argument crystallizes the nationalistic hearth-love so prevalent in Christmas books:

> "Dear Frank, think! It may be very little you can do,—and you may never see the effect of it, any more than the widow saw the world-wide

> effect of her mite. Then, if all the good and thoughtful men run away from us to some new country, what are we to do with our poor, dear Old England?"[72]

Gaskell's heroine voices a rhetoric of stasis, arguing that the English who truly love England will bear with that nation's faults and build a better home on the motherland's shores rather than escape to financial opportunities elsewhere. As was so often the case, Christmas reading led to a discourse about the English nation, and the reading took place during a cultural moment tied up with heightened identity formation of a performance of so-called English tradition.

Gaskell frequently created a fictional England that revealed its porous boundaries. While Canadian space offers a refuge for characters like Mary Barton and Jem, and Africa presents Roger Hamley with an opportunity for scientific and social advancement, Gaskell's texts frequently include a rhetoric of warning. In Gaskell's *Cranford*, Mrs. Brown's trek to bring her last surviving child to England "functions as a harrowing, cautionary tale for those who would leave England and travel East."[73] Carolyn Lesjak finds a warning against the imperial enterprise Mary Barton and Jem undertake in the conclusion of *Mary Barton*. Job Legh buys a scorpion from a sailor and brings it home, supposing it is dead; the East Indian creature revives on the hearth and threatens Job's granddaughter Margaret, serving as "a warning of both the dangers lying dormant in the imperial enterprise and the tenuousness of the desired boundaries between colony and metropole."[74] The colonial territory actually claims a victim in *Cousin Phillis* when Phillis's faithless, émigré lover rejects her for a Canadian wife. Gaskell cautiously portrays emigration as an option for her characters in nonseasonal texts, but, as in *Cousin Phillis*, the homeland and family suffer.

Gaskell's Christmas book portrays the erosion of an English family composed of a widow and her two children, Maggie and Edward Browne.[75] Mr. Buxton, a landowner, takes an interest in the children out of respect to their dead father, and Maggie becomes a favorite with the family. In time, Mr. Buxton's virtuous son Frank proposes to Maggie, whose sweetness and patience he alone appreciates. What Frank sees as old world corruption tempts him to emigrate to a newer society, but Maggie always dissuades him. Meanwhile, Maggie's dissolute brother embezzles money from Mr. Buxton. The elder Buxton uses this opportunity to tempt Maggie to reject his son in return for her brother's freedom. Though harried, Maggie refuses to break Frank's heart; instead, she comes up with a plan to temporarily accompany her brother to America where she will try to redeem him. Maggie writes her farewell to Frank, and the siblings prepare to emigrate, but shortly after their ship leaves Liverpool it catches fire. The worthless brother drowns, and Frank miraculously appears from among the steerage passengers to save Maggie. The two return to their native town to the gratification of the contrite parents.

Gaskell's story relates the common Christmas plot of reunion, one that had been part of holiday narratives for some time. For example, L.E.L.'s "Christmas in the Olden Time, 1650," from *Fisher's Drawing-Room Scrap Book* (1836) voices the urging of family at home who want to see the wanderer return for Christmas:

> one vacant place beside [the hearth],
> Would darken all its mirth.
> At any time but Christmas
> We give you leave to roam,
> But now come back, my brother,
> You are so missed at home.
> Christmas is coming, my brother dear,
> And Christmas comes, my brother, but once a year.[76]

Dreaming the emigrant or wanderer home haunts the broken family who uses Christmas to articulate their reunion fantasy. Unlike most first-wave Christmas books that pick up on this theme—*The Snow Storm, Cricket on the Hearth, Doctor Birch and His Young Friends*—*The Moorland Cottage* does not narrativize a reunion of a colonial after many years away; rather, it tells the other side of the story by narrating a leave-taking, including the reasons for departing from the homeland and the hopes bound up in the periphery. Gaskell makes a story out of the material that usually exists only as a runaway's briefly recounted embedded text: the family strife that caused the emigrants' departure in the first place. Over and over again, however, Gaskell's narrator and the characters' dialogue undercut the possibilities of the periphery and make arguments against emigration. Three different reasons for emigration are given: ridding England of the morally wicked; renouncing the evils of the old world; and leaving to make money and start again.

Within this migration rhetoric Gaskell constructs a fitting literary metaphor for exploring the decisions of so many English emigrants. Maggie brings up the "Transmigration of Indur," referring to an eighteenth-century story in which the consciousness of the Brahmin protagonist, Indur, leaps into the bodies of different male animals upon the point of death of his last host.[77] In this way, Indur, and the readers who follow his story, experience the lives of bees, whales, mastiffs, and elephants from the inside. Transmigration means both the movement of the soul from one state to another (often death) and the movement of people from one country to another. Indur's host bodies often die at the hands of humans, but he never extemporizes about the indignity he suffers as a beast of burden. As a mastiff, he gladly dies in a fight to protect his master. The Brahmin, living within the skins of colonized species, in no way resents or protests his treatment.

Meanwhile, Gaskell's novel offers a "transmigration" of the migratory. We see into the lives of the people who contemplate leaving England for a variety of motives. The reason most purposefully depicted is kindly Frank's desire to leave England's old world corruption. Instead of using the argument that society is corrupt the world over, Maggie argues instead that it would be cowardly to abandon one's home society to the corruption one detests without working to fix the system. The novel becomes a site to practice emigrant ideas, and all the reasons for emigration become tainted with cowardice, sorrow, and dread.

Gaskell builds up Maggie's character into one that pursues goodness, no matter the cost. It follows that Maggie's antiemigration arguments are infused with her characteristic righteousness. When her fiancé suggests going to Australia to get away from the "corruptions and evils of an old state of society such as we have in England," Maggie virtuously protests: "I would go with you directly, if it were right,... But would it be? I think it would be rather cowardly."[78] Maggie redirects Frank's attention back to the home duties, and her next speech reminds him of the responsibility owed the home nation.

How does this social theme relate to emigration? Gaskell depicts colonial governments as nobler societies less corrupt than their old world counterparts. While most Christmas fiction echoes mainstream sentiments regarding the dangers of the unplumbed colonial geographies, Gaskell offers a different perspective by emphasizing their purity. Frank romantically fantasizes about the wholesome cultures of Australia, Canada, and America, and Gaskell's narrator supports this view of European-run new world civilizations. In Frank's rhetoric, the nascent states serve as a fantasyland to which the English can escape when the corrupting influences of old money and old sins burden them.

Through Gaskell's tale, the reader "transmigrates" into the perspective of the Englishperson on the verge of emigration. The time of hurried preparation rages with emotion and heartrending decisions. The siblings leave from Liverpool, where Mr. Buxton sees to their arrangements and takes cabins for them. He even sets up pastimes for Maggie by buying her books to read during the crossing.[79] The books are meant to be a comfort to Maggie, and readers could not but connect their purchase of Gaskell's book with the fictional consumption of books for the émigré. The narrative, like Dickens's *Martin Chuzzlewit*, also differentiates between the uncomfortable steerage passage and the relative comfort of private cabins. Cutting the story short of what might have been a climactic encounter with the destination on arrival, Gaskell instead walks the reader through the emotional heartache of leaving the national home during a cultural reading experience in which home has been imbued with heightened idealistic characteristics like tradition, nostalgia, and holiday expectations. On what turns out to be her only night aboard the transatlantic ship, Maggie performs that recognizable tableau, the last look: "She wrapped herself up once more, and came on deck, and sat down among the many who were looking their last look at England."[80] Throughout the story, England features as the focal homeland, and the Scottish and Irish émigrés' experiences are entirely unexplored. In fact, after the shipwreck Maggie and Frank travel through Wales to get back to England, and they encounter the Celtic Britons as foreigners. The distancing of the polite but alien Welsh highlights the national identity of the English characters returning to their native soil.

The Moorland Cottage is perhaps one of Gaskell's plainest discourses on emigration, yet her rhetoric has been wrapped in the trappings of a Christmas scene. The illustrated title page for the first edition of *Moorland Cottage* in no way depicts the events of the novel; instead the illustration—in which a man, four women, children, and a cat circle a blazing hearth—demonstrates the English family group ideal. No family group in the novel could compose this scene. Cascades of holly branches surround the title page tableau, reinforcing the Christmas expectations for the reading of this text. The collected family was the Christmas fantasy, the same fantasy that caused Gaskell to narrate a family conflict and dissolution of family ties. Illustrator Myles Birket Foster captures the hope of unchallenged stability in his image even while he instructs his audience on how to read at Christmastime. In the ensuing story, Gaskell narrates the failed emigration attempt and the family reconciliation leading to the possibility of a similarly happy fireside scene. The emigration discourse becomes a concentrated narrative marketed as the essence of Christmas reading. Instead of a plot device, emigration enters as a case study. The strain of Christmas that Hervey, Irving, and others felt invested in propagating quickly became a widespread marker of Englishness, leading to standardized narrative practices, including the Christmas utopia of seasonal fiction. Stories imagine the heart of middle-class English identity—the home—under attack from destabilizing forces. Such forces show up as poverty in *Cricket on the Hearth*, decreasing humanity in a cutthroat culture in *The Haunted Man and the Ghost's Bargain*, and broken community responsibilities in *The Snow Storm*.

Maggie Browne clearly voices fears of the domestic national home, but this theme shrinks into fears for the physical home elsewhere, like in the crumbling walls of Caleb Plummer's toy workshop and home in Dickens's *Cricket on the Hearth*. Caleb, a humble, poverty stricken, toy craftsman, verbally constructs an alternate reality for his blind daughter Bertha. She is prevented from discovering his lie ostensibly because of her disability, but her faith in his narrative also prevents her from questioning its validity. This plot point makes an excellent metaphor for the Christmas book reader's relationship with holiday consumption and the Christmas utopia. Blind Bertha lives entirely in Caleb's fictitious version of their lives: she believes her father's threadbare jacket is new and warm, that their shabby home is solid and cozy, and that their misanthropic employer respects and aids them. The Plummers certainly need a more solid home, but Caleb's mythmaking also hints at the rise in conspicuous consumption. He is able to impress Bertha with the richness of his make-believe coat, and he spends real money on gifts to further convince her of their solvency.

While Bertha's delusion has been a lifelong one, the reader of Christmas books participated in a timely, self-instigated delusion. The delusion was also self-perpetuating, and the reader could come to believe the fantasy of the Christmas utopia. Like all fiction, this genre offered a temporary escape from real life; however, the ideological forces driving this Christmas market channeled the escape-narrative into a very specific route: the fantasy of a stable home/nation. The home Bertha believes exists is a parallel for a fantasy of the English heritage and nation that the readership desired to possess, leading to an annual offering of Christmas narratives. With the English home jeopardized by exterior forces, readers desperately desired the consolation of a story that spouted a rhetoric of staying at home and righteously working for the improvement of the mother country. These timely narratives struck resonant, emotional chords that drove readers to tears.

CHAPTER 2

HOW VICTORIANS READ CHRISTMAS

The Ghost of Christmas Past reintroduces Scrooge not only to his forgotten playmates and his former self, but also to Scrooge's old imaginary friends and the comfort he took in them. When the Ghost and Scrooge take their first trip into the past, they make their way to Scrooge's schoolhouse and find his younger self alone, reading. They eavesdrop on the boy's reading, but not by peering over the lonely schoolboy Ebenezer's shoulder; rather, they look out the window to see "a man, in foreign garments: wonderfully real and distinct," who is in fact Ali Baba now materialized in the snowy, country setting. Scrooge seems unsurprised by the corporal appearance of a fictional character:

> "It's dear old honest Ali Baba! Yes, yes, I know! One Christmas time, when yonder solitary child was left here all alone, he *did* come, for the first time, just like that. Poor boy! And Valentine... and his wild brother, Orson; there they go! And what's his name, who was put down in his drawers, asleep, at the Gate of Damascus; don't you see him!"[1]

The scene continues as Scrooge reacts to visual memories of Crusoe's parrot and Friday, products of past Christmas readings that take shape before the adult Scrooge, reminding him of the efficacy of Christmastime stories. Harry Stone has argued that this evocative reading reminds Scrooge what it is to be a child; indeed, after the fantasies come to life Scrooge regrets his recent harshness to a child.[2] Of course, the tales of Ali Baba, Valentine, Orson, and Friday were not regulated to seasonal reading, but volumes like *The Arabian*

Nights and *Robinson Crusoe* comprised much of what was seen fit to give children during the early decades of the nineteenth century. When Scrooge recalls that Ali Baba "*did* come" one Christmas time, he might well mean the book arrived, perhaps from a guilt-ridden adult relative who wanted to send a lonely boy print companionship since his family denied him the real thing. There would be nothing seasonal about Scrooge's beloved volumes except the nature of gift-giving combined with the limited scope of children's literature at this period. Scrooge's own story would do much to broaden the options of book buyers. Instead of moral tales of adventure set in exotic locations, 1840s Christmastime readers could easily find holiday-themed narratives set in their own England. Scrooge became a character as real to his fans as Ali Baba was to him, as reviews repeatedly attest. Like Scrooge's unnamed benefactor, Christmas book buyers could pair December's additional leisure time with seasonal reading, but this new spate of Christmas books delicately touched emotional chords that resonated within the holiday environment. To isolate the emotional demands early audiences made on the genre, it is necessary to first define the early Christmas book audience.

Documentation as well as the placement of reviews for Christmas books (in such periodicals as *Fraser's Magazine* and *The Morning Chronicle*) suggest that they had a middle-class following. First-edition Christmas books of the 1840s with those recognizable red cloth, gilt covers were priced at 5s. This cost prevented working-class families from participating in the earliest Christmas readership at the same level as the middle class, since many working-class families survived on 10s. or 15s. a week.[3] In *The Chimes*, Trotty Veck earns just 6d. during a day of delivering messages and letters. The working-class character may be the focus of the Christmas book, but there was no way his real-life counterpart could afford *The Chimes* in addition to his dinner. However, the Chartist magazine *Northern Star* reviewed *The Chimes*, suggesting that a working-class audience would have been aware of its existence, perhaps because the working-class focus of this Christmas book in particular would have recommended it to Chartists more than most.[4] The standardization of presentation also unified the reading audience: everyone who purchased *The Battle of Life* in its first edition took home an identical, well-recognized object. This packaging not only signified that the novels were immediately ready for consumption; it also put all *Battle of Life* readers in a seemingly inclusive social group.

A percentage of the working class would have encountered the Christmas books immediately, before the cheaper reprints and abridgements, since some middle-class readers insisted on sharing their experience. J.V. Staples felt compelled to read *A Christmas Carol* to an audience of the poor. He had been spending Christmas 1843 with Mrs. Evens, who had received a copy of the *Carol*. Despite his friends' discouragement, Staples quickly arranged a public reading spread out over two nights in the Bristol Domestic Mission Institution. The audience was so receptive that Staples granted a second performance.[5] While Staples notified Dickens of the success of this earliest of readings, Dickens would not begin his own public readings until 1853 when he commenced a series of benevolent readings for the Chatham Mechanical Institute. Dickens read for personal profit only after the spring of 1858. Records of his public readings attest to the working-class familiarity with and excitement for his performance of the Christmas books.

The financial position of the Christmas audience in many ways limits the discourse to a spectrum of middle-class ideology. The story in *The Chimes*, for example, puts Trotty Veck in a position to educate middle-class readers in how to appreciate the plight of the poor. Recapturing the Christmas literature experience poses a challenge for twenty-first-century sensibilities since modern critics must avoid equating their readings of a text with that of the actual Victorian readers. It is far better to interrogate the records of actual readers, either by survey or through their autobiographies.[6] Nonetheless, the reactions of actual readers are largely limited to extant records, usually in the papers of well-known Victorians from the publishing world, and the sculpted performances of autobiography. Norman N. Holland argues for a cultural-sociological approach to audience: "whenever we read, we are associating such extratextual, extraliterary facts to the supposedly fixed text."[7] The establishment of a Christmas literature market presented readers with a chance to throw in their lot with a construction of English heritage: the celebration of the prevailing Christmas narrative. Reviews and depictions of seasonal reading best show how ways of reading and reacting to Christmas narratives also formed dominant expectations resulting in readers' performances.

Hypotheses about audience demographics pose a challenge because of the evidence of nonstandard readers who also took part in Christmas reading, but a study of a publishing phenomenon and identity formation through reading encounters necessitates categories. The Christmas literature audience was composed of English-speaking Christians or those of a persuasion willing to participate in the English Christmas as a secular celebration of middle-class ideology. Christmas readers were on the new horizon of a refurbished

Christmas that began gaining revitalized national and cultural attention during and following the late 1830s. The scope of Christmas books' reading possibilities must indeed be endless; however, evidence suggests that readers had expectations about how one read the genre, and "the conventions of reading" do indeed "relate to the behavior and thoughts of actual readers."[8] In this case, the reading experience of Christmas books set them apart from that of nonseasonal literature.

Readers brought to the Christmas reading experience their own knowledge of the everyday world plus their hope for some Christmas revelation. Christmas conferred its own text upon the reading experience, especially since the rhetoric of Christmas, be it in carols, periodicals, or novels, contained an argument for noblesse oblige and social harmony. Each genre takes a different active part in the culture, but they all demonstrate the developing rhetoric of Christmas. This ideology came to dictate publishers' requests and authors' novels because the publishing industry recognized that, once it had been unleashed on the reading audience, Christmas rhetoric informed readers' appreciation of seasonal texts. If readers chose to participate in the occasional reading audience, the filter of Christmas expectation narrowed the potential emotional encounter of the first target audience.

Early Christmas book narratives most often contributed to constructing a specifically Anglican, middle-class English identity. Readers who could not claim a part in the focal identity nonetheless recognized the identity formation taking place within the Christmas narrative, and they took part in the cultural formation with varying degrees of success. Readers outside mainstream Christianity and people living beyond the borders of England also belonged to the interpretive community of the Christmas books. Anglicans, Presbyterians, Unitarians, Methodists, and Anglo-Jews created and read Christmas fiction. Victorian Irish, Scottish, and Australian readers also read, wrote, and reviewed Christmas.

The Scots' participation in this reading community was particularly significant because, up until the end of the nineteenth century, Scots did not actively perform the rituals of Christmas as a national community. The Scots born Chambers brothers published a book, *The Book of Days*, which explained that Christmas festivity was still relatively unknown in Presbyterian Scotland. Nonetheless, an 1870 nonfiction article in *Belgravia* claims that elements of the English Christmas such as "Christmas dinners, Christmas shows, Christmas boxes, Christmas trees, Christmas cards, and so forth, are fast coming in vogue among all classes" of Scots.[9] Presbyterian Scots who celebrated Christmas ran the risk of being caught and made to do public penance, especially in the areas where elders checked to make sure the kitchens of their congregation were free of Christmas fare. When one woman tried to hide her Christmas food preparations, her dinner caused a fire and gave her away to the visiting elders.[10] New Year was the comparable winter holiday in that largely Presbyterian society. The fact that the Scots had only limited experience with the new Christmas did not stop individuals from trying to participate in the English national narrative when the opportunity presented itself. In the 1860s the Scottish publisher W.D. Latto began a Christmas and New Year story competition, and amateur Scottish authors flooded the office of *The People's Journal* with imitations of English Christmas literature. The amateur submissions showed their authors' distance from the epicenter of perceived Christmas activity since most of their compositions were set in London and demonstrated attempts at the Cockney dialect. Instead of writing about experiences and locations with which they were familiar, these amateurs enacted the performance of an ethnicity that was not their own. They appropriated the English Christmas in both their narratives and their style of composition. While the Scottish contestants must have been participating in the reading audience of the Christmas books and periodicals, they failed to adapt Christmas ritual to a fictionalized Scotland. The amateur authors instead regurgitated an English Christmas in their Scottish periodical. Latto intended the competition to revitalize the celebration of Christmas in Scotland.[11] In effect, the composition and perusal of Christmas narratives were expected to function as a training ground for Christmas performance. It turned out to be a practice for the same urban, English Christmas narrative that dominated Christmas books and periodicals coming out of London. The amateurs preferred to cast their lot with the wildly popular Christmas book authors by imagining Englishness rather than developing their own trend of Scottish occasional writing.

As a space increasingly invested with hopes of national identity, Christmas's Christian origins remained largely understated in Victorian print. Initial publishing habits suggest that only Christians who embraced the advent rites would be welcomed into the newly imagined Christmas nation. Nonetheless, people of other faiths were able to take an active part in reading and writing Christmas. While evangelical societies did print their own Christmas matter, they did not join the tide of December publication until the 1860s and 1870s.

The early Christmas books contained few direct references to Christ; however, Christian ideology formed the foundation of character motivations and social conversions. As the figurehead of the publication trend, Dickens faced accusations of removing Christ from his Christmas narratives. Dickens defended himself saying that it is "absolutely impossible" for the Christmas books to be devoid of "the Christian virtues and the inculcation of the Christian precepts. In every one of those books there is an express text preached on, and the text is always taken from the lips of Christ."[12] *The Chimes*' characters reference Christ's mercy and compassion, but Dickens's Christmas books avoid directly quoting scripture except for the rare case of *Battle of Life's* nutmeg-grater that is inscribed with Matthew 7:12, "Do as you—wold—be—done by."[13] A gospel of social reform replaces the biblical nativity story and Christ's gospel of spiritual salvation in Dickens's Christmas books, a fact that opened the celebration of Christmas to nonevangelical groups.

Just as the Presbyterians were drawn to Christmas literature, so too were Jews and atheists, groups that one would imagine felt isolated by the nationalistic tone of the Christmas narrative. Atheists may have chosen to reject Christmas traditions the way Lord Amberley did until 1871 when he and his family relented so that his young child could participate in Christmas rituals.[14] The Christian origin of Christmas did not prevent Anglo-Jews from engaging with the ideology of Christmas literature. Jewish author Benjamin Farjeon joined the Christmas book market in the 1870s with two books: *Bread-and-Cheese and Kisses* (1873) and *Golden Grain* (1874). Benjamin Farjeon had emigrated from London to Australia and then New Zealand where he ran a newspaper, but when he received a reply from Charles Dickens about a Christmas story he had sent the great author, Farjeon headed back to England to establish a career as a fiction writer.[15] Farjeon's daughter chronicled her father's fascination with participating in Christmas consumerism, and his personal interest extended to his novels' rhetoric.[16] Aware of the identity-building nature of Christmas novels, Farjeon amplified the commercial, middle-class benevolence present in the typical 1840s Christmas novel and used Christmas writing "to expand the criteria for who can be considered British."[17] Farjeon and his contemporaries read about Scrooge's consumer-based conversion, and the capitalist focus on getting and giving at the heart of so many Christmas books. He recognized that Jews could participate in this aspect of Christmas, and his Christmas books tacitly attest to Jewish inclusion in the middle-class holiday. For example, in *Golden Grain*, the Silvers' faith is not named, but they very well might be a middle-aged Jewish couple. Many of the important events in the tale take place during scenes of Christmas. The Silvers adopt an orphaned infant, name her Ruth, and raise her to be a model middle-class wife and mother. Ruth's twin sister, Blade-o-Grass, remains on the streets, and her miserable existence—a relationship with a thief, starvation, and the inability to feed her illegitimate child—contrasts poignantly with Ruth's happiness. The twins' parallel lives express Farjeon's rhetoric of active compassion toward the poor. The Silvers are the model for what middle-class Christmas celebrants should be. Farjeon refocuses the Christmas book narrative on "British capitalist industrialism" to construct "a space for Jews to claim England as home."[18]

Scots and an Anglo-Jew attempted to use Christmas narratives as tickets to English identity. Scots amateur authors failed to take possession of the English Christmas with the same flair shown by Farjeon. His Christmas books stand out for having attempted to redirect the rushing waters of Christmastime Englishness to incorporate a minority religion. Farjeon harnessed Christmas and "the music of its tender influence" to make a powerful argument for Anglo-Jewish inclusion in mainstream culture.[19] Farjeon adapted the cast of characters but maintained the sentiment expected of a holiday novel. In the decades that inaugurated the Christmas book form, texts aroused readers' expectations for sentiment and used Christmas emotionalism to make arguments for societal reform.

Much of what made Christmas literature relevant for readers could of course be found in nonseasonal novels. As a subgenre of the novel, Christmas books interacted with and imitated their parent form. The themes that overran nonseasonal novels also directed the plots of the Christmas books; however, the short length of the Christmas book form—single volumes instead of triple-deckers or long serializations—meant that many authors could only create caricatures of real-life character types and social problems. Nonetheless, "mainstream" literature was closely related to Christmas texts; the subtle differences between reading expectations among first audiences was, however, a telling distinction. Emotional appeals are far less guarded in Christmas literature, and public displays of readers' Christmas tears abound. At times, as in Wilkie Collins's *Mr. Wray's Cashbox*, teary scenes verge on the ridiculous. Collins's text shows an old actor so dedicated to Shakespeare that he nearly dies when he loses a plaster impression he had illegally made of the bard's statue. Strong family ties cause his daughter to obtain a replacement despite the risk, but throughout the story family members weep and show evidence of how deeply writing can affect a reader. A contemporary reviewer recommended the text as a "clever little tale" in which "we have a snatch of life neatly moralized, with just enough dramatic interest to create excitement and suspense (once or twice rising to a palpitating height)."[20] The "palpitating" affect of festive reading depended upon the thin veil that existed between ideals of Englishness—the same ideals that shaped nonseasonal texts in less flagrant ways—and the emotionally desirous reader.

Emotional affect and family anxieties also connected the Christmas book genre to its later relative: sensation fiction of the 1860s and 1870s. Subgenres can often serve as flash points for contemporary issues,[21] a fact that can be seen in the ways Christmas books and sensation novels take opposing approaches to the same essential social fears. Both genres explored domestic disharmony in their own way. The sensation genre was known for thrilling the reader's nerves. In their own right, Christmas books were credited with exciting emotions like compassion and hearth-love. The festive emotions sound quaint and tame until one samples the cloying expressions of overflowing emotions that frequent the poetry of the Christmas season. A poem included in *The Illustrated London News* in 1843 includes a song for Christmas: "Home again! Home again! / Home! home!" and a *Household Words* Christmas number includes a story about a single man who finds his Christmas in lodgings so miserable that he purposely secures a suburban villa near Fulham and a wife before the next Christmas season.[22] Like the Christmas books, sensation fiction of subsequent decades had a domestic focus. Festive readings portray the fantasy of the home as an increasingly stable haven, but later sensation fiction, rife with family secrets and mysterious identities, presents the family as a false sanctuary and actually the site of the home's disintegration.

Consumers who could read the material object of the Christmas book selection at their booksellers turned to the narratives within the covers to participate in cultural standards of holiday sentiment. Nineteenth-century readers' responses exist in the annual reviews of Christmas books in periodical publications, in letters and memoirs, and in records and illustrations of Charles Dickens's Christmas readings. Reviews represent atypical, professional readers, but they are indispensable, albeit public, sources that gauge and often shape readers' expectations.[23] Many of the reception texts reveal authors responding to another writer's Christmas book, and this specific audience brings an awareness of language craft to the appreciation of Christmas sentiment. Christmas readers relied on periodical reviews and scenes of reading to know where and how sentiment might be bought and commodified.

Christmas readers, whether in the reaches of the geographic empire or in Hackney, simultaneously enacted their emotional festive reading practices. Christmas literature of the 1840s was only released in the weeks leading up to Christmas and, occasionally, in the fortnight following Christmas. Twenty-first-century marketers would probably hold the release of a Christmas item that failed to beat a mid-November publication date, but the run up to the early Victorian Christmas started later (in mid-December). The holiday also lasted longer, at least in theory, as the traditional Twelfth-tide culminated on 5 January. Signs of Christmas's building momentum can be seen in the time set aside to enjoy it. J.A.R. Pimlott's impressive history of the Victorian Christmas relates that, in 1842, the Poor Law Board "ordered that no labour except housework should be done on Christmas Day and Good Friday, and in 1847 gave the local Guardians discretion to provide extra food on Christmas Day at the expense of the poor rate." In 1871 Boxing Day was named a Bank Holiday, effectively lengthening the national celebration to two full days at the very least.[24] Readers outside of the workhouse had much more leisure time during the midwinter festival. Christmas books may be subtitled "A Tale for January," and the action in *The Cricket on the Hearth* takes place in the first month of the year. January narratives were still considered timely for Christmas reading. The Victorian audience read Christmas stories in January numbers of periodicals released in late December, and reviews occasionally appeared as late as the February number. Perhaps the schoolboy's Christmas holiday was what truly extended the celebration, since boys would be home from early- or mid-December to mid- to late-January. In fact, Hervey indicates the beginning and ending of the Christmas season with the coach trips that carry boys home and back again to school.

Christmas books were clearly marked for a holiday reading experience, and reviewers treated them accordingly. G. Soane's *January Eve; a Tale of the Times*—a Christmas tale with an emigrant plot—was reviewed as "a good, cheap, easy, and profitable Christmas pastime."[25] Many Christmas book covers also marked the text within as a festive read: the most common gilt stamped decoration, holly leaves, further limited the reading experience to December and January. *Howitt's Journal* included a shrewd assessment of the uses to which Christmas book covers could be put. One poem voiced a greedy Christmas shopper's intentions to send a rich, invalided Miss Smith the latest Christmas book "though she is too ill to read."[26] A Christmas book made an ingratiating present because of the Christmas morality of benevolence known to saturate the genre. The fictional giver counts on the emotion of just the sign of the Christmas book cover. The old woman might never read the narrative, but the giver hopes that the cover alone will move her to make a generous bequest.

Both the material object and the time in which it was consumed signified Christmas, but how did the holiday experience affect the audience? Gauging first-audience expectations helps to explain how early readers processed the work and how the text itself explored the human condition.[27] Christmas reading presupposed certain aspects of the extratextual, extrinsic encounter. Much depended on a fiction itself: that the nation was for once in the same emotional state, or at least attempting to achieve one. Leisure time coincided with a reunion of the family (due to the end of term) and the holiday's expectations of a fuller, more expressive sentimentality. Dickens does not reveal how the Cratchits behave in June and July, but at Christmas they are both on the verge of tears and able to make orations about family blessings.

Christmas books were most importantly sold at the very time such narratives were in demand: the stories conferred knowledge about how the English Christmas was kept while also providing a release of emotion that the reader desired as proof of her sentimentality. Farjeon noted that during "the good season . . . the hearts of men are beating in harmony, as if one pulse of love and good-will animated them, I hope, with God's blessing, that my little book will be completed, ready for those who care to read what I have written."[28] The emotional barrier set up between a reader and the text was significantly weaker during the Christmas holiday, allowing short volumes to touch the chords of emotion. In part, the marker of Christmas caused characters and readers to grow nostalgic and look backward to past experiences and lost family members. They thus opened themselves up to emotional charges, not unlike Tennyson's persona during the three Christmases of *In Memoriam*. Nostalgia played only a part, however.

Christmastime expectations—including the force of social reform preached by such figures like Dickens, Jerrold, and the Howitts—caused a seasonal softening of the heart, or, at least, the perception of one. Christmas literature continued the process. Betty Jane Breyer notes that Trollope's Christmas story characters are aware "that the season imposes a special demand upon them to be charitable beyond the usual and at peace with those around them."[29] After all, this is the season that Scrooge's cheerful nephew Fred relishes as "the only time I know of, in the long calendar of the year, when men and women seem by one consent to open their shut-up hearts freely, and to think of people below them as if they really were fellow-passengers to the grave, and not another race of creatures bound on other journeys."[30] Vincent Newey reads Fred's isolation of Christmas time with pessimism, making Christmas an exception to the rule of self-absorbed living.[31] It might have been even worse than that. Christmas might only have been a time of a heightened myth narrative, no true cultural difference. Even if hearts were not actually softened, even if benevolent feelings found no outlet, the liminal Christmas season allowed the audience of celebrants to enjoy a communal catharsis of their normal commercial greed. Reading about Scrooge's philanthropy either cathartically alleviated one's need to do the same or encouraged one to take similar steps. The *Athenaeum* attributed to Christmas literature the ability "to soften the heart and sweeten the charities at Christmas time by the agency of pity and sympathy" because the reading encounter coincided with the cultural formation of Christmas.[32] This set Christmas reading apart: it fell in a specific, concentrated season, and it brought with it expectations of emotional affect tied to values associated with a myth of ideal Englishness.

Why would some Victorians cry over Christmas books? It has much to do with the sentiment already afloat in mainstream Victorian literature. Disagreeing with theories that connect emotional intensity with degree of mimetic illusion in characters, Richard Walsh claims that characters, such as Little Nell, are caricatures, not realistic "people" at all. Readers' "[e]motional involvement is the recognition of values" within the narrative rather than an association with the characters as real people. Readers do not self-associate with a character; rather, they self-associate with an ideology, and the character is "rhetorically charged" with that idea.[33]

Victorian readers wept over all types of literature, and the format of literature necessarily influenced the employment of emotional appeals. For example, the serial publication of *Oliver Twist* demanded recurring assurance of Oliver as a symbol of compassion and purity, which Dickens expressed through frequent tearful scenes. Seasonal literature offered a special forum for emotional performance. Christmas books represent a skeletal form of the novel formula: they are pure ideal wrapped up in a very few caricatured characters. *The Chimes*, for example, has only a dozen named characters. Christmas reading experiences welcomed readers willing to participate in the speedy transmission of emotional impetus, and back-story and detail rife in serialized novels dwindled as a result. The pure ideals of Englishness—home, hearth, benevolence (on both domestic and national levels)—took center stage as authors clothed them in social reform rhetoric or, as in Catherine Gore's Christmas novels, remnants of the society novel. Victorian scholars might say this is the case with every Victorian novel; however, Christmas novels took the nature of emotional charge and caricatured ideals to extremes that, as nineteenth-century reviewers apologetically stated, would have garnered only condemnation at other times of the year.

Contemporary accounts of the emotional affect of Dickens's Christmas writing overwhelms the rest of the genre, and it starts with the author himself who admitted that, while writing *A Christmas Carol* he "wept and laughed and wept again, and excited myself in a most exhilarating manner."[34] When John Forster read *The Chimes* to A'Beckett, A'Beckett "cried so much, and so painfully, that Forster didn't know whether to go on or stop; and he called next day to say that any expression of his feeling was beyond his power."[35] A few years later the Watsons enjoyed the author's reading of *Battle of Life*, and Mr. Watson's diary entry records how "Lavinia was quite overcome by it."[36] Not surprisingly, Dickens's Christmas books made their way into the home of Thackeray, one of the most vocal early reviewers. In a letter he reports that his mother, Mrs. Carmichael Smyth, read Dickens's *The Haunted Man* "and was very much moved. She says there's something in it will affect you personally."[37]

Emotional appeals were expected, but they also had to be balanced. Thackeray paid special attention to sentimentality within the commodification of the Christmas book, and his review of Gore's *New Year's Day* cynically describes "Tears—sweet, gushing tears, sobs of heart-breaking yet heart-soothing affection, break from one over this ravishing scene. I am crying so, I can hardly write."[38] Thackeray goes on to criticize the book's emotional outlet for being too unguarded. Later on the *Times* reviewer would attack Thackeray and his "diseased oyster" of a novel by lumping *Kickleburys on the Rhine* together with Christmas books that displayed "the ostensible intention of swelling the tide of exhilaration, or other expansive emotions incident upon the exodus of the old and the inauguration of the new year."[39]

Publishers and authors may have been aware of cloaking social ideals in the Christmas books, but readers were so engaged with their emotional response that they failed to recognize their ideal values within the texts. Thackeray included an exemplary vignette in his review of *Cricket on the Hearth* in the *Morning Chronicle*: "You hear talk of it in every company. ... at dinner, everyone had read it; everybody was talking about it; and the very clergyman who said grace confessed that he had been whimpering over it all the morning. He didn't know why... but the general effect of the writing was of this heart-stirring, kindly character."[40] The clergyman responded to the ideals of his society that were so affectingly portrayed in *Cricket.* Note how the reader—I will assume that the clergyman is an actual reader—could not even put his finger on the source of his emotional response. In his review, Thackeray applauds the clergyman's reaction not only as right, but as representative as a collective readerly response. Dickens's Christmas writing continued to affect readers for decades. In 1926 British economist (and the possible inspiration for Ayn Rand's Ellsworth Toohey) Harold J. Laski wrote "Dickens certainly had the gift of tears; and why the impossible conversion of Scrooge should make one's eyes wet at the twentieth reading when one knows exactly what is to come I don't know one bit; but there it is."[41]

Thackeray frequently defended Christmas books against critics who lambasted the lack of realism in holiday narratives. He endorsed Dickens's *The Battle of Life* and promoted *The Cricket on the Hearth*, which he called a "brisk, dashing, startling caricature," just as it ought to be for Christmas.[42] Representing Christmas-tinted ideals overshadowed any attempt to capture realism. Characters were indeed caricatures, but they were "startling" because they revealed the English community's concern for itself. As a good Christmas book critic, Thackeray writes that he "has to ask, is it a good book which so excites you and all the public with emotion?"[43] Thackeray essentially answers "yes." A reviewer in *Fraser's Magazine* complained when ideals are not clothed quite convincingly enough, as in the case of *The Doctor's Little Daughter*, because "[s]uch books are mere expanded advertisements of what their authors feel, or profess to feel, instead of containing materials calculated to awaken the feelings of their readers."[44] In contrast, the reviewer found Gaskell's *Moorland Cottage* an excellent representative of those Christmas books "calculated" to endow feelings on readers. Reviewers gave attention to judging whether texts contain properly calculated emotional charge, thus revealing that readers wanted to know how feelings might be derived from Christmas books. Readers sought advice for their palette of feelings in the pages of consumer reports: reviews.

Sentiments associated with Christmas became commodified as authors and readers participated in an exchange dependent on the identity of the Christmas participant. Emotional appeal was not only part of the commodity of the Christmas book, celebrants came to expect it as part of the performance. In a letter (dated 30 December 1850) Jane Arnold Forster describes her brother Matthew Arnold's response to *The Moorland Cottage* as a process of absorption: "Matt is stretched at full length on one sofa, reading a Christmas tale of Mrs Gaskell's which moves him to tears, & the tears to complacent admiration of his own sensibility."[45] The reading experience turned the reader inward to examine his preferred version of his own moral construct. Charlotte Bronte found the same novel "finished like an herb—a balsamic herb with healing in its leaves. That small volume has beauty for commencement, gathers power in progress, and closes in pathos. ... The little story is fresh, natural, religious; no more need be said."[46]

The commodification of morality would be the identifying marker of Christmas fiction for several decades. In a September 1874 letter to a friend, the Scottish Robert Louis Stevenson expresses the touching, galvanizing characteristic of Christmas reading:

> I wonder if you ever read Dickens' Christmas books? ... I have only read two of them yet, and feel so good after them and would do anything, yes and shall do anything, to make it a little better for people. I wish I could lose no time; I want to go out and comfort some one; I shall never listen to the nonsense they tell one about not giving money—I shall give money; not that I haven't done so always, but I shall do it with a high hand now.[47]

Stevenson's letter would make a compelling advertisement, and it attests to the singular characteristic of Christmas fiction. The Christmas utopia in Dickens's Christmas books galvanized Stevenson to action, or at least the intention to act. The texts offered the reader a chance to experience the Christmas utopia and consoled him with the hope that utopia could exist in reality if the so-called English precepts couched in the texts were carried out in real life.

Records like the one about Matthew Arnold insist upon a connection between the Christmas narrative's emotional effect and the body. Emotional responses can begin in texts and move out into reality.[48] Gesa Stedman's recent study on Victorian emotion relies heavily on Charles Bell's *The Anatomy and Philosophy of Expression as Connected to the Fine Arts* (1806), a text that enjoyed attention during the decades following its publication. While the emotion of novel-reading was so often condemned, emotion also had a positive part in reading responses since emotion "is bestowed as a boon, a mark of superior intelligence, and a source of enjoyment; ... it is the bond of the human family."[49] Such was the case in Arnold's tearful reading of *Moorland Cottage*. His tears were on display for both himself and his sister, who judged the performance with harsh reality. She was not absorbed in the Christmas story; rather, she was only aware of the Christmas context: the date, the cover, the author. Jane Forster's letter reveals how the Christmas books encouraged emotional expression. In fact, they were consumed for that effect. If readers of sensation novels desired the thrill and suspense of bigamy plots and hidden identities, Christmas book readers desired an annual test of their compassion, their kindliness, their humanity.

One scene of Christmas reading stands out from all the rest because it accentuates the emotional charge of the Christmas reading encounter. Daniel Maclise's illustration captures Dickens in the act of performing a reading of *The Chimes* for an audience of his male colleagues on 3 December 1844. The reading takes place in John Forster's rooms, and the audience includes Thomas Carlyle, Douglas Jerrold, W.J. Fox, and others. The reading came about as a result of Dickens's urgent need to visually witness the effect his narrative had on a sympathetic, reform-minded audience. He had kept Forster apprised of his progress with the manuscript in Genoa, but the distance from his ideal audience vexed him: "I would give a hundred pounds (and think it cheap) to see you read it." When he decided to return to London to oversee the book's production, he asked Forster to assemble a select audience to serve as emotional guinea pigs.[50] Unlike the majority of Christmas reading circles scenes, in Maclise's small sketch the hearth is barely visible, and none of the fire is in view. Instead, a halo gleams around the head of the young Dickens, the central figure in the image, who outshines the hearth. The postures of the listeners vary: Dyce covers his face, as if overcome with emotion; Carlyle thoughtfully props his head on a hand; Jerrold reclines very low in his chair and stares at the ceiling. Some of the figures gaze intently at Dickens, while others cast their eyes about the room, as if lost within the words and the fictional world they create. Of all the listeners, the Rev. William Harness's reaction is the most profound. In his grief he has torn his collar askew, and he clutches his face with both hands as if in prayer. One prose account of Dickens's reading of *The Chimes* in Forster's rooms is Maclise's letter to Catherine Dickens: "there was not a dry eye in the house...shrieks of laughter—there were indeed—and floods of tears as a relief to them."[51] Maclise judged the effect, not the text. The Christmas book illustrator depicted a listening audience rather than a scene from *The Chimes*, suggesting that the readers' reactions were part of the textual performance as well. Dickens had already had a taste of the performance. He had read the manuscript to Macready two nights earlier, and the letter describing the event to Catherine Dickens demonstrates how keen Dickens was to see physical evidence of his audience's emotional response: "If you had seen Macready last night, undisguisedly sobbing and crying on the sofa as I read, you would have felt, as I did, what a thing it is to have power."[52] Dickens frequently boasts about crying over his Christmas manuscripts while he writes or as he completes them, and in this letter he shows his attentiveness in the sharp, crafted, emotional sting unleashed by the text.

Dickens went on to read his Christmas books and later periodical contributions for less formal groups of friends. Eventually he began scheduled tours of very profitable public readings. Because the lecture season in the West End was April through May, Dickens's readings carried Christmas texts out of the advent season and into the springtime, although he held Christmastime readings as well. Many audience members followed the text in their own copies while Dickens performed. These readers were also necessarily affected by the inescapable authority of the reading performed by the author, and some claimed to have gained new insight to beloved characters. Furthermore, the event of the readings may have well influenced the construction of narratives for Christmas as well as its boundaries. Dickens quickly abridged his reading of the best-loved reading, *A Christmas Carol*, to two hours when he began the ticketed public readings in 1858, and the adaptation notably emphasized the sentimental and the joyous while removing the novel's social commentary.[53] Dickens had originally intended to write new Christmas stories just for the readings, but he never did. Nonetheless, Philip Collins suggests that knowledge of upcoming reading tours must have influenced the Christmas stories Dickens wrote during the 1860s since he would have seen them as potential texts for reading adaptations. For example, Dickens immediately adapted *Mugby Junction* into three separate reading texts.[54] Dickens strove to create specific emotional responses in all of his readings. He tried out one of his last readings, *Sikes and Nancy*, in front of an audience of one hundred trusted friends to see whether or not he should attempt the shocking murder scene in public.[55] Another non-Christmas reading, *The Story of Little Dombey*, combined laughter and tears, but the depths of sorrow it induced caused Dickens to cut it from the program in later years. A report in the *Spectator* said the reading of the life and death of Paul Dombey "made the most painful impression of pathos feeding upon itself." The Christmas readings drew out a more satisfactory blend of emotions, and contemporary accounts almost always reported laughter interspersed with crying. Contemporary newspaper descriptions often mentioned that audiences that listened to Dickens read *A Christmas Carol* left the assembly hall as "better moral beings; unlike the other readings, there was about this one an element of a rite, a religious affirmation." *The Chimes* reading was, according the Dickens, "[*v*]*ery* dramatic, but very melancholy on the whole." One audience member remembered a particular speech, to which the audience reacted to with a pained silence and intermittent sobs. The *Ipswich Journal* reported the emotional power of the *Doctor Marigold* Christmas number reading: "every audience before whom Mr Dickens has produced it has found it too great for self-control." This reading item would end with the title character shedding "happy and yet pitying tears" as he meets for the first time the small child of his mute adopted daughter. Examining the audience reaction to the closing scene, Kate Field wrote, "those tears steal into our eyes as well; and when Dickens steals away, there seems to be more love and unselfishness in the world than before we took Doctor Marigold's prescription."[56]

Emotion was a significant characteristic of the Christmas book subgenre. Christmas books were shorter, so a reader could not become as historically invested in the fictional community as in longer novels. She could, however, become emotionally invested. At the Christmas fireside, readers handed over their readerly reserve as they sought to explore their own emotions—to discover, and attest to their own capacity for sympathy. Christmas reading events unleashed levels of feeling that remained blocked at other times of the year and in other reading experiences. Long novels are intriguing for their realism and the complexity of life they project; they contain lives played out, which cannot be limited to the emotional charge of a single day's experience. Some Christmas books follow a single-day time frame to further heighten the immediacy of the reader's experience. Those that follow characters over the course of several months do so with such hardheaded narrowness to a specific emotional plot that they eschew realism for poignant caricatures, a plan that permitted cathartic experiences for first readers.

In his letters, Dickens hinted at the Christmas sentiment required of a Christmas book. Writing to Miss Burdett Coutts and referring to *The Haunted Man*, he claimed to "have hit upon a little notion for the book, which I hope is a pretty one, with a good Christmas tendency."[57] Just over two years earlier the Christmas book guru had written John Forster about *The Battle of Life*, his "pretty story, with some delicate notions in it agreeably presented, and with a good human Christmas groundwork. I fancy I see a great domestic effect in the last part."[58] The author's choice of words, his "good human Christmas groundwork" and his "great domestic effect" point to the spine of a Christmas narrative in this earliest wave of Victorian holiday volumes. *The Haunted Man* is a story of memory's redemptive qualities. A melancholy instructor makes a bargain to lose his distressing memories; in consequence, he becomes an unwitting memory vacuum, and he sucks the memories from all those whom he encounters. This is Scrooge's story in reverse. Redlaw learns how his past contributes to his humanity only after his memories have been sponged away. The "great domestic effect in the last part" includes several tearful scenes as the community members, who had become increasingly uncivil toward each other due to their loss of memory and humanity, reunite. The theme that runs through the story and, indeed, finishes it is "Lord, keep my memory green."[59] Authors and publishers often linked feeling to a specific ideal, such as Dickens's nostalgia. The resolution's "domestic effect" itself involves several sorrowful scenes as characters come to appreciate the pasts that have formed them and the family that surrounds them. Like *Cricket on the Hearth*, the novel ends by venerating middle-class marriage and relational harmony.

Dickens expected Christmas "effects" from his writing, but sometimes publishers contracted specifically for emotional effects. The publishing history of *The Moorland Cottage* once again attests to the "unnatural" demands placed on authors by a market that was beginning to expect Christmas books. Evidence suggests that Chapman and Hall were asking Gaskell to prepare a Christmas book early in 1850, but the author of *Mary Barton* struggled to meet the obligation this sort of writing entailed. Gaskell had already added to the Christmas literary market with a short story "Christmas Storms and Sunshine" for *Howitt's Journal* in 1848, and she would go on to write "The Old Nurse's Story" (1852) and "The Squire's Story" (1853), both for *Household Words*. In 1850 Gaskell wrote of Mr. Chapman's request for "a Xmas story, 'recommending benevolence, charity, etc', to which I agreed, why I cannot think now, for it was very foolish indeed." Because she claimed she "could not write about virtues to order," Chapman ended up with the manuscript for *The Moorland Cottage*, which recommended self-sacrifice rather than Christmas benevolence.[60]

In the short space available, Gaskell's characters become caricatures of their values, and reviews emphasize the feminine ideal of domestic long-suffering portrayed by Maggie Browne. Cultural ideals form the structure of the narrative, and readers emotionally invested in the English culture found fitting emotional release in the story. This book not only affected Charlotte Bronte and Matthew Arnold, but it also received positive reviews for its emotional content in *Fraser's Magazine*. The review finds this book better than *Mary Barton*, and classes *The Moorland Cottage*'s heroine "amongst the sweetest creations of English fiction."[61] Swinburne would later call it the "beautiful story of 'The Moorland Cottage.'"[62] Other reviews referred to it as "healthy and powerful and pathetic" (*Ladies' Companion*) and as a "strengthening little story" (*Fraser's Magazine*).[63] Although they were not what the publisher ordered, the barely clothed values manipulate readers' response to the text. It is possible that, while publishers were commodifying benevolence, Christmas book readers were open to buying and consuming narratives of that related value—self-sacrifice—during the Christmas holiday. *The Moorland Cottage*'s publishing history demonstrates how the book industry typically catered to a narrow interpretation of Christmas sentimentality, creating an artificial emotional scale.

The reading habits of the middle-class Victorian family become vital to understanding how Christmas books served to dish out English identity in annual installments. Richard Altick notes in much of his work how "[t]he fireside was the center of family life, and the products of the press were as indispensable to household custom as tableware and furniture."[64] Kate Flint shows how women's reading served as "the vehicle through which an individual's sense of identity was achieved or confirmed." Flint points out that the reading that allows for identity-building denotes the presence of leisure time, so reading itself supported the ideology of middle-class domesticity.[65] Christmas books provided an identity-forming space for both genders. Christmas reading was intended to take place in the bosom of the family, and this premise set the reader within her own understanding of one of the main ideals of the narratives: home. Location influenced interpretation because it provided the reader with a host of surrounding memories and associations that embedded her own story within the text.[66] Another expectation for Christmas reading was the family circle, and evidence shows Victorian readers brought *The Carol* to the family circle, read it aloud, and even kept it "upon a little shelf by itself, and [it] was doing them no end of good."[67]

Depictions of reading in Christmas books anticipated how Christmas fiction was being consumed. Studying fictional nineteenth-century depictions of reading helps to recover "what people thought took place" during the initial reading.[68] Christmas books certainly contain reading scenes that chronicle how readers felt they were supposed to approach sentimental Christmas reading. Reading scenes also resulted in more self-consciousness readers, since, "in reading about another's reading you can think to encounter your own."[69] The Victorian canon and Victorian art contain many images of isolated reading, but the Christmas books especially encouraged oral reading that reached out to a community of readers at an emotionally vulnerable period. Private reading is a result of "a certain construction of personal identity," and "decisions about what to read, where to read, when to read, and how to read can be understood to be determined by social, religious or political restraints and codes."[70] Scenes of reading signal the reader to consider an "adjusted orientation" to reading.[71] Such scenes force readers to become self-conscious of their habits and expectations of reading.[72] When Christmas audiences encountered scenes of tearful reading, they had the opportunity to analyze their own performance of the conventions of reading. Evidence suggests that public, tearful reactions to Christmas narratives were nothing readers needed to hide. In fact, the documentation confirms that sobbing readers exhibited their emotional reaction with pride.

The following excerpt from *The Battle of Life* resonates with details of the reading tableau that models how Christmas reading can do the reader "no end of good." The scene depicts Dr. Jeddler and his daughters, both of whom are in love with Jeddler's ward Alfred. The young man is affianced to Marion, but, before their reunion following Alfred's three-year's absence, Marion has chosen to selflessly and secretly leave home so that Alfred can turn his attentions to her sister Grace. Shortly before she runs away, Marion sits with her family by an idyllic fireside and reads aloud about a woman who realizes she must leave her "exquisitely dear" home:

> "Marion, my love!" said Grace.
>
> "Why, Puss!" exclaimed her father, "what's the matter?"
>
> She put her hand upon the hand her sister stretched towards her, and read on; her voice still faltering and trembling, though she made an effort to command it when thus interrupted. ...[Marion continues to read]
>
> "Dear Marion, read no more tonight," said Grace—for she was weeping. ...
>
> "What! overcome by a story-book!" said Doctor Jeddler. "Print and paper! Well, well, it's all one. It's as rational to make a serious matter

> of print and paper as of anything else. But dry your eyes, love, dry your eyes. I dare say the heroine has got home again long ago, and made it up all round—and if she hasn't, a real home is only four walls; and a fictitious one, mere rags and ink."

Even as Marion dries her tears, Jeddler reads a letter informing the family that Alfred will join them for Christmas. This information appears to enliven Marion, and her father quips, "The story-book is soon forgotten!"[73]

The Battle of Life narrator omits any close physical description of Marion's emotional outburst. Only the expressions of her sister and father reveal Marion's unease, suggesting once again that tears over Christmas reading are part of an acceptable performance. Marion teaches that Christmas reading can be emotional, and that it can express unspoken sentiments to one's loved ones even when the orator is unable to express or otherwise voice her devotion to family and home. Regardless of her family's ability to comprehend the significance of her words, Marion expresses an otherwise pent-up emotion through the guise of reading aloud. The text's words become her own. Dickens's first audience would have been skilled enough in the Christmas narrative to find the double meaning in Marion's tears. The first Victorian audience may not have been aware of Marion's plan to leave, but they were educated enough by 1848 to latch on to such an affecting scene as a key to the emotional punch of Christmas fiction, the emotional release they so desired for themselves.

Jeddler's final lines are tongue in cheek: fictitious homes are "mere rags and ink." After five seasons of the new, print-motivated Christmas feeling, devoted readers would have been educated to discount the doctor's caustic witticisms. Throughout the novel, Dr. Jeddler mocks the pleasures of life as "mere farce." The reader might well have shaken her head in unison with Marion who has indeed been "overcome by a storybook." The Christmas homes that appeared in print were far more than the material object of the page—they were the ideal home that reigned supreme in Christmas ideology. That rag and ink might have been a commodity of exchange, but it also allowed for the outlet of human emotion. Contrary to Jeddler's reasoning, readers did not cry over the fictional home, they cried for the connection fiction made with their own world and their experience of the home. Marion's romanticized, reading-induced tears contrast with her father's poor opinion of print.

Marion's storybook is only one of many scenes of reading in *The Battle of Life*. Elsewhere characters read auction advertisements, contracts, and, most importantly, small tools. Dr. Jeddler's maid Clemency always carries her "pocket library" of a thimble and a nutmeg grater, each bearing a motto: "For-get and for-give" and "Do as you—wold—be—done by."[74] The inscribed tools wreak a mighty change in Clemency's coworker, Benjamin Britain. "Little Britain" has been corrupted by the Doctor's "Friar Bacon" attitude, and the servant—like the nation he allegorizes—cares for nothing and believes in nothing. Britain's name pinpoints him as the caricature of the nation, and his reform is one that Dickens situates in the forefront of his Christmas books. The messages in Clemency's pocket library convert Britain to a caring, hopeful citizen. This is the hope the Christmas book offers readers. The novel's rhetoric of reform has caused Lyn Pykett to write, "*The Battle of Life*, like the other Christmas books, thus reverses the mid-Victorian grand narrative of competitive individualism, which plots life as a struggle for economic and/or evolutionary dominance."[75]

One final prose scene of reading continues to reinforce the lessons to which Christmas readers seasonally subjected themselves. In *The Haunted Man*, Dickens creates a working-class family's reaction to literature. A failed newspaperman, Tetterly has decorated a screen out of newspaper clippings, and he reads from this reconfigured text in which he finds a constant source of morality and witticism. After Redlaw's curse has fallen on the Tetterly family and loss of memory sours their domestic joy, Tetterly looks again at a story of a famished father and his starving children:

> "This used to be one of the family favourites, I recollect," said Tetterly, in a forlorn and stupid way, "and used to draw tears from the children, and make 'em good, if there was any little bickering or discontent among 'em, next to the story of the robin red-breasts in the wood. . . . Ha! I don't understand it, I'm sure," said Tetterly; "I don't see what it has got to do with us."[76]

Eschewing Tetterly's denseness, a Victorian reader would have aptly interpreted that the newspaper story, like the Christmas story at hand, certainly "has got to do with us." The novel's rhetoric engaged the reader in a diatribe about the direction of appalling national qualities: insensitivity, heartlessness, barbarism. Moreover, it reminded readers that they were engaged in just such an activity, and that communal tears might just "make 'em good."

First editions of Christmas books often depict illustrated scenes of reading entirely unrelated to the narrative at hand. Like in *The*

Moorland Cottage, frontispieces and chapter illustrations display imagined families reading around the fire, although such scenes and such families are absent in the novel's story. Illustrators depict the readers rather than the characters. Myles Birket Foster's narratively misleading *Moorland Cottage* title page illustration becomes "a measure of [the novel's] distance from its Christmas context."[77]

Such is also the case in John Tenniel's illustration for the first page of *The Haunted Man and the Ghost's Bargain: A Fancy for Christmas-Time*. A child reads to an audience of her siblings and a nurse or mother. The illustrated reader reads from a small book comparable in size to the Christmas book. Two younger siblings look up attentively at the reader, while a third child and the baby point to the monstrous shadows dancing on the wall behind them, the enlarged, disfigured shadows of their own bodies. The shadow message makes an artful narrative of the reading scene's reality. Only the youngest children are astutely able to read their reflections on the wall—the rest are engrossed in the reading. John Tenniel's illustration suggests that events in real life dictate the disproportional, even caricatured, narrated events. Tenniel frames the upper part of the page with rougher sketches of fairy-tale vignettes: a turbaned, portly Arab, a stooped, menacing old woman, a dismembered Cassim Baba looking like a marionette, and a pumpkin. Presumably the representative myths of childhood fiction emanate from the child reader's book, but the connection is not perfectly clear in the illustration. Seven pages later Dickens's prose briefly describes this tableau in a list of more than a dozen evocative wintertime scenes, and the author takes one sentence to capture the thrill of fireside reading and its attendant fantasies. In Tenniel's related illustration the fairy-tale images are rough, cartoon-like sketches, while the shadows behind the well-defined reading circle actually dominate the overall illustration. Three of the realistic figures by the fire point to the shadows rather than the line drawings (the nurse's hand appears to be pointing, although she does not look at or seem aware of the shadowy text behind her). The shadows cast by the book's audience take on a life of their own, and the Christmas book reader is forced to wonder which text deserves more attention: the mimetic, pantomime-like narrative on the wall or the tale unfolding in the storybook. The fingers pointing insistently at the wall show a child's innocent wisdom: examine one's own shadows before escaping into a story.

Thackeray's pantomimic *The Rose and the Ring* (1855) also opens with a scene of storytelling, although in this instance the orator uses no book. A grandmother tells a tale to five Victorian children and their mother or nurse. The family circle directs its attention to the speaker, but in the center of the circle the reader's attention is drawn to a scene in the fire. The shadows of a figure on horseback and its pursuer possibly draw the attention of one of the grandmother's listeners. The fire scene is reminiscent of the Christmas book at hand, subtitled *A Fireside Pantomime for Great and Small Children*, and the one child who is able to see the figures in the fire is suggestive of the successful imagination that projects the orator's story into a world of fantasy. In his prelude Thackeray recounts how the novel originated as a "fireside pantomime" he told his children during a Christmastime spent in Rome.[78] Thus, in the cover page illustration, the grandmother has taken on Thackeray's autobiographical role, but the image also recommends her as the narrator of the ensuing printed story. Moreover, the scene of storytelling without a book establishes the connection between the traditional story circle and the commodified Christmas book. Readers could buy the book and pretend they participated in a traditional rite.

Why are illustrations of otherwise unconnected family circles found in the Christmas books? Illustrators seem to have been free to deviate from the text at hand and illustrate an advertisement for the experience that readers would enjoy if they bought the book and put it to its intended use. Christmas circles in Thackeray and Tenniel's illustrations reveal a gap at the fireside. The paterfamilias, and grown men in general, are absent from the images. The Christmas reading circle is banished to the nursery and limited to the membership of women and children. *Punch*'s 1890 Christmas story-telling scene by George du Maurier shows a stately, well-dressed Aunt Marianna pausing in her "blood-curdling Ghost Story" to send the luckless lone male, a wide-eyed schoolboy, to check on a banging door. A woman and a girl have their arms wrapped around each other, and another listener leans forward, her elbows on her knees. The point here is to mock the fright a feminized story circle can engender when left without a grown male chaperone.[79] Other illustrations show the entire family. A *Belgravia* image, "January—Fireside Stories," shows the father telling a story to his rapt family audience.[80]

Illustrations of fireside story-telling idealize the relationship of the family in a way that would have appeared seductive to potential consumers skimming for the illustrations: "If I buy this volume, my family might replicate that frontispiece scene." Thus, the illustrations of reading circles offered a hope of a restabilized home embedded in a performance of a Christmas ritual. Reviews typically evaluated Christmas book prose for the emotional content. Thus, Victorian Christmas readers learned how to read Christmas from a matrix of seasonal print matter, not the least of which were the profiles, reviews, short-stories, and extra Christmas numbers of the periodicals.

Chapter 3

How Mr. Punch Stole Christmas: The Evolution of the Holiday in Periodicals

With the cultural potency of Dickens's early Christmas books and the illustrations within them, it is not surprising that *Punch* contributors occasionally kidnapped Scrooge for parody. In 1885, *Punch* cast Gladstone as Scrooge and the ghost of Benjamin Disraeli as Marley. An accompanying illustration imitates the well-known John Leech illustration of the hearty Christmas Present and his pile of goods, but this time a drunken Christmas Present meets Scrooge in Leech's original setting, with the addition of a *Punch* Almanack mixed into the cornucopia at his feet. The text then tells how the spirit takes "Scroogestone" on a journey to view the populace: "troubled Churches and perturbed parsonages, spectres of furious squires and jubilant rustics."[1] A few years later John Tenniel's main cartoon for an 1893 issue, seen here in figure 2, limits its parody to the same Leech illustration. Instead of an appetizing cornucopia, Tenniel's Christmas Present holds the torch of "Anarchy" while he sits on a small pile of foodstuff inscribed with "Eastern Question," "Irish Question," alongside containers of "Dynamite," "Combustion," and a pile of coal marked "Strike." Leech's sausages have become chains, and Tenniel turns the pole in front of Christmas Present's knee into the sword of "Strife." Scrooge will not be learning the same lesson from this Christmas Present, who waves his empty hand to encompass this sad spirit of the time.[2] Among other contemporary events, the cartoon refers to a coal-miners strike that, according to a *New York Times* report, left 86,000 idle and 300,000 people dependent on outdoor

Figure 2 John Tenniel, "The Spirit of Christmas Present," *Punch* 105 (30 December 1893): 307.

Source: Courtesy of the University of Delaware.

relief.[3] *Punch* lampooned the history of Christmas in print and satirized contemporary politics with all the immediacy of the periodical genre. *Punch* frequently adapted symbols of Christmas to criticize current events, and its unique status as a long-running comic newspaper featuring text and illustration also allowed *Punch* to contribute to the construction of Christmas while also critiquing cultural developments related to the holiday.

While readers may have turned to Christmas books like *The Moorland Cottage* to unleash physical reactions like tears, these same readers had an even cheaper recourse if they wished to access Christmas print for laughter. *Punch* creators modified Christmas to suit their comic newspaper, and in so doing, they wrote a subversive narrative of the Christmas performance, a performance that more sober texts idolized. As Christmas became an institution imbued with markers of class and ethnic identity, it became open to criticism on behalf of that identity. Comic wits attacked Christmas as a means of critiquing middle-class consumerism. *Punch* sketches also gauged what could be mocked about Christmas and what elements of the holiday were outside the bounds of polite ridicule. Unlike many of its fellow weeklies and the monthlies, *Punch* rhetoric differed markedly from the typical early Christmas book sentiment. From the very first volume in 1841, *Punch*'s contributors began shaping the cultural concept of the then unsettled Christmas. Like Dickens's Christmas books, timely *Punch* pieces contained seasonal content and heavy-handed lessons in benevolence and charity. *Punch* personalities actively engaged in the seasonal print material market both as a collective and through individual publications, and their work bears study. Focusing on the holiday work of the *Punch* team reveals the changing politics of *Punch* and Christmas benevolence as well as the ways in which the comic newspaper contributed to readers' Christmas consumerism. This vantage point also offers a striking view into the wider matrix of Christmas in nineteenth-century periodicals.

The comic newspaper began reaching for Christmas-related topics in mid- to late-December, and a surprising amount of material continued to flood issues that appeared into mid-January. The late 1840s saw a significant rise in the amount of *Punch* Christmas material when compared the first years of the decade. Even up until the mid-1850s, December and early January issues contain only a handful of articles and images relating to the Christmas holiday, but *Punch* creators more than make up for this dearth in later decades. Regular numbers of *Punch* blended Christmas articles with nonseasonal reading, so the dedicated *Punch* reader did not necessarily choose to read Christmas material when he picked up his weekly number. For example, some Christmas-themed pieces merely used festive symbols to ridicule contemporary politicians or heads of unfriendly states. Other pieces might have been entirely Christmas in context, but they ran side by side with nonseasonal items. Even when holiday material was sparse, the comic newspaper maintained a coherent rhetoric of Christmas that showed the men behind the humor trying to make sense of their culture and its changing relationship with a newly refurbished celebration of consumerism.

The editorial board began imposing *Punch* on Christmas from the start by running an advertisement in the very first number, issued in July 1841, preparing readers to buy the cloth-bound volume as a Christmas present six months later.[4] Anecdotal ads for the bound volumes (priced 7s. 6d.) dot December issues. In addition to the bound volume that was released with a Christmas preface each new year, *Punch* also marketed its Almanack for the festive audience. This Almanack, which always preserved its antiquated spelling, initially came in the form of twelve pages (later expanded to twenty-two and then thirty pages with a pull out illustration), all the same dimensions as the normal *Punch* pages. The Almanack provided a family "with ample Christmas amusement as they discovered, one by one, all the fine, waggish details the artists had invented."[5] Over the decades, the *Punch* designers altered their Almanack's layout significantly: the Almanack for 1845 shows a new format, offering a large illustration in the center of the page and smaller figures for closer inspection in the page border; the first Almanack of the 1850s centralizes comic text and garlands the page with monthly cartoons; and the 1853 Almanack has two focal cartoons plus season-related text. By 1864 the Almanack contains two main illustrations and nine or ten short comic pieces per page. It is as if text and visual images were at war in the constantly evolving Almanack that, in effect, moved from a textual to a visual ascendancy at the mid-century. To give its audience more fodder for close inspection and mirth, the Almanack would eventually pare down the larger images in exchange for closely covered sheets filled with various small cartoons and written quips. The final version developed a balance between text and image that emphasized quantity of jokes rather than the earlier focus on artwork.

The unbound Almanack was not seen as a Christmas present, but only a temporary amusement. Almanacks usually eschewed the inherently dated, political humor that appeared week after week in the normal numbers in exchange for more general puns and jokes about the turning year. The earlier pattern of featuring monthly pages complete with calendars or month-related cartoons disappeared entirely in the mid-1860s. At this point the pamphlet temporarily ceased to resemble a true almanac in any way, and instead offered only comic amusement without the pretence of usefulness. Perhaps the creative board realized that its unbound and relatively frail Almanack was only being inspected in the leisure of the midwinter holiday, and that there was no need to pretend that the flimsy paper lasted into the later months of the year. By the late 1880s the *Punch* Almanack had reverted to a format boasting a tiny calendar on the first page. Why did the calendars come and go? Were readers expected to retain the Almanacks through the year for reference? The *Mirror of Literature, Amusement, and Instruction* offered its readers a graphic calendar of the entire year on half a page in 1844, and the accompanying text encouraged readers to cut out the calendar and transfer it to a pocket-book or use it when writing in their diaries.[6] A review of *The Protestant Almanack* for 1841 told potential consumers that the almanac was "adapted either for the pocket, or for the counting house."[7] By including the calendar in the page layout, the creators marked the Almanack as a distinctly different piece of reading material, one that a consumer should buy in addition to that week's regular *Punch* number. Almanacs were certainly common enough in December, and the flood of these booklets in 1866 caused one writer to complain "The world is afflicted with almanacs . . . my illustrated newspaper has its illustrated almanac, which I am bound to buy; my comic periodical its comic almanac, which I am also bound to buy; my insurance office has a broadsheet, which I am forced to put up in my study."[8] If the overburdened consumer failed to buy all of almanacs, he could rest assured that *Punch*'s comic Almanack would be included at the front of each newly bound volume.

Unlike the flimsy Almanack, *Punch* marketed the entire bound volume as a Christmas present once it was bound at the end of the year. Presentable gift commodities became increasingly important as the commercialism of the Victorian Christmas expanded. Bound volumes, both those completed in December and June, bore gold stamps, a common signifier of the smaller, but similarly stamped Christmas volumes. The cover and stamping marked the bound volumes as more elegant print objects. Binding numbers of a periodical into a volume changed the form of the text "suggesting that *really* the periodical is a kind of book and the numbers are incomplete sections of the whole."[9]

The bound volumes open with their own preface, often the work of John Tenniel, a feature that further distinguishes them as a genre hybrid. Early prefaces to volumes ending in December during the 1840s and 1850s use a Christmas metaphor to link Christmas leisure reading and the bound versions of *Punch*, but this practice also dates the sales window of the volume. For example, Christmas volume prefaces liken *Punch* itself to a slice of Twelfth cake or plum pudding intended for Christmas consumption. The preface to the volume sold during the 1843 Christmas season revises the marketing technique for six months of *Punch* numbers to sell them as a holiday pastime. Mr. Punch tells his readers,

> The book is a Christmas pleasure; but, Reader, before you open it—ere you set your teeth in a single paragraph, answer PUNCH truly: What have you done, this "merry Christmas," for the happiness of those about, below you?
>
> Nothing? . . . Close the book: for to you, PUNCH is and shall be a dead letter. You may, indeed, scan the type, and think you understand it; you may laugh, and think the mirthfulness a pleasant reality. Alas! You have read dead words; you could not know the true spirit enshrined in them.[10]

The author draws upon the year-round social politics of *Punch* that inform the newspaper's handling of the holiday. By suggesting that only *Punch*-endorsed Christmas celebrants fully decode the humor of *Punch*—to everyone else it will be "dead words"—the preface marks the holiday season as a rite of passage for its readers. The author suggests that Christmas offers a test for readers' social ethics, and the "true spirit" presented in nonseasonal numbers aligns briefly with the national celebration at Christmas. In this preface, *Punch* positions itself squarely within the Christmas utopia that the audience otherwise inhabits only briefly during the midwinter holiday. The author argues that *Punch* politics persistently align with Christmas social reform.

While *Punch* creators crafted each holiday element (preface, articles, cartoons) during the week before a December number's printing, the same artists had been involved in readying Christmas book production earlier in the year. Many of *Punch*'s founding members, artists, and contributors were engaged in individual financial opportunities opened by the burgeoning Christmas print material market. John Leech created some of the most memorable and most parodied illustrations for Dickens's series of Christmas books.[11] Henry Mayhew carried *Punch*'s early 1840s benevolent stance into the Christmas book he wrote with his brother Augustus Mayhew: *The Good Genius: A Tale for Christmas* (1845). *Punch* authors, well-established for their abilities to amuse, wisely harnessed the Christmas market, and the *Punch* office took a lively interest in December book sales and put forth several books for the purpose. The comic newspaper did not provide a full-time job for any of the journalists, and the December market offered additional income. What Richard M. Kelly has called the "most popular and successful of all Jerrold's writings,"[12] *Mrs. Caudle's Curtain*

Lectures (1845) was bound and marketed as a Christmas present, as was A'Beckett's *The Comic Blackstone* (1845). Richard Doyle illustrated several Christmas books put out by other publishers, including Thomas Hughes's *The Scouring of the White Horse* (1859) and John Ruskin's only Christmas book, *The King of the Golden River* (1851). Doyle also illustrated Thackeray's *Rebecca and Rowena* (1854) when illness prevented the author from supplying his own illustrations, as was his custom.[13] According to the advertisements in the newspaper, *Punch* was also in the business of creating that other staple of Christmas narrative entertainment, the pantomime. Lemon, Jerrold, Smith, and A'Beckett wrote a pantomime in August of 1842 when *Punch* was one year old. The theatrical appeared in late December 1842 and was entitled *Punch's Pantomime, or Harlequin King John*.[14] Descendents of this first *Punch* pantomime were advertised irregularly throughout the rest of the century.

Thackeray, *Punch*'s most influential contributor to the escalating Christmas print market, influenced the development of the Christmas book genre through his annual reviews in various periodicals. Not one to let a chance to promote his friends' Christmas offerings slip by, some of his Christmas reviews devote half their space to assessing products of the *Punch* office. A series of reviews covering books for the 1845 season appeared in the *Morning Chronicle*, and here Thackeray includes *Mrs. Caudle's Curtain Lectures*, and *The Comic Blackstone*, both published by the *Punch* office, as well as *The Fairy Ring*, a Murray publication illustrated by Richard Doyle. Thackeray not only prepared the way for Christmas literature in his reviews and essays, he also contributed six volumes to the Christmas market: *Mrs. Perkins' Ball* (1847), *Our Street* (1848), *Doctor Birch and His Young Friends* (1849), *The Kickleburys on the Rhine* (1850), *Rebecca and Rowena* (1854), and *The Rose and the Ring* (1855).[15] His early Christmas books carried *Punch*-like sketches into the Christmas market, and these texts show a marked difference from the narrative-based Christmas books put out by Thackeray's seasonal competitors. A striking similarity exists between Thackeray's *Punch* series "The Physiology of London Evening Parties" (1842, vol. 2) and the first Thackeryan Christmas book, *Mrs. Perkins' Ball*. Both picaresque narratives poke fun at the types of people who frequent social events, like the quiet Mr. Larkin who lives to dance; the poetic, if gluttonous, Miss Bunion; and the pompous, prematurely bald Mr. Ranville Ranville of the Foreign Office.[16] Thackeray's work for *Punch* was a rehearsal for his solo undertakings in the Christmas market, and, although his last two Christmas books deviated from his periodical sketches, they still showed the unmistakable marks of *Punch* humor. As pantomime-inspired fiction, *The Rose and the Ring* is a pantomime far more comical than any other 1850 Christmas book. Similarly, Thackeray's burlesque sequel to Ivanhoe, *Rebecca and Rowena*, drolly refigures Wilfred's middle age by reconnecting him with a converted Rebecca after Rowena's death. Christmas books by other authors typically champion social values with gravity, but Thackeray's holiday novels offer comical escapes.

While Thackeray was helping to shape the Christmas book genre, the comic newspaper that employed him was shaping symbols of a nationalistic Christmas and employing them in political cartoons. *Punch* developed a Christmas symbolism that told an increasingly festive nation that Christmas stood for a particular myth of patriotic, traditional Englishness. The nature of the image in *Punch*'s discourse allowed the comic newspaper to construct the conflation of Englishness and Christmas. Illustrators mixed icons of Englishness like Britannia and John Bull with emblems of the season, especially Christmas food items and, after the 1860s, the Christmas tree. The plum pudding often featured in the full-page political cartoon in late December. In the revolutionary year 1848, one Leech cartoon shows John Bull and Mr. Punch relishing a dish of a Constitutional Plum Pudding bearing the words "Liberty of the Press, Common Sense, Order, Trial by Jury, Religion."[17] Meanwhile, other heads of state look on, dolefully aware of their own errors and their implied failure to match the English values symbolized. A decade later, a Tenniel cartoon reacted to Parliament's May 1859 authorization of a Volunteer Rifle Corp. John Bull holds a rifle and defends a gargantuan plum pudding inscribed in cloves with the words, "Old England Forever."[18] The Christmas pudding had become synonymous with John Bull's Englishness, but it was here displayed as a sign for traditional "Old" England itself.

Other print material might have been paving the way for readers to equate Christmas fare with a representation of Englishness, but *Punch*'s proclivity for image-based symbolism transmitted the sign almost instantaneously and without room for debate. Both Thomas Hervey and Charles Knight reference the Christmas pudding as a British-dominated globe in their respective works, *The Book of Christmas* (1837) and "A Christmas Pudding" (*Household Words*, 1850). The prose examples of food-based symbolism pale in rhetorical comparison to the immediacy of the cartoon. Now the ingredients of the pudding have become the signs for global trade and colonization. For example, the poem that accompanies the rifleman John

Bull illustration uses the plum pudding metaphor to depict John Bull guarding his pudding from other colonizers who want "such plums as Gibraltar, such currants as Malta."[19] An 1885 Tenniel cartoon shows "Greedy Boy" Otto von Bismarck not only helping himself to a huge pudding slice marked "Angra Pequena," but also stealing John Bull's pudding piece of "New Guinea." The accompanying text is barely needed to explain John Bull's dismayed expression, but it offers his poem:

> "The World's my—Pudding," Otto;
> Or at least that used to be
> My unformulated motto,
> One accepted tacitly,
> Though other chaps were welcome to small slices—after ME!

The poem goes on to prophesy German failure resulting from fast-paced imperialism.[20]

Why did *Punch* artists frequently depend on food's ability to transmit ethnic identity within political discourse? Food dominated periodical descriptions of Christmas, and the blatancy of food production rituals—animals herded to Christmas markets, the months-long preparation of the Christmas pudding, and the exchange of rurally raised food between kin-groups—heralded the midwinter feast. Seymour's frontispiece to *The Book of Christmas* anticipated the anthropomorphized Christmas foods that populated *Punch*'s seasonal numbers by personifying elements of traditional Christmas feasting. *Punch* illustrators, however, converted Christmas fare into a symbol of English global dominance. One illustrator parodied the proposed removal of captured foreign flags during the Duke of Wellington's funeral in "Too Civil by Half!" in which a butcher commands his boy to hide the beef and plum pudding from the window rather than offend foreign pedestrians with such obvious markers of English power.[21] The plum pudding took on a textual life of its own in *Punch*. It became a sign for Englishness, and, occasionally, its globe-like form fit into a cartoon about British government. As cooks and politicians baked and served the Christmas pudding, they handled a conveniently shaped packaging of English democratic values. It is notable that while Christmas food came to stand for the English nation, artists refrained from mocking the signified national identity through depictions of food. Instead, the plum pudding became another incarnation of the anthropomorphized John Bull and, at times, Britannia.

Punch also employed visual imagery to construct a discordant narrative about Christmas cheer. More than the prose contributions, the illustrations of *Punch* most successfully argued that the holiday was a construction, something that the comic newspaper recognized and disclosed to its readers. Meanwhile, most Victorian periodicals merely contributed to the Christmas fantasy, blinding readers to the ideologies that contributed to the constructed Christmas. In a December 1876 number the focal full-page illustration shows Mr. Punch mixing such magical ingredients as a wet umbrella, a Christmas number, and a stack of bills to conjure a host of translucent images: Harlequin, a Father Christmas wrapped in sausages and drinking from a goblet, and a cornucopia all balanced atop a huge plum pudding. The artist has taken the symbols of *Punch's* version of Christmas (the bills and wet blanket) and constructed a more central, although less solid image of what idealistic readers may desire to see at Christmas (abundance).[22] While the large Father Christmas and Harlequin figments seem central, the reader can follow their origins to the cauldron full of unwelcome Christmas responsibilities at the bottom of the page. Even the illustration's spatial organization suggests that readers were more willing to view the fantasy embedded in Christmas than acknowledge the day-to-day realities that accompanied the ritual. In volume after volume, *Punch* cartoons cut through the construction of the rituals associated with the holiday in the interests of revealing the consumerism at the heart of the English Christmas.

Even before localized customs had been replaced with the politics of national Christmas rituals, the London-based *Punch* represented elements that came to be seen as Christmas standbys. Through visual propaganda, *Punch* contributed to the movement to standardize Christmas. The cauldron-brewing Mr. Punch example represents many illustrations that interweave the growing regard for Christmas with the readership's mythic ideals of a national identity. Perhaps in keeping with the newspaper's ironic sense of humor, *Punch* journalists were also in the forefront of undermining the newly established national rites. Thus, their critique led to the formation of an alternative Christmas narrative. As Christmas became more ingrained in middle-class Victorian society over the course of the 1840s, *Punch* turned to the stand it would take throughout the remaining decades of the long nineteenth century: satirizing Christmas rituals. Hardly a holiday season passed without a cartoon bemoaning the Christmas waits or post-Christmas bills. More often, this brand of jesting dominated the seasonal numbers. The seasonal street music credited with annoying rather than entertaining its audiences suggested an annual column, "Christmas Waits", which mocked political parties, groups, and personalities awaiting some event as in the 1849 case of "Mr. Disraeli waiting for something to turn up. The Farmers waiting for Protection."[23] Seasonal literature and songs may have mused that Christmas springs from hearth-love and benevolence, but *Punch* almost never fell prey to that mawkish December rhetoric. Instead, the comic newspaper candidly disillusioned its audience: Christmas equaled consumerism, a topic about which *Punch* was uniformly depreciatory. As it gained distance from its radical roots, *Punch* became a family paper, and its "solid and dependable readership wanted to see itself mirrored week by week; they wanted to absorb every detail of their own day to day lives and the humour that was in them."[24] Multiple pieces over the years gave voice to the ridiculous nature of middle-class Christmas culture. For example, one full-page illustration represents a miserable Father Christmas hiding from a pack of vicious dogs with collars marking them as "Waits," "Xmas Bills," and "Dinners."[25] Elsewhere articles imitate a curmudgeon with a quarrel against Christmas ("Christmas, in my mind, is simply associated with duns"), or a sadly disappointed Christmas idealist who bemoans the commercial depravity of the holiday.[26] In an 1877 piece, Mr. Punch outlines his plan to create a fictional Christmas number titled *A Dreary Christmas*, which will show the holiday "as it is," complete with the otherwise silenced scenes of the holiday: a family feud, a man beating his wife, and a debtors' prison.[27]

Through the periodical's portrayal of Christmas, *Punch* offered a new niche in the Christmas print market: the perspective of a Christmas cynic. Margaret Beetham has written that "each periodical positions its readers in terms which construct for that reader a recognizable self."[28] *Punch* instructed its audience to recognize the unrealistic hopes many Victorian celebrants blindly held about the new Christmas. For disillusioned readers, and for the readers who recognized the failings of the festivity on their own, *Punch* created an underworld of Christmas and a space in which Christmas cynics could revel in their identity. Meanwhile, non-Punchian Christmas fiction constantly rejected any derision of Christmas by redeeming the Scrooge-like cynics. In Anthony Trollope's "Christmas Day at Kirkby Cottage," first published in *Routledge's Christmas Annual* for 1870, Maurice Archer shocks and alienates Isabel, the girl he loves, when he says "Christmas is a bore" because it only consists of people eating more than usual and going to bed early. Maurice reduces Christmas to the iconic beef and pudding, a definition that the spiritual, idealistic Isabel abhors. When Isabel subsequently rejects Maurice's suit, the rash young man plans to abandon his estate and country in favor of a bachelor's life in Africa. Maurice must recant his *Punch*-like perspective before he can marry Isabel and gain access to the domestic setting that her Christmas performance epitomizes.[29] One imagines Maurice will henceforth only find relief for his Christmas complaints in the pages of *Punch.*

Punch used its particular interest in middle-class consumerism to ridicule the rise of Christmas literature. "Christmas Books for Men of Business" is a short sketch that comically inverts the values of the Christmas conversion story so often found in the maudlin Christmas book narratives. In the story, an uncle has just convinced his nephew to marry a wealthy widow rather than her young, penniless rival. The uncle chuckles over his nephew's financial success: "A hundred thousand in the Three Per Cents., eh? Thirty ditto in Railway Shares, eh? The whole of Bullion Terrace and Sterling's Rents—eh? Ha! ha! ha. A little better than ANGELINA and Camden Town—eh!"[30] The uncle's greed reverses the early Christmas book plot in which a compassionate uncle return from India in time to aid his noble but poor nephew to a marriage of love. *Punch* calls out the fantasy of the Christmas book here by mocking its financially disinterested marriage plot. The parody exposes a sensitivity to the real insecurities behind typical 1840s Christmas stories in which characteristically mushy narratives involve audiences emotionally and then cathartically cleanse readers from everyday greed without fully addressing practical solutions.

While *Punch* represented the growing, mid-century fascination with the employment of holiday symbols, the journalists made an early contribution to the tone that would characterize the Victorian Christmas. *Punch*'s Christmas rhetoric can be traced in a December 1841 *Punch* piece. Douglas Jerrold's "How Mr. Chokepear Keeps a Merry Christmas" is a short story about an Englishman who celebrates all the rituals of Christmas without the obligatory benevolence. After listing the businessman's festive routine, the piece mentions his estrangement from his adult child. The short story ends without the reunion scene that would become typical of subsequent Christmas stories. In fact, Mr. Chokepear reads like an unrepentant Scrooge, and the common motif of selfishness has led Richard Altick to write that Douglas Jerrold's Chokepear "harmonizes perfectly" with Dickens's *A Christmas Carol.*[31]

The 1849 "Preface" identifies Mr. Punch as "the embodiment of Christmas."[32] This self-styled title could more accurately pinpoint *Punch*'s role as a driving force in the ideology of charitable reform that came to be associated with Christmas. After all, *Punch* was the "first popular English periodical of any lasting consequence to wholeheartedly enlist itself in the humanitarian cause."[33] *Punch* creators made the most of Christmastime to advance their rhetoric. *Punch's* Christmas satire frequently attacked the uncharitable middle class by showcasing the voice of a misanthropist and allowing the reader to judge the unattractive effect for herself. In "Christmas in the Workhouse," one fictional, middle-class skeptic fears workhouse inhabitants will get too accustomed to roast beef after their relatively indulgent Christmas dinner and will steal from him to maintain their new beef craving. The speaker suggests scuttling ships full of paupers rather than risking his own roast beef's welfare.[34]

Punch led the way in identifying the workhouse as an ironically imperfect icon of mainstream Victorian Christmas practices. In 1843 Douglas Jerrold railed against the Poor Law and those who had opposed a plan to share holiday food traditions with workhouse inmates: "There had been talk . . . to regale certain workhouse people with a gill or so of ale, and a slice of pudding that Christmas might be to their senses something more than a name—that they might feel that a recollection of the Advent of CHRIST yet throbbed in the hearts of their richer fellow-Christians."[35] If Jerrold felt that a one-time inclusion in food rituals would envelop the pauper in an inclusive identity with his "fellows," other reformers disagreed. Many pieces began with workhouse voices anticipating their one-day holiday, followed by an editorial narrator descrying such short-lived charity. Printed just weeks before Jerrold's appeal, Thomas Hood's 1843 "The Pauper's Christmas Carol" is an empathetic meditation on the plight of a workhouse pauper for whom the one day of Christmas plenty and good spirits stands in stark contrast to the rest of his year:

> Treated like a welcome guest,
> One of Nature's social chain,
> Seated, tended on, and press'd—
> But when shall I be press'd again,
> Twice to pudding, thrice to beef,
> A dozen times to ale and beer?[36]

Hood's message—that the poor were typically unwelcome, hungry, and outcast for all but one day a year—changed the nature of the common refrain, "Christmas comes but once a year." Instead of an excuse for personal excess, Hood's pauper uses the platitude to note his one-day pass into a world of comfort and the brotherhood of man that is otherwise denied him.

Later in the century and outside the pages of *Punch*, George R. Sims took an even harsher look at indoor relief in his "Christmas Day in the Workhouse," a catchy poem that has inspired many parodies, both bawdy and otherwise. Sims's original poem attacked the middle-class mindset toward relief of the poor, which was institutionalized with the Poor Law of 1834. Sims employs a dramatic monologue, ostensibly given by a widower who shocks the well-dressed observers who have come to watch the poor enjoy their Christmas meal. In Sims's poem, the narrator accuses the heartless system of relief for his wife's Christmastime death since she had been denied outdoor aid and subsequently starved. Sims's narrator John resists being adopted by the culture of Christmas because he rejects the hypocrisy within the routine.[37]

Punch was not the only periodical to meditate on the workhouse's holiday celebrations. "Christmas-Day in the Workhouses" became the title of an annual section in *The Times* in which the newspaper synthesized information from various London workhouses to display the "comparative increase or decrease in pauperism," although one reporter notes that Christmas day hardly offers representative figures, "inclemency of the weather and the certainty of a Christmas dinner being a strong incentive to persons to claim parochial relief."[38] When two workhouses were left out of the statistical report in 1851, apologetic guardians wrote to the editor in defense of their unions' holiday "generosity." They did not want *Times* readers to think their unions were "unmindful of a generous feeling toward their poor at the season of the year when charity and beneficence are looked for on behalf of all those who are unable to help themselves." *The Times* also reported that it had indeed become a Christmas custom for some ratepayers to visit workhouses like the City of London union and St. Marylebone, which were open for an audience of curious onlookers. So, while Christmas served as a liminal space in which charity gained heightened status, guardians encouraged a tourist approach to class-based goodwill by opening union doors for voyeurs seeking the spectacle of benevolence and gratitude. During the 1850s, a pauper not "enjoying" indoor relief might look forward to this inducement to come indoors for Christmas: 6 oz. roasted beef, 13 oz. baked potato, 4 oz. bread, 1lb. plum pudding, 1 pint porter. Fruit, tea, tobacco, and snuff were added to the menu by the 1870s in some unions.[39]

Much may be said about the demands of the English Christmas food rituals that caused guardians and ratepayers to extend this identity-building performance to the destitute. When poets and satirists gave the poor any type of agency, they showed the poor rejecting rather than embracing the supposedly inclusive net of holiday custom. Reformers who blended social arguments with Christmas settings repeatedly argued that when the middle class tried to project Christmas rituals onto the poor, the attempt backfired. It is not enough, such pieces claimed, to begrudgingly invite the poor to the holiday feast. Middle-class champions of the poor, whose opinions were recorded far more frequently than those of the poor themselves, did not want to see the poor merely participate in the identity-building nature of the holiday; rather, they wanted a true reform that offered respectful assistance regardless of the day. Records like Eliza Cook's poem "Christmas Song of the Poor Man" point out that the performance of the holiday was beyond the reach of the pauper who was perhaps intentionally excluded from the frequent refrain "Merry Christmas, *Gentlemen*":

> 'Tis thus the ancient ditty runs;
> No tongues shall sing, no bells shall ring,
> For Poverty's low, haggard sons;[40]

Texts that explored the performance of the workhouse Christmas argued that, for the poor, the day did not signify the epitome of English charity; rather, it was only a once-a-year performance that underscored their status as social outcasts for the rest of the year. The frequent portrayal of the poor house Christmas attests to the brittle nature of the construct of mainstream Christmas.

Punch rhetoric encouraged a dream of a Christmas utopia in which the middle classes would reach out to the poor all year long. While noblesse oblige became a common cry once the new Christmas got going at the mid-century, *Punch* was among the public voices critiquing the nexus of the two topics from the start. The satirical posturing of *Punch* allowed the newspaper to construct a rhetoric of shame that compelled its middle-class readers to look beyond their own comfort during the season of indulgence.

Christmas celebrants in *Punch* either starved or overindulged. Gluttony took many forms, and overstuffed children often represented the nation's unleashed seasonal consumerism. In fact, *Punch* focused on the risk to children. For example, *Punch* commonly quipped that eating mince pie was only lucky for the doctor called in to help the overly indulged celebrant.[41] Sketches often depicted the day after the revel, reminding readers that Christmas luxuries could leech into everyday culpability. Christmas bills especially featured in the newspaper's cynicism for the season. Other periodicals would occasionally look forward to Christmas bills, but in *Punch* the bills were more prevalent than the presents that preceded them. While Christmas literature typically championed the rites of the holiday, *Punch* belittled them, saying, "at Christmas what man, with a proper respect for his stomach, can accept an invitation without making up his mind to heartburn, nightmare, and all the other horrors of indigestion?"[42]

Punch pieces regularly warned against overconsumption. For example, a "Song of the Festive Season" reminds a young woman that her new dress will be old next year, and "Choosing Christmas Toys" offers dialogue overheard in a toy shop in which greedy children whine for toys and an overly indulgent mother and grandmother give spoiled little Percy a toy to silence him.[43] Elsewhere *Punch* redirected celebrants to the abysmal conditions of workers involved in the production of their Christmas treats:

> That gorgeous velvet, that makes pale all tissues where they've laid it—
> What if the weaver's passing by, whose wasted fingers made it?
> Oh, richly broidered are those scarves; but think of her who, sighing,
> Drew the sore stitches—o're her work for hunger slowly dying.[44]

Punch authors occasionally broke from the cynical Christmas mold, but the most conspicuous deviation came as they began to foster a Christmas-used-to-be-better rhetoric in the 1880s and 1890s. Despite the consistent ridicule of Christmas habits all along, pieces in the last two decades of the century began to look fondly upon previous Christmases, even as they bemoaned the season at hand. For example, "The Fiction of the Season" describes two Christmases. The piece casts an 1869 Christmas as merry, calling it "Yesterday's Geniality." Meanwhile, a character in the contrasted sketch of the dismal Christmas at hand, that of 1889, concocts a poison from holly berries and ends his own Christmas suffering.[45] *Punch* enthusiasts who had faithfully bought the bound volumes could refer back to the 1869 Christmas season to review that this recent past was in fact no ideal holiday. In fact, *Punch* had run an 1869 article in which a Professor Jorks refused to keep Christmas rituals properly, echoing earlier letters from anti-Christmas curmudgeons.[46] In the last decades of the century, *Punch* rewrote its own history of Christmas in print so that the genial Christmas of the past always stayed within living memory but outside of current accessibility.

Authors added a new, late-century complaint to the score against Christmas as sketches and articles repeatedly referenced the traditional family quarrel. "Christmas on View in 1988" narrates a futuristic family's attempt to replicate the "antiquated" Christmas traditions of 1888. While the celebrants cannot fathom the use or amusement of Christmas cards, pantomimes, or live church services ("it seemed rather senseless leaving our telephones idle"), they do manage to perform one aspect of the traditional Christmas correctly: "We are just as good as our forefathers were in carrying out a fine say-what-you-like do-what-you-like jolly old Christmas family row!"[47] The comic newspaper took advantage of the liminal quality of Christmas to explore times past and present, taking care to limit imaginative time travel to Christmas scenes. Because Christmas was a time set apart from the normal working year, a time filled with heightened expectations of family, the season allowed texts to magnify the nostalgia expected of normal celebrants.

Despite its frequent position as the Devil's advocate of Christmas, *Punch* actively encouraged a particular type of midwinter festival in which the middle classes fulfilled their duty to the poor and enjoyed a minimalist celebration that decentralized consumerism. In one 1859 piece a contributor for once drops the satirical posturing to candidly appeal for a different sort of celebration. He writes,

> I believe, the fact is, that we try to be too demonstratively jolly on that day, and that if we were only to let ourselves alone, and not overdo and force the hilarity and joviality quite so much as we try to do, we should get on much better, and Christmas Day would be socially, as it ought to be and naturally is, the happiest and most blessed day in all the year.[48]

Such a message of simplicity is only rarely found in other periodicals like *Household Words*, the *Illustrated London News*, and, later, *Belgravia*, because they followed the trend of catering to ideal versions of the powerful celebration of middle-class Victorian ideology wrapped up in Christmas. To the twenty-first-century ear, *Punch's* slightly less idealistic take on seasonal expectations sounds refreshingly frank amid the more typical hymns venerating hearth-love and nostalgia.

Thumbing its nose at its own consumer cautions, *Punch* blatantly marketed its bound volumes specifically as Christmas presents. *Punch* catered to the December need for Christmas reading even before the publishing industry developed a new December focus to put out Christmas numbers and Christmas books. So, between bashing excess and advocating consumption of Christmas reading, *Punch* educated its middle-class readership on Christmas spending. Modern Christmas Victoriana seems to have settled into a distinctly Dickensian mold. However, many mid-century personalities gained access into a Christmas market after *Punch* paved the way by instructing the reader in Christmas consumerism.

A staple of other periodicals, the Christmas profile appeared often enough to warrant *Punch*'s 1877 mockery of the genre. The *Punch* profile fictionalizes outlandish regional superstitions like not being able to add codicils to wills or marry second cousins with false teeth during the holiday season.[49] More factual profiles were a common approach to Christmas in periodicals. Profiles on Christmas in other countries initially ran free of nostalgia in the early decades of the century, but they eventually became rife with expectations of melancholy longing. Dozens if not hundreds of profiles appeared in print throughout the nineteenth century, and the approach authors took to Christmas abroad demonstrates the evolution of the English possession of the holiday. The issues of *The Mirror* from the 1830s repeatedly included short profiles such as "Christmas in Mexico" (1832) and "Christmas in Italy" (1833), offering the schedule of Christmas in the title location without comparing it to any version of the English Christmas, which was itself in a nascent state. Even English locations received the same antiquarian treatment, as in "Christmas in Hereford" (1832), which was treated just like the exotic Mexican profile, at least in *The Mirror*. Regional profiles continued sporadically throughout the century. By 1850, the Christmas profile for the most part switched focus to how English people celebrated Christmas abroad. Profiling articles and short pieces of fiction were never called "An Indian Christmas," but rather "Christmas in India," as if the author could not expect a colonial location to absorb Christmas since Christmas was so entirely identified as English. *Belgravia* pieces belittled Christmas in America for copying the English Christmas and noted that Christmases in Canada were losing their local color but resembled English rituals.[50] Profiles maintained that Christmas could at best be imperfectly transported to India, Africa, Egypt, and other colonial and emigrant destinations. The holiday underscored the celebrants' distance from the inspiration for the holiday.

As conductor of *Household Words*, Charles Dickens reinforced the Christmas profile in 1850 when the weekly's very first Christmas number featured a collection of profiles in poetry, fiction, and nonfiction. With a well-developed Christmas narrative in place by 1850, the profilers could ask their reader to imagine nonstandard Christmases such as "Christmas at Sea," "Christmas in India," and "Christmas in the Bush." Contributors did not limit the nonstandard Christmas to exotic locations. "Christmas among the London Poor and Sick" profiles the experience of London workhouse inmates on Christmas day, and Richard H. Horne's "Household Christmas Carols" imagines the voices of disabled children with "The Deformed Child's Carol," "The Sick Child's Carol," and "The Deaf and Dumb Child's Carol." The middle-class Christmas had enough clout that atypical Christmas encounters presented a constant contrast with the ideal narrative, the one that *Punch* simultaneously mocked. Considering that less than two decades earlier print matter had focused on developing that ideal narrative of Christmas, the ideal very quickly became the standard contrast to the deaf and dumb child's experience with the holiday.

Exotic Christmas profiles, both fictional and nonfictional, follow three common tropes. The first, the sensory differences between the English Christmas at home, emphasizes the presumed failure of the performance abroad. In one piece, a freshly landed gentleman cadet hears the muezzin call instead of English church bells and cannot make sense of the disconnect between his perception of Christmas and the reality of an Egyptian climate: "Christmas-day! why there ain't no snow upon the house-tops, neither is there any frost, no more than there is the phantom of one of those dear, muddy, muggy, murky, dank fogs of loved old England."[51] The celebrant has so completely accepted the 1850s English Christmas narrative, he expects the narrative to enact itself regardless of his setting.

Articles frequently follow the second pattern, telling how, when faced with the discrepancy of 25 December and the philosophy of home the holiday espouses, celebrants force English custom on their new location. Profiles repeatedly emphasize this second trope: the lengths to which English immigrants, perhaps even second generation immigrants, go to reenact their ideal Christmas narrative down to the holly-like greens, fires in the grates, and holiday foods. Food is especially valuable in the locations deficient in English cultural currency, as one article shows via the reception of plum puddings and mince pies in India: "All the way from England they come in carefully closed tins, and bilious men and women on that occasion eat of them valiantly, and defy their livers."[52]

The Victorian home cry at Christmas, a third approach to the profile, often blends the semblance of nonfiction with a heightened emotionalism more in keeping with fiction. An 1843 poem reminds readers that Old Christmas "loves to see old comrades round, in their accustomed places, / And kindred kindly meeting,"[53] and, like a year-long game of musical chairs, Victorians caught up in new migration patterns would imagine rushing to fill their traditional seats in time for the midwinter festival. Christmas books like *The Moorland Cottage* and *The Snow Storm* emphasized the symbolic nature of home/nation during the Christmas reading experience, but periodicals allowed for journalism-influenced profiles that focused on nonstandard Christmases to highlight the traditions of the home Christmas. Exotic profiles depicted celebrants using Christmas to worship the English home, as in the case of polar exploration parties, in which "Englishmen have read the prayers of Christmas Day, and have drunk to friends at home, and sung home songs."[54] In *Household Words'* "Christmas in the Navy," a young sailor "got maudlin, and cried at the sight of some preserved pears, which reminded him of home. Several fellows became sentimental, and wondered whether their relatives in England were 'keeping it up.' "[55]

Regardless of its setting, the standard holiday short fiction in periodicals was rife with scenes of family reunions, but émigrés were often beyond the call of a Christmas homecoming. Instead of a physical reunion, periodicals showed émigrés and civil officials enacting one-sided emotional exercises rather than physical reunions. Christmas offered the nation that liminal moment to pause, like a mother of grown, emigrated children, to wonder how well the offspring continued family traditions. In an 1894 article in *London Society*, the Christmas Eve moon peeks into Indian narratives that testify to the faithfulness of motherly love. With Christmas turning the emigrants' thoughts home to mother England, the moon plays the role of the panopticon watching and evaluating England's children. One cadet decides against suicide when his Christmas thoughts remind him of his loving, far distant mother. The piece ends with another sorrowful mother meditating on the sons she has sent to the safer English climate. She thinks about them so intently she awakens one youngster from his Christmas Eve sleep, and he lisps, "I thinked it was mother, but perhaps I only waked because it was Christmas Day."[56] This was the expected role of the fictional emigrant at Christmas: to reminisce about friends and Christmases of the past, and to worship the English Christmas by regretting one's absence from that brightest hearth-flame. Being able to imagine the loved ones engaged in annual rituals was seen to comfort the homesick who used the liminal space of Christmas to reconnect emotionally with their homeplace identity. Like the Christmas novels that used emotion to cathartically repair middle-class guilt, shorter pieces imagining immigrant longing used tearful scenes of homesickness to alleviate fears of a splintered national family. Fears of forgetting and dangers of obsessing haunted these ubiquitous profiles, but they typically propped the vitality of home identity wrapped up in Christmas. Christmas was a locus point, a touchstone for reasserting who a person was in his family, how he saw himself, and how he reacted to separation from the nourishing home community. Christmas was sold as a tie back to the home, even for people thousands of miles away.

If fictional émigrés and servants of empire were anything like their real counterparts, they might be imagined to have imbibed their expectations of a home Christmas from print matter that taught them how to celebrate and how to read Christmas. Periodicals provided that vital component of Christmas in print: the review. Periodicals like the *London Times*, the *Graphic*, the *Morning Chronicle*, and *Fraser's Magazine* informed the reader about what to expect in Christmas books, numbers, and annuals, and many periodicals also advertised Christmas books for sale. Some advertisements listed the components of other periodicals' Christmas numbers so consumers could feel forewarned about the contents of their periodical purchases. *Punch* joined in by parodying and thereby adding to the institutional quality of well-worn Christmas narratives by Dickens; the comic newspaper also regularly mocked Christmas audience fads, including the ubiquitous Christmas ghost story, a seasonal phenomenon to which I now turn.

CHAPTER 4

GHOST STORIES AT CHRISTMAS

In terms of genre, ghostly tales at Christmas knew no bounds. Christmas ghosts flitted into novels, poems, periodical short stories, and even collections of nonfiction history. An 1873 *Belgravia* ghost story opens with one entrepreneurial character, Tom Chester, and his plan to commodify a haunted house: "Rejoice with me . . . Yes, rejoice with me; I have discovered a new sensation."[1] Editors of magazines had been counting on this very sensation to support Christmas sales for some twenty years by the time *Belgravia* printed Maurice Davies's story, but the print tradition goes back even further and into other genres. Tom has discovered a haunted house, and he plans to investigate the ghost with the intention of renting the space out for séances, since "[s]pirits are decidedly looking up just now."[2] Haunting spirits and manor-house ghosts had been "looking up" since the 1820s when annuals relied on ghosts, but a new spate of magazines and journals of the 1850s turned to the oral tradition of Christmas ghost stories as publishers sought to fill special Christmas numbers. Creators of the different genres of Christmas print material sought to harness the ghost story and channel its cultural appeal into new and profitable formats.

All of the Christmas genres I have discussed so far regularly exploited the early association between the holiday and the ghost story. In their helpful overview of book history, John O. Jordan and Robert L. Patten state that "future historians will have to cope with the ambiguities of a print culture—the ways in which it supersedes without erasing oral and visual cultures and spawns its own imitations, rejections, and assimilations."[3] Studies of English ghost stories like Julia Briggs's *Night Visitors* trace the explosion of the genre to periodical literature. Before they found a home in nineteenth-century periodicals, ghost stories had a vibrant oral existence during the eighteenth century, although, by its very nature, oral tradition is difficult to trace. E.J. Clery has investigated written accounts of eighteenth-century ghost story telling, and she argues that oral ghost-story traditions led to a late-eighteenth-century trend in published ghost stories.[4] Tradition suggested that the Christmas fire was an excellent setting for sharing ghost narratives, but tradition offers few clues to the longevity of this particular Christmas custom. David Parker has identified the earliest published item that blended ghosts with Christmas as *Round about our Coal Fire* from the 1730s.[5] Washington Irving celebrates this English custom in *The Sketch Book of Geoffrey Crayon, Gent*: "I found the company seated round the fire, listening to the parson . . . dealing forth strange accounts of the popular superstitions, and legends of the surrounding country."[6] Thomas Hervey's *The Book of Christmas* could not overlook ghostly tales in his chronicle of Christmas-keeping. While Seymour illustrates a gothic interior, Hervey connects the ghost narratives to the ballads of long ago: "The song and the story, the recitation and the book read aloud are, in town and in village, mansion and farmhouse, amongst the universal resources of the winter nights now, as they or their equivalents have at all times been."[7] While other elements of the seventeenth- and eighteenth-century Christmas were cast aside in favor of the dominant London midwinter narrative, ghost stories survived and, in print at least, multiplied. References to ghost stories at Christmas became much more numerous after 1800, and the ritual was both accepted and well practiced by the end of the 1830s.[8]

Ghost stories continued to be a popular genre for Christmas publication throughout the nineteenth century. The annuals of the 1820s employed ghosts as a staple element to their refined commodification of literature, and two of Walter Scott's ghost stories appeared seasonally in the very first *Keepsake* (1828). With the revitalization of Christmas in the 1840s, the old oral tradition that had smoldered in the annuals burst into a flame that would light the midwinter print market for the rest of the century. Dickens and his audience were well aware that *A Christmas Carol*, a "Ghostly little book," was built on an oral tradition, but their historical perspective faded enough over time to require a critic's reminder in 1869: "The season and spirits were allied long before Mr. Dickens's 'Carol' "[9] Nonetheless, Dickens had enough of an influence on expectations of the genre to cause an astounding ratio of uncanny elements in the first wave of Christmas books. All of Dickens's Christmas books except *The Battle of Life* involve some sort of ghostly interference or a spiritually viewed space set apart from normal time, what Harry Stone has called "a magically telescoped survey of the protagonist's life."[10] Dickensian Christmas ghosts include Scrooge's Christmas spirits, *The Chimes*' goblins of the bells, *Cricket on the Hearth*'s Household Spirits, and the ghost's bargain that first removes then returns Redlaw's memories. Other authors occasionally use the supernatural to enact change in their characters. In the Mayhews' Eastern tale for Christmas (1846) the Good Genius of Industry teaches the protagonist a lesson, and in *The Faces in the Fire* (1849) the Spirit of Good rebukes a writer for doubting its existence during the climax. Like the fairy in that other Christmas genre, the pantomime, supernatural agents enter the narrative to alter reality and, in the books, to bring about a Christmas utopia of reunion and spiritual redemption.

Christmas annuals and post-1840s books for sale at Christmas wildly expanded the market for ghosts, but these were less soulful ghosts. Nonetheless, they were beloved as a part of Christmas in print, causing one reviewer to write in 1869 "if they have ceased to teach touching morality and only turn their attention to the discovery of lost wills and the elucidation of the mysteries of murders! if they have deteriorated—no matter, they are ghosts still for all that." The reviewer also remarks on the prevalence of ghosts: "it is pleasant . . . to rejoice that the Christmas 'Annuals' and 'Numbers' contain a plentiful supply of good seasonable ghosts and kindred horrors. Let Midsummer monopolize her fairies; she cannot deprive Christmas of her ghosts."[11] Christmas issues were "one of the main sources for the Victorian ghost story."[12] Dickens's Christmas numbers were the best known of the bunch, and they provided an outlet for the ghost stories of several women writers, including Amelia B. Edwards, Elizabeth Gaskell, and Rosa Mulholland. Perhaps because of the sensations related to spiritualism, 1873 seems to have been a high point in Christmas ghost story publication in books as well as periodicals, and this year saw Richard Bentley and Son publish Rhoda Broughton's *Tales for Christmas Eve* (1873), a collection of five stories previously published in *Temple Bar*. Despite the title, not one of the stories mentions Christmas. It is rather the genre of the ghost story that makes this text occasional reading. Ghosts became so ubiquitous that a humorous piece in *Once a Week* quipped, "[t]he man who writes an interesting ghost tale is a general benefactor, but he should have mercy upon those poor old ghosts who have walked their legs off in our service, and whose horrors are worn threadbare by this time, and give us in their stead something that may make us shudder and not laugh."[13] Familiarity was breeding contempt in one reader, at least, but this did not stop the march of the ghosts in print.

Despite the popularity of the Christmas ghost, the midwinter did not own the patent on ghostly tales, and plenty appeared in periodicals throughout the year. The ghost narratives I deal with here all come from print made available for midwinter reading unless otherwise specified. As Srdjan Smajic has written, "ghosts evidently belong everywhere in literature—and consequently one might say nowhere in particular."[14] Ghosts certainly belong in a study of Christmas in print, but narrowing down precisely how they function there poses challenges. Tennyson's *In Memoriam* shows how Christmas serves as an annual moment to connect with memories of those who no longer meet at the Christmas reunion, and Christmas offered additional and, moreover, traditional leisure reading rituals that allowed celebrants to consider how the supernatural functioned in their increasingly technological environment. According to the Howitts' biographer Amice Lee, William Howitt vehemently believed that "spiritualism mitigated against the fierce materialism of the age."[15] For those who believed as Howitt did, and even for those whose ideas about spiritualism were not as extreme, the uncanny offered an escape from modernity and consumption. Christmas, with its conflicted consuming/giving narratives, embraced the uncanny as a defense against overwhelming materialism.

As a result of the growing interest in spiritualism, Christmas stories were not the only means of comodifying ghosts in the nineteenth century. The phantasmagoria spectacles, in which illusionists used magic lanterns to replicate a ghostly experienced, arrived in England in 1801. By the 1860s the middle classes could buy their own magic lantern complete with directions for "How to Raise a Ghost" for their own domestic amusement. Moreover, the phantasmagoria effect was used in an 1862 theatrical version of Dickens's *The Haunted Man*, leading to "one of the longest theatrical runs of the time." Consumers could blend Christmas tales with the visually uncanny experience either in their homes or at the theater.[16] The effect of amateur spectral encounters would have been very different from the type of emotionalism of the virtues-to-order style of Christmas books. Instead of thrilling to cathartic plots, readers of ghost stories shivered at the potential for the uncanny.

Although uncanny, midwinter stories were a folk tradition that Hardy went on to commemorate in *Under the Greenwood Tree*. However, not everyone had a willing audience or such an able storyteller. During the 1849 Christmas season, a narrator entertains his perfect holiday "visitors" who cost him nothing and leave as soon as he desires: "In a word, they are a few favourite red-edged, round-cornered, musty old books."[17] He delves into his seventeenth-century books to experience a tradition of ghosts "at this their own season."[18] The scene of a bibliophile celebrating a solitary Christmas with his costly and therefore limited library of ghost-filled books anticipates the explosion of cheap, accessible Christmas numbers in the following decades. Within the next twenty years, a reader in a similar situation could turn to newly manufactured ghost narratives in periodical Christmas offerings rather than those found in moldering old books. Ghost stories led to narrative adaptations of the reading circle, and they often opened with a frame that represents the story circle.

The print market altered what had been celebrated as a locally based, often oral tradition of performance into a narrative structure: the frame tale. Unlike the bibliophile's rare old books, periodicals tended to adapt ghost tales into frame-tale narratives as a way of capturing the eighteenth-century story-telling circle in print. It now became the custom of an individual reader accessing a national "fireside" to open a Christmas number and read about fictional ghosts rather than entertain the local legends common to oral tradition. This allowed the urban middle-class and working-class reader to escape into the idealized Christmas of the nobility, about whom many ghost stories—especially those in the 1850s and 1860s—were written. Ebenezer Scrooge's lonely existence represents what must have been a reality for many a Victorian reader. Scrooge exemplifies how mid-Victorian capitalism and industry had broken down the extended families and communities of the past. As a child he read exotic fantasies, but had the adult miser decided to find Christmas cheer without the help of the three spirits, his most accessible means of doing so would have been to enhance his bowl of gruel with a Christmas number. Therein he would instantly have found himself enmeshed in an artificial community like the ones the ghosts reconstruct for him. Frame tales narrated and commodified the practice of family reading. Richard Altick calls the middle-class Victorian reading circle "the most familiar and beloved of domestic institutions,"[19] but urban living led to splintered families among the working-classes and middle-classes. The avalanche of Christmas literary periodicals showcased a trend toward commodified, printed versions of ghost stories, replacing the oral or ballad tradition with a prepackaged version of a Christmas custom.

The family story-telling circle was idealized, but the cheap Christmas numbers of magazines made ghost stories consumable and allowed for a single person's participation in the custom. Illustrations of ghost-story-telling circles appeared in *Punch* and *Belgravia* and informed audiences' reading realities. An 1867 illustration in *Belgravia* shows a happy family circle, drawn closer together by the paterfamilias' presentation of a ghostly narrative about,

> the ghost of Lady Clare,
> Or the phantom on the stair
> Near the panel where the stains
> Reveal'd the crime,[20]

The shadow springing from the mother's chair suggests a haunting figure lurking just outside the circle. The consumer has adapted to eavesdropping on story-telling circles. Illustrations of ghost story-telling in *Belgravia* and *Punch* do not show the orator reading from a book; instead, the print medium lionized the oral tradition, while at the same time and within just a few pages the periodical commodified that tradition's printed descendant.

The frame tale, as it initially appeared in Christmas numbers like *Household Word's The Seven Poor Travellers* (1854) offered a chance for contributors to create characters who volunteer stories to pass the time in some constructed situation, the creation of the editor. After experimenting with a frameless series of stories exchanged by a group in *A Round of Stories by the Christmas Fire* (1852), Dickens instituted the frame tale as a holiday staple in his Christmas numbers. The narrative format of a framing situation became a common one in periodicals' ghost tales and continued to be the most memorable aspect of Dickens's Christmas numbers throughout the rest of *Household Words* and *All the Year Round.*[21] Narrative frames were markers of the holiday season, and they were modified to incorporate various types of print into the reading season. For example, an 1859 *Once a Week* piece contains ghost-free embedded stories told by several men doing honor to the Christmas season.[22] Imitators often failed to sustain as many embedded stories as Dickens's original pieces, and the frame could also introduce a single tale. John Sheehan wrote a ghost story for *Temple Bar* that begins by introducing Paddy MGauran and his Christmas story circle before moving into the sole embedded ghostly narrative.[23] "Old Hooker's Ghost; or, Christmas Gambols at Huntingfield Hall" from *Bentley's Miscellany* (1865) chronicles Christmas pastimes including a story circle and an embedded ghost tale.[24] In this and dozens of other ghostly tales, a frame with a holiday setting leads into the often Christmas-free embedded narrative.

Because of the ghostly nature of the Christmas story-telling circle, Christmas book sales also became involved in the debate over Victorian spiritualism. For example, Rhoda Broughton ended many of the tales in her *Tales for Christmas Eve* with statements asserting the truth of the stories. If they did not end that way, they often opened with assertions of truth: "the incident...however improbable, is, I have reason to believe, strictly true."[25] Catherine Crowe, author of what Vanessa D. Dickerson calls "a Victorian bible of supernaturalism," marketed a volume of frame-tale ghost stories specifically for Christmas consumption.[26] In the preface of *Ghosts and Family Legends: A Volume for Christmas* (1859), Crowe situates herself as narrator of a text that recounts her last country house Christmas. The holiday party had taken a planned format of ghost story telling, and Crowe promises to record the tales as nearly as she can to the original manner of their telling. As a result, the embedded stories exhibit particularly inelegant writing, but, since this only grows out of Crowe's attempt to capture her real experience as a lucky member of a communal circle, it models what a lonely reader may not have an opportunity to enjoy. The reader becomes a legitimized eavesdropper. More important to the debate over spiritualism is the second half of Crowe's *Ghosts and Family Legends: A Volume for Christmas.* This otherwise Christmasless section focuses on "real" legends associated with people with enough pedigree to also have a supernatural death notice or a haunting. This need to authenticate ghost tales may derive from the evolution of local legends into mass-marketed printed stories. Regional stories passed down through oral storytelling would come with an element of authenticity because they were connected to nearby locations and told by trusted family or friends. How could ghosts be as scary when they had become entirely separated from any real location or teller? Authors' weak assertions of truth reminded readers that ghost stories were not only holiday rites, but they also attempted to explain peoples' perception of their spiritual world.

Ghost stories cannot be defined as narratives with supernatural appearances because so many of the ghost tales conclude by undermining the reality of ghosts when characters discover a completely natural explanation for a supposed haunting. Dickens's periodicals contained both types of ghosts. Compared to *Household Words, All the Year Round* notably featured an increase in fiction and nonfiction pieces about ghosts, and Dickens used this forum to enter the Christmastime debate about spiritualism. One frame tale Christmas number of special relevance to this study, *The Haunted House* (1859), required contributors to write ghostless ghost stories because Dickens wanted to underscore his critical skepticism of spiritualism. The premise of the frame narrative developed out of an earlier *All the Year Round* article Dickens wrote criticizing spiritualism and the resulting epistolary dispute William Howitt took up with the novelist. Dickens wrote back: "if you know of any haunted house whatsoever within the limits of the United Kingdom where nobody can live, eat, drink, sit, stand, lie or sleep, without spirit-molestation, I believe I can produce a gentleman who will readily try its effect in his own person."[27] Dickens went to one of the houses the Howitts suggested, but he only ate one dinner there before calling his experiment a success. Much of the 1859 frame tale goes toward mocking spiritualism and the belief in any ghosts outside of paper covers. The host-narrator encounters a "google-eyed" Rapper in his train compartment and depicts spirit writing as a ridiculous pastime.[28] In a cool, always confident tone, he recounts the communal imagination that goes toward turning a dreary house into a supposedly haunted house, and he lays the lore of the ghost by dismissing the impressionable servants, using a gun to threaten a meddling youth, and inhabiting the house with his rationalist friends. Unlike Dickens himself, the characters in *The Haunted House*'s frame tale prolong the test for several months, and they tell the tales of their ghost-free hauntings on Twelfth Night. In keeping with *A Christmas Carol* philosophy, the company enjoys the redemptive quality of the past. For example, the narrator/host explains he has been haunted only by "the ghost of my own childhood."[29] Maurice Davies would play over the same testing of spiritualism in the 1873 Christmas ghost story that heralds a haunted house as a sensation. Two men who doubt "dancing tables" and "Mr Home's 'levitation' and spiritualistic ladies' drawings, &c." wish to ascertain the reality of ghosts set apart from commercialized spiritualism, so they spend "A Night in A Ghost-Chamber."[30] What they end up proving is that a draught can scare a roomful of young men just as successfully as a visible apparition. Dickens's and Davies's stories represent the many emphatically ghost-free hauntings that take place in the pages of Christmastime periodicals. Such stories adopt the ghost tradition but deny the presence of ghosts in the real world.

Ghost stories emanate from aristocratic, middle-class, and working-class characters, but a large proportion of the story-telling circles represented in the Christmas numbers take place at a country house, and the prevalence of rural, gentrified settings in the ghost stories found in Victorian periodicals suggests an idealization of the country house Christmas. Crowe's country house frame tale, subtitled *A Volume for Christmas*, epitomizes the practice. In the country house ghost story so common at Christmas, the detective figure and, at times, the ghost, police aristocratic bloodlines. The middle-class readership aspired to Christmas in the country and, moreover, Christmas with the wealthy, but readers depended on the ghost genre to give them this invitation. Meanwhile, the early Christmas novels rarely take an aristocratic setting, and non-supernatural Christmas stories and poems featured in periodicals range across the economic spectrum, frequently giving attention to middle-class benevolence to the poor. Christmas books by Catherine Gore (*The Snow Storm, New Year's Day*) and Mary Elizabeth Braddon (*The Christmas Hirelings*) are notably aristocratic exceptions. Christmas books by authors such as Farjeon, Gaskell, Thackeray, Trollope, Dickens, and Ruskin follow the actions of middle-class or working-class characters.

The concern with gentility and ghosts appeared in the early annuals that were designed for conspicuous consumption and the upward-looking middle classes. The 1829 *Keepsake* contained Walter Scott's "The Tapestried Room" in which a homesick soldier returning from the war in America finds an idealized castle estate, but is shaken in his belief in the purity of England when he discovers a murderous and incestuous ghost in his chamber. This ghost narrative is unsettling because it places incest and moral decay in the heart of aristocratic, romanticized England. Scott develops what will be a prototype for ghost stories when he keeps any supporting details for the proof of a haunting vague in the interest of remaining intentionally ambiguous about the spectral.[31] If the uncanny remains indefinite, the typical setting is never in question.

Richard Altick finds a largely middle-class readership for the shilling monthlies, and offers escapism as a reason for the proliferation of aristocracy-based stories in family papers like the *Family Herald* and the *London Journal*.[32] Ouida's "Holly Wreaths and Rose Chains, or How We Spent Christmas at Deerhurst" (*Bentley's Miscellany* 1859) exposes the cultural superiority of a country house Christmas:

> Deerhurst was a capital house to spend a Christmas in. It was the house of an English gentleman, with even the dens called bachelors' rooms comfortable and luxurious to the last extent: a first-rate stud, a capital billiard-table, a good sporting country, [and] pretty girls to amuse one with when tired of the pink.[33]

This "capital" Christmas leads into a narrative that involves an education in ghost stories as a coquette learns to appreciate her truest admirer, a man headed for Balaklava, when she meditates on the failed love story of the house's legendary ghost.[34] The interest in the aristocracy took on a national importance during the Christmas season as the readership base sought to enjoy the festivities on a more genteel level through escapist reading.

Stories feature aristocratic ghosts as ethereal imprints of high-born privilege. Margaret Oliphant's "The Lady's Walk" shows to what lengths a ghost will go to retain her family's access to the country house. In this story, published in *Longman's Magazine* for Christmas consumption in 1882, a kindly family ghost who inhabits a favorite walk keeps prophesying danger for the family, and, when catastrophe strikes, the ghost lady helps to save the family home by encouraging a guest to pay off the debt with his new inheritance. The final part of the story takes place during a Christmas visit. The ghost lady serves as a parallel for the narrator's love interest in the story, the oldest daughter of the otherwise motherless family. Like the daughter, the ghost feels a deep but helpless responsibility for the family's welfare; both are also tied to the family, the ghost by her haunting and the daughter by her inability to marry or otherwise leave the family due to a fear that, if the angel in the house leaves, the large family will lose its stabilizing element. The narrator and savior of the ancestral country house depicts his travels from London up into the Scottish countryside for traditional holiday recreation. By narrating his adventure, he allows readers to accompany him on his flights from the metropolis. The reader's interest in the country house Christmas saves the idealized space for posterity as much as the ghost's warning saves it for her descendents.

Belgravia editor M.E. Braddon specifically chose the magazine's title for the snob appeal associated with the wealthy London neighborhood, and the majority of Christmas ghost stories that appeared under her editorship maintained that tactic.[35] As one would expect of a magazine whose "*raison d'etre* was sensation fiction and constructions of 'high society,'" elitism informs numerous *Belgravia* Christmas ghost stories, especially those that exhibit a fear of degeneracy through questionable marriages.[36] Under Braddon's editorship, *Belgravia* printed "Jack Layford's Friend; With an Account of how he Laid the Ghost, A Christmas Story" (December 1869), in which not a ghost but a governess haunts Jack, the heir to a landed estate. The deceptive governess hopes to scare him into marrying her. Fortunately for Jack, a good friend takes a break from enjoying the country rituals of Christmas and unmasks the "ghost." This faux-ghost narrative shows how the educated laborer is not allowed into the inner sanctum of the country house family. However, the story also expresses a tension concerning incest; Jack's mother had been against first cousin marriage, and the governess chooses this theme for her haunting to scare Jack out of his devotion to his beautiful cousin. The ghost narrative both denies the middle-class and working-class entrance into the sanctum of the landed family while also revealing the fear of inbreeding among the upper class. The theme pops up in many aristocratic ghost stories. Ada Buisson contributed a ghost tale to *Belgravia* in which a wealthy man awaits the death his family ghost has announced, and the doctor who accompanies him to his mansion and sits by his deathbed is shocked to discover that the spirit's claw-like hand (missing the third finger) is replicated in the haunted man's otherwise dazzling widow. There is no question of foul play, but the family curse physically inhabits the woman's body.[37] Her beauty turns foul as the reader is left pondering the mystery of why the man's family banshee resembles his wife.

Thomas Anstey Guthrie, who eventually became a writer for *Punch*, published "The Curse of the Catafalques" under his pseudonym F. Anstey. The story replays the theme of degeneracy in a sardonic way. Although *Cornhill Magazine* ran the story in August 1882, the Christmas setting suggests that it was written within the holiday ghost tradition. A young, unsuccessful Englishman comes from Australia, impersonates a relative of the Catafalques to gain entrance to their home, and then woos the baronet's daughter. The Catafalques tell him that, as a suitor, he must enter the gray room on Christmas Eve and face the family Curse, a vague yet terrifying presence. He runs rather than face the Curse. The Catafalques represent everything that a middle-class urban or colonial British citizen could desire: pedigree, wealth, and a fine London home. What the narrator realizes is that impersonating the gentry and invading their home at Christmas—as millions of readers were doing via the Christmas numbers—allows him to immerse himself in the much-desired aristocratic ghost narratives. Ironically, the Curse is the administrator of the Catafalques patrimony, a type of ghostly accountant. Anstey's story shows a astute awareness of the tropes of Christmas ghosts: the family mansion, the family curse, and, occasionally, a stranger who may "lay the ghost." Anstey makes fun of the common scenario from the inside. His portrayal of the morbid, impotent Catafalques and their inability to marry off their daughter and continue the family patrimony shows Anstey undermining the trope of the ideal upper-class Christmas. Here Christmas among the affluent has taken on an atmosphere of decay, reverting to gothic sentimentality rather than a healthy and invigorating hospitality of Hervey's baronial halls.

If the aristocracy was the standard subject, laboring characters were often the conduits for ghostly tales. For example, in one brief framing device the ladies of the house access ghostly tales through their cook, who tells her story during her Christmas dinner preparations: "But, if I take up the morning with story-telling, how will my mince-meat get done?"[38] Fictional middle-class renters and homeowners often rely on their servants to tell them about the local hauntings, even those about their own house, causing Jennifer Uglow to call it a "class conspiracy": "the butcher knows, the grocer knows, the caretakers, nursemaids, cooks and servants certainly know, but the prosperous families who move into haunted spaces are kept in the dark until the crisis comes."[39] Time and again renters looking for a bargain end up with a haunted house that not only destroys the domestic sanctuary, but also leads to death by shock and the uncanny.

The home was threatened in ghostless Christmas tales as well as in the spookier variety of midwinter stories. In so many of the early Christmas novels—including *The Cricket on the Hearth, The Snow Storm*, and *The Good Genius*—emigration breaks down the domestic circle. The typical periodical Christmas profile depicted a fascination with the unattainable return to home. As the inescapable backbone of the ghost story, haunted house narratives attacked the domestic from yet another angle, one especially relevant in the Christmas print context. Ghosts thwarted human inhabitants' attempts to create a domestic shrine.

Bad reputations and even an inexplicable, sinking feeling of wrongness could destroy a home's domestic well-being. Dickens's female protagonist of the frame narrative in *A House to Let* (*Household Words* Christmas Number, 1858) becomes haunted by the supposedly empty house opposite her London rental: "I have heard, as everybody else has, of a spirit's haunting a house; but I have had my own personal experience of a house's haunting a spirit; for that House haunted mine."[40] In the end, the house that haunts her mind ends up containing a hidden, abused orphan, an heir and distant relation to the protagonist. The child becomes her ward, and she buys the house and makes it a hospital for children, cleansing the home of its previous propensity for child abuse. A haunted house story by Charles Ollier reminds readers that an uninhabited house can gain the "fatal reputation" of being haunted.[41] And what can be "fatal" to a home if not the failure to exist as an emblem of hearth-love?

While other types of hauntings exist—such as dead spirits returning from abroad to notify family of their death—haunted places are a mainstay of the genre, and they often explore the dark side of property and wealth. Haunted houses make troubling assets, as tales by Charlotte Riddell display. Riddell's "Old House in Vauxhall Walk" depicts a large city home that cannot keep its renters because of the ghost of a murdered miser who, like the once human ghosts in *A Christmas Carol*, bemoans her poor use of her gold. The message is clear: greed taints a home and makes it unfit for domestic peace. The young man who lays the ghost learns a lesson and reunites with his father on Christmas Eve.[42] Haunted homes, especially those created by women authors, depict male characters helplessly unable to oust the uncanny from their hearth. Men bothered by ghosts must rely on "virtues which the age prescribed to the feminine sphere."[43]

Riddell collects many of the dominant themes present in Christmas ghost narratives in her novella *The Uninhabited House* published as Routledge's Christmas Annual for 1875. This notable text concentrates fears of social degeneracy and modernity on the domestic space, and it also depicts devotion trumping materialism. Altogether, the narrative offers a domestic thriller in the literal sense, in which the home becomes a character corrupted by a glaringly modern greed. As such, *The Uninhabited House* must have struck many readers as the perfect ghostly tale for a cozy Christmas reading. Routledge certainly liked it enough to continue ordering narratives from Riddell for subsequent annuals. Riddell published her first novel in 1856 and became known for her abundant knowledge of the business of the City. Her protagonists are "clergymen, civil engineers, chemists, accountants, medical practitioners, architects, and office clerks." Patricia Thomas Srebrnick argues convincingly that Riddell wrote for the middle and lower-middle classes—including junior and senior clerks, technicians, tradesmen, authors, and female office workers—just the class of readers who purchased cheap reprints, used "Free" libraries, and bought 1s. Christmas annuals. The *Saturday Review* wrote confidently of Riddell as an expert: "She is at home in City offices, and lodgings, and warehouses. . . . her country or West-end readers must be ready to assume that this is the way they manage matters in the City."[44]

In *The Uninhabited House*, Riddell's readers had to look west of the West-end to learn how the taint of City business could haunt the domestic peace of a suburban home. In this ghost story, two figures haunt the house: a ghost of the murdered Robert Elmsdale and Mr. Harringford, his murderer. Elmsdale had vindictively called in the debts Harringford had incurred speculating as a builder, and Harringford shot the moneylender and took the money. The murdered man's haunting occasionally takes the form of his incorporeal spirit, but more often, doors open or close and gas lights go on and off inexplicably. The servants are, of course, the first to express concern. They see the gaslight under the vacant library door, but they meet only darkness when they enter the room. Similar experiences scare away a line of renters and bring about suits between renters and the owners. The narrator, a law clerk named Harry Patterson, agrees to explore the haunting and find the "secret of these strange lights" in an effort to redeem the worthless real-estate for his clients, the frumpy, elderly Miss Blake and her beautiful ward.[45] Patterson moves into River House and experiences all the haunting—gas lights going on and off by themselves and even a ghostly figure on the stair. On a hunch, Patterson brings Harrington into the library, the scene of the murder and the epicenter of the gas light/ghostly activity. In the climactic conclusion, the gas and the murdered man overlap into a single entity: "Standing in the entrance to the strong room was [the dead] Robert Elmsdale himself, darkness for a background, the light of the gas falling full upon his face."[46] The manifestation of the haunting has been through the gaslight for so long that Elmsdale's climactic, corporeal presence appears to embody the technological innovation.

Riddell employs gaslight as a ghostly form of technology, a symbol of modernity that may otherwise be seen as a ghost repellant. Patterson's employer, Mr. Craven, "would not believe that where gas was, any house could be ghost-ridden," suggesting that gas, as a symbol of modern city planning, safety, and reliability, chases away the antiquated traditions of ghosts.[47] The narrator in an 1849 article similarly expresses the modern dearth of ghosts, blaming technology: "In the country they would shun spots where the gleam and scream of the mail-train might disturb their importance; and in London they would hate the gaslight shining through the bedroom blinds."[48] No one ever funded gas lighting in the interest of laying ghosts, but the technology did radically affect street crime when it came to London. An innovative Mr. Murdoch had first illuminated his home in Cornwall with coal gas in 1792, and he brought the lighting system to Soho streets in 1802. Parliament licensed the London and Westminster Chartered Gas-Light and Coke Company in 1810, and gas lighting crept into factories, streets, and private residences. In 1822, the average number of lights included 10,660 private lights, 2,248 street lamps and 3,894 in theaters.[49] Moreover, phantasmagoria technology would evolve to show even better phantoms using gas-powered magic lanterns.

By the 1870s gas had entered the newly built urban and suburban home, and it permeated the nightly experience of domesticity of certain classes since "for much of the nineteenth century, gas lighting literally illuminated the differences between wealthy and poor; it was an expensive urban luxury."[50] Graeme J.N. Gooday has traced a gender divide in opinions about gas installation at the mid-century when middle-class women argued against the innovation their husbands wanted. An 1854 *Punch* pieces shows the paterfamilias eager to have gas in his home, but his wife cautions against it, citing the danger of explosion, ammonia leakage, smell, and corrosive destruction of furniture and books.[51] Indeed, in 1861, when the British Museum considered introducing gaslighting, the superintendent of the London Fire-Engine Establishment cautioned against it, citing "the danger of explosion, to which every place where gas is used is liable."[52] *The Times* contains many notices of gas explosions throughout the second half of the century, suggesting that homeowners well knew the threat of allowing the technology admittance.

Despite its risk, gaslight became a lens through which people viewed the home and the self. The gaslight impacted Victorian visuality. Riddell's novella shows how dependant her culture was on gaslight as a means of experiencing the visual world. Miss Blake follows gaslight clues to find the body of her dead brother-in-law; gaslight inhabits the home just as the ghost and the living characters do; the narrator shares the house with the gaslight, which pervades most scenes that take place indoors. When he is being tailed by the murderer, the narrator uses gaslight in his office to show his presence in one room, then slips into another, darkened room to spy on his stalker. The home as a holy outpost for domesticity and idealized values has been breached, and the gaslight's presence warns the reader that individuals must come to terms with this new "company," since it is around to stay. Consider the reading experience of the Christmas audience. Many readers probably perused Riddell's tale by the same gaslight that haunted her Uninhabited House, and they would have to turn down the light, now imbued with ghostly characteristics, before retiring to their Christmas sleep.

In the glare of the gaslight, Riddell depicts male capitalism endangering the sacrosanct domestic space. Ruskin describes the home in "Of Queen's Gardens" as "the place of Peace; the shelter, not only from all injury, but from all terror, doubt, and division."[53] Home, by extension, should be a retreat from the injuries of an increasingly capitalist society. This ideal fails, of course, as Thad Logan's study of the parlor shows how ubiquitously consumerism infiltrated the parlor. Logan describes an "empire of things," noting how the home became an "arena" for the visual display of colonial possessions, testifying to a global market.[54] However, the ideology of home resisted the relentless tide of capitalism. In *The Uninhabited House*, one of the few complaints against the murdered man is the fact that he brought his moneylending business into the home. Such a contaminating action necessarily leads to the home becoming the Uninhabited House. In Dickens's last Christmas book a lawyer's wife avers that she has been "long accustomed to connect the office with everything opposed to domesticity."[55] The two spaces may be at odds ideologically, but fiction often joins them together so that readers can stand back and admire the resulting fireworks. Like *Cricket on the Hearth*'s Caleb Plummer and his toy factory/home, Robert Elmsdale, the murdered man who later haunts his daughter's inheritance, "brought his business home."[56] Miss Blake, the Irish caricature and guardian of the orphaned heir to the house, expresses the general Victorian distrust of business in the home when she says her dead sister would not have tolerated it in her lifetime, but, as the deceased wife's sister, she was in no position to put a stop to the unfortunate practice.

Part of the problem between the Elmsdales was their class status. Mrs. Elmsdale had been a poor woman with pretensions to good family connections, and Mr. Elmsdale had a working-class background. Lara Baker Whelan finds that suburban ghost narrative structure is concerned with "ordering and 'normalizing' domestic space"; the suburban ghost regulates lower-class intruders in middle-class neighborhoods.[57] As the son of a builder, Elmsdale was out of place in his own impressive estate before his death, and he is dangerously out of place when he haunts it. In Riddell's story, the ghost remains connected to his office, and the heir only wishes she could sever the haunted office from the now-ruined home. Notably, his well-educated daughter considers becoming a governess to alleviate her financial problems, but her friends forbid what they see as a degrading step. This next generation of Elmsdales has moved so far beyond the builder-grandfather that she becomes financially useless until she can come into her father's haunted property.

Commercializing home sales and the status symbol of the home initiates the haunting of the house that eventually fails as a home. Elsmdale's greed leads to his death in his home-cum-office and the eventual obliteration of the house. His home had from the first been tainted with conspicuous consumption when Elmsdale attempted to pacify his forbidding wife's decorative expectations: "for her sake, he, who had always scoffed at the folly of people turning their houses into stores for 'useless timber,' as he styled the upholsterer's greatest triumphs, furnished his rooms with a lavish disregard of cost; for her sake, he, who hated society, smiled on visitors, and entertained the guests she invited, with no grudging hospitality."[58] As the builder's son who grasped at middle-class respectability, Robert Elmsdale becomes a deviant male engaged in thwarted domesticity. Elmsdale's wife never returns his love, and he dies only to haunt his home and decrease its value. In the end, the narrator lays the ghost by finding out its secret, but he then tears down the tainted house and uses the space to build not an antiquated square—which had been the ghost's plan—but a space-saving, modern terrace, the home of successful doctors and businessmen.[59] Because the uninhabitable home represents "misappropriated social worth," it must be destroyed and replaced with a suburban estate "that is, presumably, responsibly planned and represents a good middle-class investment opportunity."[60]

Riddell's novella also adds to the Christmastime debate about the authenticity of ghosts when it literally puts ghosts on trial. This writer of the City creates a court scene in which the swindled renter, Colonel Morris, defends himself and his decision to abandon the rental contract because he was not informed of the house's resident ghost. Patterson and his fellow law clerks go into the court case confident because they "could find no precedent for ghosts being held as just pleas upon which to relinquish a tenancy."[61] However, the colonel's lawyer forces an appalling court room confession from Miss Blake, the guardian: she and her ward had experienced evidence of a ghost in the house, and even they refused to live in their rental property. Patterson's head clerk comments that, "I don't think ghosts have ever before come into court." Riddell not only brings them to court, she brings them into the world of City business and exchange, and they come heralded as a "new sensation" worthy of drawing an audience of court spectators.[62] In the end, the colonel decides he would rather pay a half year's rent rather than enter the witness box and face the public ridicule of admitting to being frightened by a ghost, and, in so doing, the colonel resorts to financial measures rather than replicate Miss Blake's humiliatingly feminine confession of fear on the bench.

There is nothing spiritual about the figure of Robert Elmsdale that haunts the front cover of Routledge's Christmas Annual; the ghost has become less spiritually moving, less personal. As time passed, the ghostly characters of Christmas books became harder, colder, and far less interested in the redemption of the living. The popular ghost story of the second half of the nineteenth century blotted out the redemptive ghost Dickens installed in Christmas. The ghosts that populated short stories and novels sold for Christmas consumption after 1860 had more fears about their own souls, and they cared little for the souls of others. Perhaps this shift was caused by the non-seasonal popularity of ghost stories, which often featured in literary periodicals. The cultural fascination with the occult may also have introduced the concept of the individual, selfish spirit. Such character traits were entirely lacking in the spirits of Dickens's early Christmas books and other fairy story Christmas materials. The fairy gave way to the ghost of spiritualism.

Within the range of Christmas reading, ghost stories offered readers a chance to access an English cultural past, a romanticized custom of community and country house hospitality underpinned with tensions concerning class status and the degeneracy of the upper class. They also provided a culturally sanctioned space in which to become a part of fictitious reading communities and a judge of the supernatural. The necessary invitation to such a perfect Christmas? The price of a magazine.

Chapter 5

The Expansion of Christmas Consumerism: Gifts and Commodities

It did not take many years after the resurgence of a standardized Christmas before colorful booksellers' windows became an expected part of the Victorian experience. Articles recording the Christmas marketplace touch upon the evergreen stalls, the food stalls, the toy shops, and the rainbow of volumes:

> Not a tradesman but lays a trap for us, as if the public were sparrows in the frost. We might go through the whole category of tradescraft, from the butcher, with his prize oxen from the Cattle Show, to the booksellers and stationers, alive with coloured plates, Christmas numbers, and Christmas cards of every shape, size, variety, and price. How we must pity the large hearts with small means, suffering the allurements of the tempting windows.[1]

As the Christmas reading audience became adept at the cultural performance of Christmas, the print matter served up for holiday consumerism transformed to meet new needs. In the decades after the 1840s, much of the population willingly adopted the rituals associated with the cultural Christmas. As a result, the bulk of December texts became far less invested in Christmas ritual and sentimental instruction; nonetheless, December book sales continued to climb. As critics did not tire of mentioning, the Christmas book label had broadened to embrace a wider flood of volumes put forth for the holiday season. The new designation explains the divorcing of Christmas narratives from Christmas print expectations, and it also represents the decisive move to a child-focused, gift-centered market.

During the 1840s, the amount of Christmas material and festive scenery in the Christmas books varied widely, but by the end of the decade, the term "Christmas book" became a marketing slogan rather than an indication of holiday content. Reviews still recommended collections of Christmas carols and the *Punch* Almanacks, but the *Times* reviewer of "Decorated Christmas-Books for 1848" seems to have been confused by the onslaught of ornamental books that "have nothing in common, save the time of their publication. . . . they look as if they stoutly defied being coaxed under one heading."[2] Another reviewer calls them "original works of solid literary merit . . . well adapted for illustration," noting also that they take part in a carnival of commerce requiring "festive costume"—cover design and color.[3]

Stories translated from the German, often reminiscent of the Grimm brothers' work, were also a popular category of Christmas books, which is probably why Eleanor Hervey wrote one set in Germany (*The Pathway of the Fawn*, 1852), and why John Ruskin's father and publisher decided to print Ruskin's *The King of the Golden River, a Tale of Stiria* (1851) as a Christmas book. In Ruskin's case the German setting, fairytale narrative, and short, illustrated format gained his novel access to the holiday market. The publishing phenomenon opened the market to a wide range of Christmas books, as one 1850 review attests: "It may be a fairy story; it may be a story of real life; it may be a piece of broad humour; it may be a social satire."[4]

Nonfiction dominated the Christmas catalogues. By the 1860s, titles listed as "Christmas Books" were often ornately illustrated table-books such as *Examples of Chinese Ornament* (1867), a work with little text but over a hundred plates of Chinese designs procured from objects in English museums. *Japanese Fragments* (1866), a text that satisfied the reviewer that Japan boasted of comic illustrators on par with Richard Doyle, also featured in the lists. Collections of English literature, nonfiction histories of various cultures, travelogues, and biographies appeared under the category of "Christmas Book." While they had nothing else in common, *Russo-Turkish War* (1880) by Edmund Ollier, *An Unsentimental Journey through Cornwall* (1884), and *The History of Lace* (1864) all shared the distinction of being Christmas books. Volumes eventually shrank from their ornamental, 1860s extremes. The larger table books went out of style in the 1870s because "drawing-rooms ceased to contain tables capable of holding such tomes, and, as a result, there was no place for them."[5] As they were weeded out of the drawing room, so too were they weeded out of the book catalogues.

Reviewers concentrated their reactions to the all-important material object of the Christmas books, including the obnoxious smells of leather bindings (*Miracles of Our Lord* and *Good Shunamite*, both of 1847), the appeal of gilded borders by Owen Jones (*Paradise and the Peri*, 1860), and the unexpected accomplishments in the new art of chromolithographs (*The English School of Paintings in Water Colours*, 1861).[6] *Life of the Queen* (1884), published by Virtue and Co., contained "type and paper . . . [which] make it admirably adapted for either a Christmas or wedding gift."[7] A review of *The Princess Nobody: A Tale of Fairyland* (1884) followed a common trend by giving more attention to Richard Doyle's illustrations than the text.[8] Bringing a boon to illustrators' incomes, the Christmas book trade demanded images, many of which were influenced by the German Romantic style so beloved by publishers like James Burns.[9] Lorraine Janzen Kooistra has argued that Christmas packaging—illustrations and cover designs—altered the way the popular market responded to poetry. For example, by packaging Tennyson's poetry as an illustrated Christmas gift book, the publisher Moxon undermined the laureate's desire to maintain the highbrow purity of his art: "There could be no pretence of 'pure' poetry when it was tricked out in the elaborate trappings of an illustrated gift book for Christmas consumption."[10]

Consumerism rituals began to dominate the rites of the developing English Christmas narrative right alongside Scrooge and his walk through Christmas Present's food market. Periodicals and seasonal books continued to serve the interests of a commercial Christmas with frequent marketplace descriptions that overwhelmed readers with visual details of "large English pine-apples, pomegranates, brown biffins from Norfolk, and baskets of soft medlars; Kent cobnuts, filberts and foreign nuts of outlandish shapes" and "rich ripe plums and tempting grapes; luscious foreign fruits in natty little boxes set round in paper lace; sparkling white sugar; and glistening tea with the bloom upon it."[11] These excerpted cornucopia-like descriptions from *Chambers's Edinburgh Journal* and a Dickens's look-alike Christmas book, *The Faces in the Fire*, demonstrate how lists of commodities were paired with holiday markets. Writers not only captured a written snapshot of the food for sale, they also lovingly detailed the appearance of holiday bookstalls. One reviewer expressed how the visual imagery of the market overwhelmed the imprudent consumer: "They not unfrequently bear marks of haste, and seem designed to carry off the purchaser's eye by a showy outside, or mere profuseness of ornamentation."[12] Thackeray pairs London's Christmas fare with "Mr. Nickisson's library tables in Regent-street, blazing with a hundred new Christmas volumes, in beautiful bindings, with beautiful pictures."[13] Victorian adults and children approached the altar of the bookseller to venerate the colorful codex. *The Book of Days*'s (1873) entry for 24 December noted the common visual display of a Christmas publishing sensation by the third quarter of the century:

> Christmas books of all shapes, sizes, and subject-matter blaze forth magnificently in booksellers' windows, decked in all the colours of the rainbow, resplendent in all the gorgeousness of modern bookbinding, and displaying the grandest trophies of typographic and illustrative skill. The publishers of the various popular periodicals now put forth the "extra Christmas number," and the interest and curiosity excited by this last are shared with the graver and more business-like almanacs for the ensuing year.[14]

Reviews often started by referring to the physical commodity of the Christmas books rather than any holiday sentiment, and "the vast and glittering array of Christmas books" became "an infallible sign" of Christmastime. Another *Times* reviewer said of the bright, enticing books for sale, "Christmas would not be recognized without them."[15]

How did this transformation to a ritual of conspicuous commerce take place during a holiday touted two decades earlier for its sentiment rather than its materiality? Consumers were learning to mitigate guilt about new wealth by allowing consumption practices new entry through the family-focused portal of Christmas giving. When Hervey and Seymour coded *The Book of Christmas* as a Christmas present in 1836, they were continuing the preannual and literary annual gift-giving tradition. Books may have been frequent Christmas and New Year's gifts before the literary annuals, but previous to the 1820s children who received books could, at best, expect educational volumes of history, philosophy, science, and a relatively limited range of fictional titles. New titles were relatively scarce and bindings received less attention, but children had worshipped at earlier market displays during the first few decades of the century. Those children flocked to flat, heavily illustrated poster sheets. Back then "Christmas pieces" were enthrallingly colorful single sheets of paper printed on both sides, usually with Bible stories, meant to be inscribed with the gift recipient's name in the middle. This fad for printed broadsheets trained maturing consumers to relish visual images as gifts, causing one reviewer to write, "[w]hen the men of the present generation were little children—say, some forty years ago—they were wont to regale their eyes at the windows of the stationers' and booksellers' shops," and when they became the joyful recipients of a Christmas piece, they spread them out on a table and "clatter[ed] over them comparing notes amongst the incredible apples that hung down out of labyrinths of boughs, and the antediluvian animals."[16] *Punch*'s closely drawn Almanacks must have reminded many adult readers of the Christmas pieces of their youth. The earlier broadsheets also prepared the book-starved children for a visually driven Christmas marketplace that would replace their single-sheet consumption. Improvements in technology, paper prices, and literacy rates contributed to a revolution of the children's print market. According to one 1851 review, the annuals "displaced the whole of the Crusoes, and Gullivers, and Sinbads, so far as the holydays were concerned," and, with new annuals out every year, "the Juvenile Library looked forward to become as grand in the course of time as the drawing-room table."[17] Scrooge may have reveled in his childhood library consisting of *The Arabian Nights* and *Robinson Crusoe*, but, decades later, a bountiful, child-focused book market altered gift expectations.

The early, Dickens-inspired Christmas books were certainly exchanged as gifts in some households, but reviews attest that the consumer was also the expected reader of Christmas narrative books. From the 1830s on, advertisements appeared in the days around Christmas, heralding short lists of books as presents, and periodicals did not fail to tout their own seasonal Christmas numbers. Reviews began to shift away from counseling what the consumer should read himself to what he should buy for others. As the new, post-1840s Christmas accelerated, advertisements appeared earlier and earlier, and they took up more and more of the periodicals' advertising space as books enjoyed special status as ideal Christmas gifts. The custom caused one reviewer to write in 1883, "presents very generally take the form of gift-books."[18] The new style of illustrated, gilded books of poetry—best represented by Vizetelly's *Christmas with the Poets* (1851) and Routledge's "heavily illustrated editions of the poets in their equally heavily gilded and embossed bindings"—forced the annuals out of the market in less than five years.[19] These new presentation editions, volumes marketed as Christmas gifts, necessitated yearly review articles in periodicals. *The Times* expanded its Christmas book reviews from one installment from 1860–1866, to lengthy three-part installments beginning in 1867. In 1883 the *Times* needed six days' worth of Christmas book reviews, and readers found eight installments of reviews just two years later. Victorian print genres began to create a culture of Christmas book consumerism that eventually developed gendered, age-specific categories. By the end of the 1850s, Christmas books were intended for use by an informed audience participating in the performance of Christmas and, as such, in need of presents.

Informed Christmas-keepers did not always buy into the new consumer-based performance. Those who held onto the radical work Christmas had done in the 1840s resisted the change to gift-giving consumerism. In the autobiography he was writing in 1875–1876, Anthony Trollope famously praised the earliest Christmas books: "A Christmas story, in the proper sense, should be the ebullition of some mind anxious to instill others with a desire for Christmas religious thought, or Christmas festivities,—or, better still with Christmas charity." He went on to argue that Dickens's Christmas stories did this, but the Christmas tales that ornamented 1870s magazines "all of which have been fixed to Christmas like children's toys to a Christmas tree" had "no real savour of Christmas about them." Trollope bemoaned the loss of the radical narrative of Christmas that used to characterize much of Christmas in print. By comparing his contemporaries' work to toys hung on a tree, Trollope belittled the blatant commodity economy of Christmas publishing.[20] Trollope's own short stories for Christmas emphasize biblical precepts like sacrifice in "The Widow's Mite" and Christian unity in "The Two Heroines of Plumpington." His Christmas characters often analyze sermons as a way of propagating the Christian "savour of Christmas" Trollope chose to glorify. Merciless reviewers could have still accused Trollope's Christmas tales of ornamenting the Christmas periodical; the only difference was that he sought to redirect consumer readers toward a socially responsible, rigidly middle-class Christmas narrative.

According to Anne Lundin, "[t]he concentration of children's book publishing at the Christmas season promoted the notion of the book as commodity."[21] However, books were well-recognized Christmas commodities two and even three decades before children's books came to dominate the market. Present-giving took a solid position beside ritual foods as an expected performance of the dominant Christmas narrative. The collision of the Christmas season and the book market had long invited comparisons to different types of consumption, as Trollope's toy simile suggests. Decades earlier Thackeray had called books "mince-pies," and his 1847 review maintained the metaphor as his assistant hands him a "dish" by Mrs. Gore with "plates" by Cruikshank.[22] Elsewhere Thackeray likens the books to plum puddings, and Christmas authors, who finish writing months before Christmas, to the cooks who awaken at midnight to start cooking preparations for everyone else to enjoy at a more seasonable hour.[23]

Books at Christmas became as expected as the traditional dishes, and periodical pieces often labeled them as heralds of the season: "[t]he advent of these pretty volumes upon our table tell us, if nothing else does so, that Christmas is coming."[24] One *Times* reporter wrote of the books that, "Christmas would not be recognized without them."[25] Another *Times* reviewer wrote, "The English manner of celebrating Christmas has a distinct influence on the development of popular English art."[26] The 1883 article serves to show how Christmas habits had progressed from regional wassailing rituals to adopted German Christmas tree traditions (as a result of the life of Christmas in print) and, finally, to the commercialism of gift-buying as a ritual. The revitalized Christmas of the 1840s had generated a Christmas narrative that focused on "the central problem of the new materialism," which was finding a balance between embracing commodification of goods and avoiding materialism.[27] By late century the status of materialism at Christmas had shifted, and commodification in the guise of gift-giving absorbed the Christmas-keeper. Christmas book giving contributed to the national identity since it "reinforced Victorian values" of instruction and usefulness rather than the hedonism less educational luxury goods would convey.[28] Reviews were widely available to help inform givers about what gift theorists have identified as "the actors' own understanding of their acts and motives," a crucial element in the act of gift-giving.[29] Lists of presentation editions eschewed the earlier Christmas mantra of benevolence and instead encouraged rampant, but informed, consumption. *The Bookseller* ran a double Christmas number in 1864 so that it could list two hundred pages' worth of volumes for sale.[30] Thackeray, who had been the victim of a reviewer's attack on Christmas book commercialism, would not have had to redirect accusations of selling Christmas books for profit after 1860. The practice was too accepted to question. Furthermore, Christmas books were no longer destined for the unified family reading circle, but for the individualized, age-appropriate audience.

The *Fortnightly Review* was among the periodicals noting the shift in December publications, and its reviewer could only pause to express amazement before becoming complicit in the commercialization of Christmas books for children:

> Whoever undertakes to write the literary history of England during the latter half of the nineteenth century will be confronted by a force

> hitherto almost non-existent. The approach of Christmas now heralds a flood of juvenile literature unknown five or six decades since.[31]

Portrayals of Christmas and reviews of presentation editions marked the transition from a celebration of Englishness to a consumption-obsessed holiday centered on children. For example, *Punch* became increasingly sensitive to the child focus that infiltrated the season, and the 1880s and 1890s frequently saw Mr. Punch gamboling with youngsters, as in two 1885 cartoons. One shows Mr. Punch tossing Christmas books under review to a crowd of reaching children and another shows children, referred to as "the Only True Home-Rulers at Christmas Time," hanging on his coat and coaxing presents out of him.[32] Christmas book markets began to link Christmas presentation fiction with juvenile reading, and authors seeking midwinter profits readjusted their writing to entertain a younger audience.

It is no coincidence that the child focus of Christmas books corresponds with what Peter Hunt has called the "first golden age of children's literature" beginning in the 1860s and lasting until the First World War.[33] The Victorian period celebrated the child in books about children, which might be for children but also presented a version of childhood attractive to adult consumers.[34] Later reviews and marketing habits exhibited a cultural shift toward book consumption by children or on behalf of children. An 1874 review of new books in *London Society* listed *Whispers from Fairy Land* by E.H. Knatchbull-Hugessen as a volume "to be very often read aloud this Christmas" to children.[35] F.E. Weatherby's *Elsie's Expedition* (1875) garnered some contempt for being a Christmas book for children that plagiarized Carroll's *Alice's Adventures in Wonderland*, but this was just the type of book that flooded Christmas reviewers' tables.[36] In 1907 a *Punch* piece facetiously reviewed titles of children's presentation editions and introduced readers to a child reviewer who wanted more "stories like *Peter Pan* and *Alice*" and unabashedly claimed a insatiable consumption of books: "I cannot have too many. I read twenty a day."[37] The continual output of fairy stories for children's Christmas consumption built on the imaginative foundation of Victorian children's literature.

The evolving children's book market coincided with heightened Christmas consumerism, and Christmas became the season of children's books. Publishers stretched the Christmas market to absorb huge numbers of Christmas books, and reviews often bemoaned the falling quality of the mass quantities. Where Hervey's *The Book of Christmas* appeared the day after Christmas, its later descendants came out in October. In mid-November Juliana Ewing was able to write that "more than 2/3 of the 1st edition of my new Xmas book was taken by the trade in about 3 days."[38] The decades after the 1860s also saw increased gender and age division in books, with girls' books serving as preparations for social roles and boys' books favoring adventure.[39] Presentation catalogue listings at the back of *Routledge's Christmas Annual* segregated the illustrated and fanciful books that best delighted young children from a special section devoted to boys' books. Niche market children's books also benefited from the increased aestheticisms of the 1880s and 1890s, although reviews had been noting the quality of children's book illustrations since the 1860s. In an 1881 *Punch* sketch, Linley Sambourne drew Mr. Punch offering a version of Kate Greenaway's Christmas book *Birthday Book for Children* (1881) to Beatrice while the three giants of children's publishing, Crane, Caldecott, and Greenaway, float in the background as spirits of the holiday.[40] While children's book artists were busy throughout the year, Christmas turned into an annual fashion show for children's book couture.

The blaze of Christmas publications functioned as just one visual testament to the Victorian mania for literature at Christmas, and Victorian biographies record how children relished their gift books. Molly Hughes recalls her 1872 Christmastime expedition into the booksellers and the joy her family took in illustrated volumes:

> I can remember mounting the stairs at Bumpus's amid what seemed to me thousands of books—a land of Canaan indeed. . . . Mother chose *The Story without an End*. . . . it is impossible to describe the endless pleasure given us all by those full-page pictures, whose colours are as fresh and beautiful to-day as when Charles received them.[41]

New books were rare for Molly Hughes's middle-class family, but she and each of her siblings gave her father a book for Christmas 1878: "There he sat, gazing at the pile of five books—too pleased to speak, too pleased to touch them."[42] During the thirty years covered by her autobiography, Hughes often gives or receives books at Christmas. As exciting as the visual displays were in the stores, they were clearly thrilling to have in one's home. Lady Sybil Lubbock's autobiography reveals her childhood appetite for a yearly infusion of books:

> Sleep indeed!—when we each of us had a new bound Annual, provided, it would seem, for just such an occasion, bursting with new stories and absorbing articles on varied topics, home millinery and

> confectionary, the keeping of white mice, the real origin of thunder bolts, the domestic habits of black beetles. . . . Those who, like us, had always drained their books dry in the course of the year, such a feast was joy indeed, flanked as it also was by new volumes of Sir Walter Scott or Dickens, at least one new poetry book and a whole library of school stories.[43]

Lubbock recalls how she and her siblings only reluctantly left their books in the days after Christmas.

The new market of Christmas books altered the style of seasonal book reviews. Whereas reviewers once included long excerpts of Christmas books for adult readers to sample, the amount of later print material as well as the new approach to isolating audiences prevented this old practice. Instead, reviewers attempted to anticipate responses from the child recipient of each book. Late 1890s reviews in periodicals like the *Academy* and *Review of Reviews* used new printing technology to reproduce illustrations from reviewed texts so that consumers could sample the delightful images reviewers had so long attempted to translate into words. Especially festive Christmas books gained special recognition for continuing the instruction of holiday performances in a specialty market otherwise glutted with nonseasonal narratives. Christmas training and festive feeling fell more and more to the periodicals, whose dated material more readily suited the temporary scope of Christmas reading.

Like the literary annuals that had once served as school gifts throughout the year, Christmas books became institutionalized as school prizes. After recommending Barbara Hutton's *Tales of the Saracens*, an 1870 review notes that "[s]tories such as these require to be carefully written; children imbibe from them many historical and ethnological ideas, which, if right, are so much gain, and if wrong are a double loss, as they have afterwards to be unlearnt."[44] Evidently Sir George Monoux Grammar School, Walthamstow appreciated Hutton's text as a presentation edition. The school bound copies with covers displaying the school seal, and they were still presenting this volume for special prizes in general progress during Christmases of the 1890s. *The Practical Teacher* specifically reviewed pleasure-volumes intended for school prizes. Louise Pickard chose to present her nephew Walter S. Mitchell with a book reviewed as a Christmas presentation edition, *The Legendary Ballads of England and Scotland*, for Christmas 1881. So many presentation editions afford the reader a new perspective on their position in the global world—they either celebrate an English or British heritage (as in *The Legendary Ballads*), or they confer knowledge about a distant and exoticized land, such as *Tales of the Saracens* and *Vikram and the Vampire, or Tales of Hindu Devilry* (1870). Many other now faded nineteenth-century volumes bear witness to the Christmas presentation edition phenomenon on their flyleaves where presenters inscribed the recipient's name and the Christmas occasion.

The increased options for consumers meant heightened stress for publishers and authors who came to see late November as a cutoff date for productive sales. For many forgotten Victorian authors, the run up to Christmas might well have been the most stressful time of the year. By the 1880s Christmas cards were not the only missives to clog the mail in the season leading up to Christmas. If Lewis Carroll's relationship with his publisher Alexander Macmillan is any indication, authors and publishers increased their correspondence in October and November as they pressured each other for pre-December release dates. Carroll's publishing career offers a chance to conduct a case study on Christmas publishing in the decades that saw the expansion of the Christmas book market via presentation editions.

The origin of *Alice in Wonderland* cannot be separated from Christmas book consumerism. Carroll initially conceived *Alice in Wonderland* as a Christmas present for Alice Liddell. He presented a manuscript version of his tale, subtitled *A Christmas Gift to a Dear Child in Memory of a Summer Day*, to his child muse on 6 November 1864.[45] During the same season, Macmillan was preparing *Alice* for sale as a Christmas book. Carroll's subsequent volumes would also sell as presentation edition Christmas books. When *Punch* reviewed *The Snark* in "Some Christmas Books," the reviewer remarks that it was "by Lewis Carroll, who, as he never appears in print except at this festive season, ought to be known as the Christmas Carroll."[46]

Carroll would initially have resisted the title "Christmas Carroll" with all of his eccentric might. When he feared that Macmillan was compromising aesthetic beauty by rushing the pre-Christmas publication of *Through the Looking-Glass*, he wrote in his characteristically deprecating style demanding a later, January release: "You will think me a lunatic for thus wishing to send away money from the doors; and will tell me perhaps that I shall thus lose thousands of would-be purchasers, who will not wait so long, but will go and buy other Christmas books."[47] Macmillan had by this time a clear picture of Carroll's weaknesses, and on 6 November 1871 he appealed to his author on the grounds of the children: "Why, half the children will be laid up with pure vexation and anguish of spirit. Plum pudding of the delicatest, toys the most elaborate will have no charms. ...The book must come out for Christmas."[48] Although Carroll had not intended *Looking-Glass* for a Christmas book, he eventually wrote a little Christmas address to be pasted inside the cover. The letter would be inserted in all of his subsequent work on sale during the Christmas season. Macmillan was able to print enough copies of *Looking-Glass* for the volume to sell briskly before Christmas 1871 despite Carroll's complaints.

Time and decreased popularity taught the naïve author the power of the Christmas book market. In 1875 Carroll calculated booksellers' profits and complained about the bookseller discount. Macmillan responded with a lesson about Christmas book sales, explaining that the average bookseller, John Smith, needed to get discounts because Christmas shoppers would disregard the tattered, handled, last-year's-volume: "John Smith's two copies [left over from Christmas] may be on hand for many months, till he is obliged to offer them for 6d. or 1s. under the ordinary price so that at next Christmas he may have quite *fresh copies*."[49] Macmillan oversimplifies the situation. In 1852, following the dissolution of the regulating body, the Booksellers' Association, publishers depended on booksellers who had no fixed prices. Profits dropped as booksellers competed for customers in a war of low prices, and from the 1860s through the 1880s first booksellers then publishers felt the financial crunch that drove Carroll to fight back with math.[50] In the end, Carroll demanded his books be treated differently in Macmillan's contracts with booksellers. The Macmillan publishing house was the first to require all his booksellers to sell at a fixed retail price as of 1890. The Net Book Agreement went into effect for the whole market in 1900 and lasted until 1994, when mammoth booksellers had the power to ignore the Agreement and return to competition based on price (mainly in the form of special title discounts and "three for two" sales).[51] Although the reduced discount put Macmillan in a compromising position initially, other publishers soon saw the benefit of increased price control, and the Net Book System that went into place in 1900 was based in part upon Carroll's shrewd calculations.[52]

Carroll eventually came to rely on Christmas sales with a wholehearted desperation. In 1877 Carroll wrote Macmillan, "How has the *Snark* sold during the Xmas Season? *That*, I should think, would be a much better test of its success or failure than any amount of sale at its first coming out."[53] While Carroll at times repeated his early carelessness about Christmas sales, the 1880s saw him embracing the marketability of Christmas. For example, he pushed Macmillan to publish his neighbor W.W. Synge's book as a Christmas book. Carroll initially planned to publish his own *Sylvie and Bruno* for either Christmas 1886 or Christmas 1887; however, the belabored text did not come out until Christmas 1889. A non-Christmas publication did not seem an option at that point. Two months before Carroll's death, the author wrote Macmillan to bemoan the impossibility of getting *Three Sunsets* out by Christmas.[54] While the altruistic author had come to respect the market demands of Christmas presentation editions, he could not learn the lesson of many writers and tame his writing to the seasonal schedule.

Two of the powerhouses in Christmas book publication who were enforcing the seasonal schedule were Routledge and the Society for Promoting Christian Knowledge (SPCK). George Routledge's publishing house, which had begun by distributing reprints, eventually included illustrated books among its wide ranging specialties, a strong trait for Christmas publishing. Routledge put out a Christmas Annual, which packaged the fiction of writers W.S. Gilbert (*On the Cards*, 1867), Anthony Trollope (*Christmas Day at Kirby Cottage*, 1870), Charlotte Riddell (*Fairy Water*, 1873; *The Uninhabited House*, 1875; *The Haunted River*, 1877; *The Disappearance of Jeremiah Redworth*, 1878), and Oscar Wilde (*The Green Room*, 1880). Routledge targeted boys and girls with juvenile annuals as well as publishing presentation editions for Christmas sales, books like *Gems of Modern French Art* (1870). This house "published virtually all of the major Gift books," and the strong collaboration between Routledge and his engravers, the Dalziel Brothers, led to the fine caliber of illustration in ensuing texts.[55]

Reviewers of Christmas books regularly devoted a section of their review to the SPCK's holiday offerings, occasionally noting the wide interpretation of what contributes to "Christian Knowledge."[56] If the SPCK's offerings did not always espouse overtly Christian views, their fiction for children regularly moralized about good behavior and personality traits expected of the English national character. Presenters of post-1850 children's editions, which were often 1s., were instructed to use the texts to influence working-class children as well. For example, the review of *Fan: A Tale of Village Life* was described as a "story of a little waif, who develops noble qualities in a hard life, and overcomes evil with good. The book will be a useful present to servants and school-children."[57] When not choosing books to instruct the working-class reader, middle-class parents might have been browsing the SPCK catalogue for just the right "antidote" for their own child's shortcomings.[58]

Although SPCK offerings were not always overtly evangelical or theological, they did generally possess a definite tone of morality.

After the mid-century, the SPCK and other similar societies became noticeably less religious in instruction due to the revival of the moral tale and an upsurge in sentimentality.[59] Nonetheless, authors occasionally had qualms about joining forces with the SPCK. Anthony Trollope entered into negotiations with the SPCK for a manuscript. He offered to charge them half of his usual copyright fee, and the Society would have the right to edit anything it found unseemly in Trollope's text. The publisher's identity as a charity won them that much from Trollope, but the author baulked at being called "one with the Society," as an editor said he should be called if Trollope wrote for the SPCK. Despite his investment in the Christian narrative of Christmas, Trollope could not agree entirely with the philosophy of the SPCK, so, in the end, negotiations broke down amicably.[60]

Juliana Ewing had none of Trollope's compunctions. The SPCK published several of Ewing's Christmas-themed narratives in the years after her 1885, but by then her stories had come to light several times, both in periodical and book form. Most of Ewing's writing first appeared in *Aunt Judy's Magazine*, a periodical with high intellectual expectations for children. Ewing's mother and editor, Margaret Gatty, titled the magazine after Ewing's pet name among the family. Ewing's tales include the most famous *Jackanapes* as well as *Daddy Darwin's Dovecote*, and *Snapdragons*. Upon her death she was said to be only equaled by Louisa Molesworth and Louisa May Alcott.[61] Writing Ewing's obituary, Molesworth insists that Ewing's "exquisitely quaint, humorous, and yet often pathetic verses for children, with their lovely illustrations, are—surely?—in every nursery."[62]

While her work initially appeared in her mother's periodical, Ewing also knew something of the Christmas publishing schedule that harassed Carroll. She wrote to her brother saying her first publisher, Bell, "announced that he wanted a volume, and that for the Christmas market one must begin in July! Such is competition!" Since Bell assured her something new would be more successful than a reprinted piece, Ewing produced *Lob Lie by the Fire*, illustrated by Cruikshank, and sold it for Christmas 1873.[63] A decade later, and with the negotiating help of her illustrator, Randolph Caldecott, Ewing undertook the production of *Jackanapes*, her most famous text. The SPCK merely functioned as distributor. The effort cost her much anxiety, especially with a busy and procrastinating illustrator and frequent negotiations and renegotiations with the printer (Evans) and the SPCK, who were known as "dreadful screws."[64] More than a year after Ewing began negotiations with Caldecott, *Jackanapes* was published in October 1883 for the holiday market. Ewing writes that copies sold "at the rate of 500 a day, 19,000 have been ordered already, and the printers can't get them out fast enough. This of course, is not likely to go on after Christmas." She would earn one half penny per one shilling copy of the novel.[65]

While other previously periodical tales appeared in volume form during Ewing's lifetime, my interest is in the series the SPCK brought out after Ewing's death, which included *The Peace Egg and a Christmas Mumming Play* (1887 edition). This series of cheap, 1s. editions show the continuity of the children's literature author, but, unlike many of the volumes on sale for children in the late century, Ewing's narratives continue the work Seymour, Hervey, Irving, Dickens, and others who educated readers in the rituals of the English Christmas. Furthermore, *The Peace Egg and a Christmas Mumming Play* introduces yet another genre to the variety of printed texts available for Christmas sales. While printed dramas did not dominate holiday book lists, they did make notable inroads into the consumable print matter of the season.

In *The Peace Egg*, a mother of five is estranged from her father because she chose to marry a captain in the army. The young family has been living quite happily abroad, where Mama tells her children all about her Yorkshire Christmas traditions. The couple eventually becomes homesick for England, so, when the wife inherits a house in her old hometown, her husband sells his commission. They settle just down the street from the wife's father, who refuses all attempts at reconciliation. The couple's oldest son, Robert, sees some mummers practicing, and he decides it has enough of the military style for his taste, so he buys a copy of *The Peace Egg* and musters his siblings and their two dogs into the play. On Christmas Eve the siblings decide to take their show on the road, and, unbeknownst to them, chose their own grandfather for an audience. The grandfather is so taken by his well-behaved grandchildren and their little play that he returns home with them and reconciles with his daughter and her husband. Since the mumming tradition does not exist widely worldwide, it may be well to explain, as Ewing did, that mummers were traditionally adult men, dressed in fantastic costumes covered in "flowers, feathers, bugles and coloured streamers" as they enacted the traditional roles of St. George, the Valiant Slasher, the Doctor, the Fool, and other heroes or enemies of the contemporary current events.[66] The play typically contained various battles, deaths, and some resurrections as symbolic heroes fought national enemies. The mumming play, with its long tradition and new surge in village popularity following 1780,[67] would be acted in kitchens (as in Ewing's experience) or, as in

Hardy's *The Return of the Native*, before a local Christmas party, and the actors expected gifts of money or drink.

In the 1884 reprinting of *The Peace Egg* in *Aunt Judy's Magazine*, Ewing added the script for a bowdlerized mummers' play, also titled *The Peace Egg*, saying she had received many requests for the play Robert and his siblings perform. Once joined, the narrative and the script would be packaged together and reprinted by the SPCK in 1887, 1895, and by Bell and Sons in 1928. I will refer to the prose narrative as *The Peace Egg*, the play as "A Christmas Mumming Play," and the two texts together as *The Peace Egg and a Christmas Mumming Play*. "A Christmas Mumming Play" is a series of six sword fights: St. George challenges and slays the dragon; St. Patrick of Ireland slays the black Prince of Paradine and mortally wounds the Egyptian King's champion Hector, but the Doctor heals Hector; St. Andrew of Scotland wounds Slasher, but the Doctor heals him; St. David of Wales fights and kills the Turkish Knight; Saladin enters, fights, and wounds the brave Little Page; and the play ends with "God Save the Queen" and a sword dance. The text would have far-reaching effects. Peter Millington has proved that Ewing's piecemeal mumming play came to be adopted as the traditional mumming play performed by troupes in Nevis and St. Kitts of the West Indies and were still being performed in the 1960s.[68]

As with Christmas ghost stories, Ewing's text shows that oral tradition in the form of mumming plays were translated into commodified print. At the experienced mummers' recommendation, Robert pays his penny and buys the chapbook of the play from the post-office shop. The term "chapbook" comes from the Old English "céap-mann," the bartering peddler who sold the cheap books. Although the chapbook's heyday had passed by the nineteenth century, this term still accurately represents the very inexpensive texts used by working men for their holiday rituals. Robert's copy was most likely the text Millington identifies as "The Peace Egg" published by J. Johnson of Kirkgate, Leeds.[69] The pamphlet of eight pages contained five woodcuts, and a stationer told one consumer that he only sold copies of the play at Christmas despite its Easter-time title.[70] Ewing's own adaptation includes an illustration of a girl helping a boy into a dragon costume, an extensive history of mumming plays, and Ewing's defense of her reworking of the traditional lines. The history of mumming Ewing provides speaks not to the child reader, but rather addresses the adult who still requires this Christmas education more than fifty years into the revitalized Christmas because mumming is not part of the typical performance of Christmas, at least not that standardized

London print version of Christmas. Ewing bemoans her inability to capture the lines used by "Peace Egg" mummers she had seen, and instead she pieces together sections of multiple chapbooks.[71] The oral tradition is thus thrice commodified by Ewing: as a bought text within her volume; as an embedded text the children perform; and in the addendum to the story. Like young Robert, nursery children would learn about mumming as a pastime for children rather than as an adult tradition, but, to be safe, children needed to consume a censored, written version of the ritual.

In Ewing's *The Peace Egg*, Mama censors the original chapbook play in the same way Ewing expurgates her chapbook sources for her readers: "It was a very old thing, [Mama] said, and very queer; not adapted for a child's play. . . . so in the end she picked out some bits for each, which they learned easily, and which, with a good deal of fighting, made quite as good a story of it as if they had done the whole."[72] Mama also makes the children leave out "another character," which she refuses to name, but which is obviously the Devil since Robert points to the woodcut of a figure with horns. Millington's exhaustive, line by line comparison of Ewing's "Christmas Mumming Play" shows that she, too, censored the chapbook plays according to religious preferences. She erased the common mumming character of the Devil, and Ewing went to lengths to show that such a character was not welcome in polite homes. She also deleted or changed "[a]ny lines mentioning God, the Devil, anything vaguely rude or anything with a hint of blasphemy." The lines she did add have a "moral or maternal tone."[73] Early folklorists had already been at work bowdlerizing mumming plays and histories. George Ormond's *The History of Cheshire* (1818) excerpted a mumming play rather than include its unabridged coarseness, in this case calling a character "nasty, dirty Whore" and referring to "the Devil's A-se H-le."[74] Recorders of real mumming plays were rarely performers and could not claim to be immersed in the language and folk culture, and bowdlerization went on into the twentieth century. Tragically, earlier, "coarser" versions have disappeared while edited versions have taken their place in historical annals. In *The Peace Egg and a Christmas Mumming Play* Ewing played Mama to the nation, cutting out what she did not want children to know about the oral tradition even as her version of mumming history sculpted expectations. The older Christmas narrative was augmented through print so that it was child-friendly and empty of the uncouth elements that Hervey was already bemoaning in 1836.

Drama at Christmas can be traced back as far as the eleventh century and its mystery plays. However, the availability of printed scripts for private consumption began with mummers' plays of the eighteenth century. Mumming plays were inscribed in one penny chapbooks published and used in Yorkshire and southern Lancashire. Evidently they were not well circulated, since in 1835 a Wiltshire bookseller reported annual local demand for seemingly nonexistent mummers' books. As northerners became reliant on printed scripts, they "lost control of the ceremony and handed it over to publishers who were more concerned with profit than with maintaining tradition." Ironically, these same publishers garnished mumming plays with respectability and kept the tradition going as the increasingly sophisticated working class began to drop the playful tradition, and it shifted to a pastime for children.[75]

The other drama of Christmas, the pantomime, also changed throughout the nineteenth century and became commodified in print matter. Dickens wrote in 1838 of the great joy bills describing pantomime furnished readers who "still fall down upon our knees, with other men and boys, upon the pavement by shop doors, to read them down to the very last line." In 1861 Thackeray wrote of a similar addiction to the "delicious" *Times* articles describing pantomimes: "perhaps reading is even better than seeing. The best way, I think, is to say you are ill, lie in bed, and have the paper for two hours, reading all the way down from Drury Lane to the Britannia at Hoxton."[76] Like descriptions of the tangible display at booksellers stands, Dickens's and Thackeray's reactions border on worship. Dickens and Thackeray respond to the written word, the printed descriptions of visual wonders. While depictions of bookstalls contain lush language, in both Thackeray's and Dickens's examples the authors eschew vivid examples of visual imagery and merely attest to its presence in the bills. Words capturing theatrical magic unlock nostalgia for childhood, and Thackeray turns to deception to evoke the leisure of childhood via a morning in bed.

Pantomimes were not just for the public theaters since books made pantomimes available for amateur performers and fans. One of the most prolific pantomime playwrights, E.L. Blanchard, would see three or four of his pantomimes performed in different high profile theaters each year. Many of these were put into print by J. Tuck of London. The periodicals that Thackeray loved to read kept journalists busy late into the night after Boxing Day performances; George Augustus Sala reviewed pantomimes, as did E.L. Blanchard himself, who often reviewed his own productions for the *Daily Telegraph* and *The Era*.[77] Even a young W.S. Gilbert sold a pantomime script for £60 and had its script published by the Music Publishing Company of London.

The book of Horace Mayhew's 1847 pantomime *The Plum-Pudding Pantomime; or, Harlequin and the British Lion* could be had for 6d. Other texts were produced with a family performance in mind. Eliza Keating wrote many abridged pantomimes for children's theatricals, such as *Aladdin: or, The Very Wonderful Lamp! A Fairy Extravaganza in Two Acts* (n.d.). This script included elaborate suggestions for set designs. Home theatricals had increased with expanding print media in the late eighteenth century, and, by the mid-nineteenth century, the home theater book market targeted various niches including charade dialogue, volumes for children, scripts solely for women, and texts for home recitation.[78] Since Christmas recollected families at home for long periods of time, scripts and advice books about acting were packaged for December sales. In 1860, for example, Routledge, Warne and Routledge advertised *Acting Charades* by Miss Bowman and *Acting Proverbs, or Drawing-Room Theatricals.* Other titles from which parents could pick included *Games for Family Parties and Children* (1876), *Plays for Young People* (1878), *The Children's Musical Cinderella* (1878), and *Beeton's Christmas Annual* for sale for Christmas 1860, which contained "Robin Hood: A Christmas Burlesque" as well as charades. Memoirist Molly Hughes recorded how her brothers staged *Box and Cox*, a one-act farce often featured with professional pantomimes, for the Christmas of 1878. A magic lantern show and present opening followed the family performance.[79]

Despite the overwhelming number of holiday-free narratives for sale in December, Ewing's *The Peace Egg and a Christmas Mumming Play* was not alone in the continuing work of combining dramatic form with Christmas performance. *The Christmas Mummers* (1858) by Charlotte Yonge contains a partial script inserted in place of dialogue when working-class boys revive a mumming tradition that they have had to write down from memory. Far from idealizing mumming, the moralistic novel ends with a chat with the local clergyman who explains that the pursuit of pleasure is never the goal of a Christian. Yonge sets up rules for polite mumming, should the readership take it up: never allow mumming to interfere with church attendance at Christmas, and never mix alcohol with mumming. Yonge's rhetoric firmly affixes the clergyman as the authority for Christmas keeping while preaching against the dangers of bad company.

Mary Elizabeth Braddon's text *The Christmas Hirelings* (1894) revisited the theme of Christmas reunion and offered instruction on traditional foods and the English identity. Moreover, it opened with a prologue in the form of a script in which three adults discuss the insipidness of a childless Christmas and the possibility of hiring children to make them merry. Subsequent chapters appeared in regular prose, and the opening script was not intended to be acted out by readers; rather, it reinforced the performative nature of Christmas. The adult characters liken the hypothetical hirelings to "mummers" and "a conjuror for a juvenile party," language that immediately equates the children to performers.[80] The hirelings' employer, Sir John Penlyon, is perhaps less self-deluded than the typical Christmas celebrant. He deliberately seeks to construct the ideal holiday and surreptitiously gain access to its emotions. Adult Christmas-keepers like Penlyon, who were otherwise well-versed in the national narrative signified by holiday rituals, chose to adopt consumerism as an answer to the Christmas blues.

Through the character of Penlyon, Braddon explored the adult disappointment in Christmas. As the holiday moved from regional rituals to a national narrative well-supported by a print market, adults could not help noticing that the date on the calendar did not automatically whisk them into a Christmas utopia. Many book reviewers of the 1890s also expressed a disconnect with the emotional aspect of Christmas. A handful of texts dared to explore the adult difficulty of accessing Christmas's supposed cathartic powers. When they sought to end on a happy note, the best these glum authors could recommend was turning to children. Braddon fictionalized this approach and romanticized the outcome. In the last two decades of the century, book reviewers less frequently recommended cathartic reading experiences. Instead, some lamented a falling off in the literary merit of the glutted Christmas marketplace while others fixated on the material object of the volumes up for review. One 1899 reviewer, for example, lovingly reminisced about the good old days of splendid Christmas numbers during the 1850s and 1860s: "But how different those Christmas numbers of two-score years back were from the Christmas numbers which are laid before us now! . . . The wonder rather is that the form should have survived so long after its spirit has fled."[81]

Adults gravitated to an evolving dependence on gifted print materials. This was in part encouraged by printed reviews that privileged the vibrant displays of books over the textual content. As consumers felt escalating pressure to provide material gifts at the mid-century, Christmas print became even more enslaved to the physical object of the book. With such devotion to the material object of the book, it becomes no surprise that a reviewer would call the December books "pretty things, such as Christmas times always produce—the winter flowers in the garden of literature."[82] Books by Lewis Carroll and

Juliana Ewing, Routledge's various Christmas annuals, children's books, printed scripts, and a host of delicately illustrated poetry, nonfiction, and classics sprouted in the fertile soil of the Christmas market, both a product of the more cohesive Christmas performance and, at times, an instigator of the heightened identity-building narratives of the holiday. One can imagine publishers and booksellers relishing book sale expectations of the holiday season, and more than one must have echoed Macmillan's cunning letter to Lewis Carroll: "Plum pudding of the delicatest, toys the most elaborate will have no charms. . . . The book must come out for Christmas."[83]

Chapter 6

The Poetry of Christmas

The Victorians have a reputation for being a society invested in religious devotion and debate, yet thus far the genres of Christmas literature defy that character. Victorians readers would have had to read between the lines or turn inventive to glean scriptural messages from the Christmas books and nonfiction descriptions of Christmas customs. The poetry of Christmas, however, stands on a different footing. As a descendent of a healthy eighteenth-century tradition of devotional poetry, religious poetry came to embrace the topic of Christmas not as a renewed, nineteenth-century entity, but rather as a scriptural touchstone. While much of the poetry of Christmas expanded on older traditions of faith and the English cultural celebration, Christmas poetry and its inherent connection to Christianity caused many poets to designate this genre as a battleground in the debate about faith that had developed in a society prone to the very loud rumblings of science, Higher Criticism, and doubt. As a holiday associated with the spiritual world, leisured Victorians could do some soul searching during the liminal space of Christmas. Poetry offered a field in which Christmas celebrants could turn contemplative and introspective.

One poem attests that the holiday was "the festive time / So loved and celebrated by each poet, / So often lauded up in prose and rhyme."[1] Poets did extol the delights of Christmas, but publishing traditions limited where their poems could appear, especially early in the century. Despite the December marketing of early literary annuals, the poems within the gilded covers of those 1820s and 1830s volumes rarely made any mention of the holiday for which they were consumed. Christmas poems were perhaps most available in December periodicals, especially the weeklies and monthlies. The *Household Words* Christmas numbers Dickens edited frequently contained a poetic narrative by Eliza Griffiths and, more often, Adelaide Procter. Like the prose that surrounded them, periodical verse narratives overflowed with emotion. They sometimes succeeded in Dickens's frequent goal, his carol philosophy, to have the past soften one's present outlook. While most characters in the framing story circle told their narratives in prose, at least one fictional character would choose to entertain his or her companions with a tale in verse. By the end of the century even daily newspapers ran brief sections of classic Christmas poetry by Wordsworth, Thackeray, or Longfellow.

Christmas poetry also filled the collections of carols such as those by William Sandys and John Hotten that became increasingly popular as antiquarians' zeal coincided with a rising interest in the English Christmas. Like Hervey's early readers, Victorian celebrants hoped to trace a noble lineage in their performance of the traditional, if evolved, Christmas, and poetry was their sanitized, convenient method of access. Victorian poets occasionally put forth entire volumes of verse intended solely for the Christmas market, like Horatius Bonar's *Verses for Christmas and the New Year* (1885) and the Chartist Thomas Cooper's *The Baron's Yule Feast* (1846), a small volume that used red cloth and gold stamping to blend in with the prose Christmas books of Dickens. Henry Vizetelly first published his anthology of Christmas poems and lore in 1851, and the decorated gift book *Christmas with the Poets*, illustrated by Miles Birket Foster, contained several centuries' worth of holiday poetry. Reviewers loved it, and one assured consumers that the 1861 edition "being printed on the smoothest vellum paper and bound with especial elegance, forms a Christmas Gift Book that will be always at this season in request."[2] The first edition was, moreover, chosen to represent illustration and printing practices at the Great Exhibition of 1851. Other books of verse were prepared for gift-giving but skirted the topic of the holiday. For example, *The Poetical Works of Oliver Goldsmith* was repackaged with new designs in 1868, and *Two Centuries of Song* featured as "[o]ne of the most handsome" volumes for sale in 1866.[3] Emily Faithfull's Victoria Press put out a joint-stock volume, *Victoria Regia*, in 1861 that contained the work of poets like Tennyson and Patmore and was edited by Adelaide Proctor. Many big name poets feasted on Christmas sales since "the poetry market was primarily a giftbook market centred on Christmas" with volumes selling for the same 5s. Dickens's prose books cost. In fact, the craze for annuals destroyed the market for single-author volumes of new poetry during the 1820s, and that legacy was still affecting poets' publishing habits in the mid-century.[4]

Lorraine Janzen Kooistra claims that during the Golden Age of Illustration "wood-engraved books of poetry dominated Christmas sales," but such a claim is overly generous.[5] Books of poetry did make strong showings in the fourth-quarter market, but reviews in the *Times* and elsewhere confirm that new poetry and beautifully bound reprints of classics stood in the shadow of the many volumes of nonfiction, books for children, and collections of colorfully bound engravings. Volumes of poetry did claim their place on the reviewers' December tables, however, allowing poetry to reposition itself as an element of popular culture. The focus on the objectified Christmas volume—exterior descriptions receive more note than interior ones—certainly supports Kooistra's adroit labeling of poetry's transition as an erosion of "the poet's autonomy and authority" during a "highly charged moment in publishing history." Poets whose books joined the Christmas rush suffered the "taint of trade," and both poetry and the poet were "feminized, and this feminization foretold the marginalization of poetry's prestige and power by the end of the century."[6]

Many verse texts that built the construction of the Victorian Christmas bypassed fourth-quarter, elegantly-bound sales. Poems about the experience of Christmas featured in the collected works of poets. Readers of Keble's *Christian Year* should have been able to anticipate a Christmas poem, but in other collections of verse the holiday poem would have come as an unanticipated, inherently dated reading experience. Criticism most often used to understand the reading of periodicals may inform this genre, since readers could jump around the table of contents in a book of verse to suit their interests. The poems about Christmas may have been written with the seasonal reading experience in mind, but by the time they were collected and bound, there was no guarantee that the season still held sway over the consumer's imagination. Instead, the consumer might read the Christmas poem at any time of the year, and the sentiment would inform the building, annual expectation of that holiday.

One final venue for holiday verse, the Christmas card, was far more closely linked to the holiday experience. The Christmas card blended popular art with large-scale printing, and, like the Christmas books, periodicals reviewed Christmas cards for potential buyers. At the behest of Henry Cole, John Calcott Horsley designed the first card in 1843, and it cost 1s. The custom did not thrive even though celebrants were in the custom of embellishing their own calling cards with Christmas greetings. Printers eventually began to capitalize on this older habit, and Christmas card sales grew during the 1860s and boomed in the 1880s. Until the 1870s, Christmas cards were sold by bookseller and stationers, but eventually tobacconists and toy shops carried them as well. In 1883 an exposé of the Christmas card ran in the *Times*: "It has created quite a new trade, and has opened up a new field of labour for artists, lithographers, engravers, printers, ink and pasteboard makers." A large percent of the verses came from amateurs. Consumers preferred to remain ignorant of the authors of their cards' verses unless they were well-established poets. The competition in the trade during the 1870s caused publishers to vie for famous names to help sell their cards. For example, one publisher offered Tennyson one thousand guineas for a Christmas card poem.[7] Tennyson's "Christmas Bells" and "Ring Out, Wild Bells" were used as card sentiments. Verses by E. Nesbit, Alice Meynell, George MacDonald, D.M. Craik, George Eliot, Juliana Ewing, and E.B. Browning all found their way into Christmas cards.[8]

Victorian recipients frequently cherished their cards in albums they would review during subsequent Christmas seasons, and a verse written by Helen Marion Burnside for a card from the early 1880s wishes its receiver will use the card to access memories of the giver "[i]n some hereafter / Christmas." Verses sometimes adapted traditional carols or expanded on Burnside's theme of good feelings across a distance. The religious approach to card design only ever comprised a small percentage of Victorian cards, despite the prevalence of Christianity in the society. Exchanging Christmas cards was seen as a social function, not a religious one. Subsequently, Christmas card historians remark on the dearth of nativity images and religious sentiments in Victorian albums.[9]

The reader of Victorian Christmas literature may be surprised by the vacuum of overtly Christian material intended for Christmas reading. Dickens tried to convince others that the gospel dripped from every Christmas text he wrote, but the values appearing in his holiday novels and those of his fellow writers depicted English values rather than a gospel message. There is nothing about hearth-love and family reunions in the nativity account; rather, nineteenth-century prose adapted the celebration to its own evolving social needs. Novel and short story characters may attend church on Christmas day, but outside of Trollope's seasonal short stories, the reader remains ignorant of the text that was preached or the spiritual significance of the holiday to the characters. Unlike the other genres that suited the Christmas reader, the bound poetry of the season contains the religious heart of the Victorian Christmas. Poem after poem retells the Bethlehem nativity scene, often with little variation of the details offered in the New Testament.

It may seem like any celebration of Christmas is inherently Christian. Indeed, there is the assumption that a culture that encourages Christmas is at least tacitly Christian; nonetheless, people of other beliefs at times found it beneficial to take part in what they saw as a celebration of middle-class values and English identity. The poetry of Christmas may presume a Christian understanding of the nativity story that the Christian church celebrates during advent, but many poets instead chose to meditate on the cultural celebrations of the holiday. Others intentionally sidestepped the contemporary cultural Christmas to tackle Christian doctrine that was often far removed from the rituals of the English Christmas.

Much of the religious poetry of the season gave voice to nineteenth-century evangelicalism, a movement that had a significant role in shaping middle-class culture. This category of bible-believing Protestants had their roots in the reaction against eighteenth-century deism and the religious revival of the 1730s, which has been attributed to John and Charles Wesley. Evangelicals would hold sway over the "moral tone" of nineteenth-century society, and they led the way in many social reforms, including the officious policing of working-class values and behaviors.[10] They encouraged the salvation of as many people as possible since only a belief in Christ's sacrifice and the redemption of believers would gain one entrance into heaven. Christmas marked the beginning of that sacrifice since it celebrated Christ's arrival on earth and the beginning of his human quest toward the cross. Hannah More's "A Christmas Hymn" was among the many nineteenth-century poems to preach this very sermon: "O how wondrous is the story / Of our blest Redeemer's birth!"[11] Evangelicals were supporters of the revived Christmas and its cultural access to the hearts and hearths of potential converts, but evangelicals also populated the small, anti-Christmas camp. John Castillo, who converted to Catholicism, had a problem with the cultural rituals of the English Christmas. One of Castillo's poetic personas lists the excesses of the early-century Christmas, ending with "Yes, a New Zealand chief would be hard of belief, / Of our Christian Christmas carousing."[12] Decades later Edmund Gosse remembered how his evangelical father refused even the symbols of Christmas entrance into his home because he saw it as a tainting influence: " 'The very word is Popish,' he used to exclaim, 'Christ's Mass!' pursing his lips with the gesture of one who tastes assafoetida by accident. . . . He would denounce the horrors of Christmas until it almost made me blush to look at a holly-berry."

During the Christmas of 1859 Gosse's two maids covertly cooked a pudding, and the scene ended with Mr. Gosse violently smashing the "idolatrous confectionery" into the ashes.[13]

That many evangelicals disagreed with the Gosse family's take on Christmas is evident in the number of poems and hymns dedicated to a faith-based look at Christmas. Religious poetry came in several varieties, including that which is "designed to advance a particular religious position." Much of Victorian Christmas poetry fell into this category as it attempted to argue the need for salvation through a contemplation of the Christ child's divinity. Others took a step further and made pacifist arguments through meditations on the nativity scripture. Devotional poetry, like Keble's *The Christian Year*, was "tied to acts of religious worship," as Keble's volume was tied to the liturgical year.[14] Some Christmas verses, such as those by Keble, Hopkins, Christina Rossetti, and the many Methodist hymn writers, served this purpose.

Keble's "Christmas Day," which appears early in the liturgically structured *Christian Year* (1827), sets a fine example of what much of the religious verse of Christmas would continue to be. Twenty-first-century readers with their postmodern expectations may find Keble's poetry, and much of Victorian Christmas poetry, "unadventurous and unimpassioned, so dutiful and formulaic,"[15] but the development of doctrine through devotional verse offers an insight into the development of what the holiday meant to evangelicals. Much of *The Christian Year* displays Keble's style of blending scripture with the poet's own words in a collage rather than a paraphrase. While poets like Hopkins "dissolve the original unmetrified material and reconstituted its essence (but not its verbal form)," Keble and many devotional Christmas poets keep the original, biblical prose intact.[16]

The Christian Year's "Christmas Day" avoids imagery of holiday pageantry so common in the character of Christmas poems, inaugurating a tradition of evangelical Christmas writing.[17] In fact, "Christmas Eve: Vespers," which appears in Keble's *Lyra Innocentium* (1846), argues against the rituals of church decorating at Christmas. In the poem, a girl comes to church expecting to see greenery and holly, and when she is disappointed in that visual feast, she says "There is no Christmas here." Rather than apologize for failing cultural expectations, Keble's persona engages in a theme of vegetation as he imagines the types of fruit and spiritual growth that Christ expects to find in his worshippers:

> Where are the fruits I yearly seek,
> As holy seasons pass away,

Eyes turned from ill, lips pure and meek,
A heart that strives to pray?[18]

Bemoaning the sparkling veneer of Christmas that can outshine any religious celebration of the nativity, Keble points inward. In fact, Keble depicts the evangelical idea of Christmas inhabiting the celebrant rather than the secular, cultural expectation of the celebrant performing Christmas.

The Book of Common Prayer guaranteed that Anglican celebrants could count on a Christmas Day reading of Isaiah 9:8–10:

> The people that walked in darkness have seen a great light: they that dwell in the land of the shadow of death, upon them hath the light shined. ...unto us a child is born, unto us a son is given: and the government shall be upon his shoulder: and his name shall be called Wonderful, Counsellor, The mighty God, The everlasting Father, The Prince of Peace.

That theme of peace is repeated in the New Testament scripture for Christmas Day in which the angelic multitude pronounce that often recited message: "Glory to God in the highest, and on earth peace, good will toward men."[19] The evangelical priority of scripture can be seen in poets' repeated recapturing of the angels' message, the biblical text most often at work in religious Christmas poetry. Poets were not the only ones to latch onto the celebratory declaration the angels' heralded. Reinscribed as a message of "self-congratulation," technological advancement, and the cohesion of the Atlantic English speaking communities, the angels' biblical message supplied the content for Queen Victoria's August 1858 Morse code communication to President Buchanan: "Europe and America are united by telegraph. Glory to God in the highest. On earth peace and good-will toward men."[20] Here the technology replaces Christ's birth. Neither Victoria nor Buchanan could know that the same technology would shortly malfunction. Nonetheless, Victoria, with the help of her transmitters, replays the angels' role.

Scores of poets, from Tractarians like Keble to the Methodist hymn writers, also felt the need to adopt the direct scripture from the chorus of the angelic multitude. Their texts served as devotional verses about the nativity rather than a transatlantic declaration of progress. As the culture of the English Christmas took on a vibrant life of its own, evangelicals turned back to the original source of the biblical Christmas where they could be sure to find a plum-pudding-free narrative. Furthermore, the song of the angels serves as a lyrical inspiration for the Christian seeking to worship God in a biblical manner. As much of the Victorian society turned to honoring the performance of the English Christmas that was being taught in the periodicals and Christmas novels, evangelicals added their unique voices to the throng through an observance of the holiday that featured an English perspective of the Holy Land rather than overt Englishness. Ellen Thorneycroft Fowler's poem in the *Wesleyan-Methodist Magazine* exemplifies how Christian poets felt they were picking up the role the angels had initiated:

> Though the angels ceased their singing
> Eighteen hundred years ago,
> Still its echoes sweet are ringing
> Down the years of want and woe;
> While through all life's weary yearning,
> And through all life's bitter wrong,
> Slowly, surely we are learning
> How to sing the angels' song
> . . .
> We shall learn the Christmas Carol
> Traced by an immortal pen—
> Sung by those in white apparel—
> "Peace on earth, good will to men!"[21]

Many of the religious poems were in fact hymns for Christmas, which commonly ran in the Wesleyan periodicals and made appearances within poets' collected works. Hymns entered mainstream culture via the Dissenters, especially the Methodists, and it took some time for the dissenting "taint" to wear off this form of religious expression. A Wesleyan could proudly name her poem "Christmas Hymn" decades before mainstream poets began to adopt the common title. Hymns and carols expressed human longings and questions "in a public and accessible form," which often made for clearer reading than the poetry of the great Victorian poets.[22] Victorians began rediscovering the tradition of medieval hymns, and the study of hymnody coincided with the recovery of the Christmas carol. J. French imagined a triumphal entry of a soldier savior in his "An Hymn for Christmas" (*Methodist Magazine*, 1804), and J. Chapple also overlaid the Hosannas of the triumphal entry in his 1809 "Hymn for Christmas." Another favorite theme of the hymns was the savior's poverty:

> If prest by poverty severe,
> In envious want we pine,

Oh may the Spirit whisper near,
How poor a lot was Thine![23]

Most of this poetry lacked any indication of the tune to which it might have been sung, but the cadence of the hymns remained consistent, suggesting their accessibility for the common reader. While the inherently repetitive nature of devotional poetry may cause this genre to pale beside that which has been treated more kindly by the canon, this was the poetry of the people. Made accessible in periodicals and invoked for daily religious contemplation, the hymn offered printed words for its first audience to tender back to God.

The renewed interest in antiquated carols led to the revival of many that coincided with the evangelical spirit. Carols by eighteenth-century hymn writers Isaac Watts ("Joy to the World") and Charles Wesley ("Hark! The Herald Angels Sing!" "Come, Thou Long Expected Jesus") continued to find favor with Victorians. Many volumes and collections of carols contained what John Hotten called "perhaps the greatest favourite of all the Carols now sung at Christmas," "God Rest Ye Merry Gentlemen," which must have satisfied many evangelical readers and carolists as it exhorted Christians not to let anything cause them alarm.[24] Christ's birth was his first earthly step to his death on the cross, and so Christians who are sure of their eternal salvation need "let nothing you dismay." To them, the heavenly existence was almost tangible. J.M. Neale's collection of Christmas carols from 1854 included an explanation of the cultural relevance of a bell-tolling tradition in Yorkshire that signified the gospel message inherent in the evangelical advent. The bells of Dewsbury would ring the passing of the devil on Christmas Eve as a proclamation of Christ's "death-blow to the Empire of Satan."[25] Carolists on both sides of the Atlantic produced many long-lasting nineteenth-century carols: William C. Dix, a Glasgow insurance salesman, wrote "What Child is This"; Philadelphian pastor Phillips Brooks penned "O Little Town of Bethlehem" for his congregation; and James Montgomery printed "Angels from the Realms of Glory" in his newspaper, the *Sheffield Iris*, in 1816.[26]

The overtly Christian precedent of many Christmas poems opened the genre to the debate between traditional Christianity and scientific, technological, and social advances of the century, a debate that left a wake through much of the century's literature. According to Richard Altick, the animated nineteenth-century "response to growing anti-religious forces constitutes a high, sometimes tragic drama of the national soul."[27] Robert Browning depicted just such a spiritual drama when he put forth a rebuttal to what was at that time the dominant intellectual debate about Christianity. Browning's "Christmas Eve" written in late 1849, offers a "poetic triptych" of how that holy day might be celebrated by three different types of Christian gatherings: a dissenting English chapel, the mass at St. Peter's in Rome, and a German university lecture. Browning's structure might well be based on the German Frederick Schleiermacher's Christmas dialogue of 1806, *Die Weihnachtsfeier*. The typical markers of the contemporary English holiday—waits, holiday foods, the marketplace—are entirely absent from Browning's poem, perhaps in part due to the fact that he wrote the poem in Italy, but, more importantly, because the poem has less to do about the social Christmas and everything to do with "how one discovers the meaning of Christmas (or any other Biblical event)." The narrator surveys the "three dominant modes of Biblical interpretation" available at the mid-century.[28] First, the narrator disdains the "immense stupidity" he hears coming form the pulpit in the Zion Chapel Meeting, and the experience is further tainted by the exclusiveness of the chapel-goers who glare at him, a visitor.[29] Disgusted, he flings himself out the door into nature, the church and biblical text he most understands. There he encounters the person of God, and the narrator recognizes that "folly and pride" made him unable to see God being worshipped, however imperfectly, by the evangelical chapel-goers. Newly contrite, he catches hold of God's garment to travel with him to see other scenes of Christmas Eve worship:

> He suffers me to follow him
> For ever, my own way,—dispensed
> From seeking to be influenced
> By all the less immediate ways
> That earth, in worships manifold,
> Adopts to reach, by prayer and praise,
> The garment's hem, which, lo, I hold![30]

While Dickens's Christmas Past conveys Scrooge through scenes by a touch of his hand on the miser's heart, God's mantle is enough to carry the inquiring narrator to Rome, where he is left on the threshold of St. Peter's Basilica. By the end of the poem the narrator has christened the Catholic Christmas Eve celebration a "buffoonery, / Of posturings and petticoatings."[31]

Browning's harshest judgment comes upon the third scene, where the narrator and God confront a German lecturer bringing an intellectual message on Christmas Eve. He represents higher criticism, the belief set forth in Coleridge's posthumous *Confessions of an Enquiring Spirit* (1840) and David Friedrich Strauss's *Das Leben Jesu* (1835), the text that had such a defining impact on George Eliot. Higher criticism relabeled the Old Testament as "a mixed bag of human documents—tribal histories, genealogies, digests of law, erotic songs, biographies, and folk myths." While higher criticism sanctioned the "spiritual and ethical significance" of the Bible, it clashed with evangelical beliefs in the inherent accuracy of everything set down in scripture.[32] Browning's German professor, possibly inspired by Ludwig Feuerbach or David Friedrich Strauss, rejects the biblical Christ as a fable, and the narrator reacts to what he terms a vacuous doctrine. The narrator decides that this group of humanists cannot be Christian when they divorce Christ from deity. This monologue represents one of several in which Browning voices his high regard for Christianity's essential truth.[33] It is perhaps ironic that Browning turns to a German university for this scene. Along with being the source of Higher Criticism, Germany also provided the only other culture of Christmas that English writers responded to with deference. Profiles of the holiday in Germany describe the ritual of the continental other with more respect and awe than outside nations typically receive. After all, Germany provided the Christmas tree that was being absorbed into the English Christmas. Browning follows a Victorian trope by tracing Christmas to its supposed cultural source, but in this case the rituals of the holiday are entirely absent and have been replaced with a lecture, a cold experience meant to pale beside other English representations of the German Christmas.

In the end, Browning's narrator awakens in the Zion Chapel and reevaluates the English, low church form of imperfect worship. He analyzes the dream vision and his resulting spiritual growth that took place while he slept through the nonconformist Christmas Eve worship service. Browning's poem holds the chapel meeting as the holiest of the imperfect options, expressing Browning's disregard of higher criticism and Catholicism. The Christmas Eve setting serves as a different type of liminal space in this poem: it is a time in which God interacts with this seeking narrator and lifts him into a new perspective about man's attempts to worship. The Christmas Eve chapel meeting is unique in its setting for Christmas Eve. Prose pieces, and even poetry with contemporary settings, often limit the setting to outdoor scenes. Here Browning brings his thoughtful narrator into the crush of the chapel with its tubercular worshippers and their human smells and wet clothes. Browning had purposely switched publishers for the

1851 publication of the volume, but the devotional readers who he imagined would buy religious Christmas gift books were nonplussed by the emphasis on intellectualism the poem offered.[34]

W.H. Mallock goes a step beyond Browning's German professor when his dramatic monologist assumes the voice of an atheist in the satire "Christmas Thoughts, by a Modern Thinker," an 1893 poem. Known as the "last Victorian voice of orthodoxy,"[35] Mallock's atheist narrator ponders his intellectual mentors, Rousseau, Goethe, and the fictional Obermann, while he observes the rituals of Christmas. Rather than join the festivities, the straw man narrator attempts a Byronic, if impotent pose: he sighs, makes "a mournful, atheistic face," and runs directly from the church to have a portrait taken to capture his exquisite misery.[36] If Christmas is the celebration of the nativity, the narrator uses it to worship the founders of his intellectual atheism. Mallock mocks free thinkers by juxtaposing his narrator's wistful posturing with the activity of village fiddlers and blooming, happy girls intent on the rituals of the Christian Christmas.

Thomas Hardy reverses the evaluation of Mallock's sad, self-conscious atheist and Christmas's rituals by looking toward an eventual breakdown of the dominant Christian faith. "Christmas in the Elgin Room" includes the Christmas bells that resound through so much of Victorian Christmas poetry, but Hardy undercuts any power this holiday ritual possesses. In keeping with the nineteenth-century trend of attacking Christianity through the more vulnerable Greek pantheon, Hardy carries the celebration out of the church setting and into a temple of culture and history. "Christmas in the Elgin Room" appeared in the *Times* on 24 December 1924, while Hardy lay dying. Ironically, the brief note Hardy sent in response to Edmund Gosse's praise of the poem included an expression of Hardy's relief at evading the demands of his servants' plum pudding that year.[37] The poem itself depicts the dethroned Greek gods, the trophies from the Parthenon, meditating on Christianity's temporary victory over their own religious culture. The poem argues that the fervor of Christianity, as represented by the emphatic midnight bells, will one day be cast aside like the Greek pantheon.[38] Margot K. Louis has followed a similar rhetoric in Swinburne's poetry, in which "the attack on the Olympians implicitly includes a harsh critique of the transcendent Christian God," or any god that withdraws from the travail of human suffering.[39] Hardy's poem does not offer any sustaining hope for Christianity's survival, but treats it like a fad that will one day be limited to a merely historical interest.

Perhaps no one more facilitates the debate about Christianity within the scope of this high feast day than Augustus Swinburne who structured his "Christmas Antiphones" as a rebuttal to the typical evangelical hymn for Christmas. An antiphon is a musical composition with two choirs alternating their singing. Swinburne's poem, however, consists of three voices. The first part, "In Church," is expressed as a prayer to God and imitates the evangelical style of preaching salvation through Christ alone within a retelling of the nativity story:

> As this night was bright
> With thy cradle-ray,
> Very light of light,
> Turn the wild world's night
> To thy perfect day.

While the opening section's content may have lulled early readers with its very mundane approach to the Christmas story, the cadence of the stanzas, which use an *abaab* rhyme scheme, throws up a red flag that this is not the traditional meditation on the biblical account of the nativity. The first line of each stanza contains internal rhymes that quicken the pace: "God whose feet made sweet" and "Brotherhood of good."[40] Indeed, the devotional lyrics of "In Church" might well have grown out of his "quasi-Catholic" family's reverence for Keble and Swinburne's early education in church doctrine. He wrote the first part to please his devout mother.[41]

The second part begins to undermine the fundamentalist perspective by voicing the discontented view of the poor, those "Outside Church." They recount how the wealthy bid the poor to pray when the poor have no hope of enjoying the "light" of God's glory or even a comfortable life. The first part is full of images of light, but the second underscores the inconsolable pauper's prison of darkness through stanzas that parallel the initial Christmas experience:

> In what hour what power
> Shall we pray for morn,
> If your perfect hour,
> When all day bears flower,
> Not for us is born?[42]

While evangelical Christmas hymns depict the holiday as an entryway into the second coming of Christ, Swinburne's answering chorus claims no part in that hope.

Finally, "Beyond Church" offers a revision of the Christmas carol so familiar to the Victorian reader. The rationalist atheist rejects salvation through Christ's name through a direct rebuttal to the rhetoric represented by the "In Church" section; instead, this final voice touts equality and humanistic universalism as the new Christ. In place of Christmas, Swinburne creates an expectation for a Rationalist Brotherhood of Man Day:

> All shall see and be
> Parcel of the morn;
> Ay, though blind were we,
> None shall choose but see
> When that day is born.[43]

That celebration obliterates the Christmas opening of the poem. In fact, the second and third parts "criticize and reinterpret the terms employed in Part I."[44] When all religion ceases and when mankind reaches a classless society, then, the poem argues, citizens of Earth will face a future day worth celebrating. This concluding part becomes the atheist's parallel prayer to the platitudes of the typical Christmas hymn, which Swinburne revises enormously. Swinburne's poetic attack on Christianity was well established by the time "Christmas Antiphones" came out in his volume *Songs before Sunrise* in 1871. His *Poems and Ballads* of 1866 openly opposed Christianity following his loss of faith at Oxford in 1858 or 1859.[45] "Christmas Antiphones" subverts the typical use of the Christmas hymn by turning it into a musical devotion to a zeal for social justice devoid of Christian doctrine. Swinburne does more than claim a new Christmas for atheists; he attacks the Christian Christmas as a fraud.

Swinburne, Hardy, Browning, and Mallock brought the debate about faith to the season that served for many as the religious and spiritual highpoint of the year. Like the *Punch* creators who found much to mock in the cultural celebration of the holiday, Browning and Swinburne locate foibles and contradictions in Christmas celebrations and, in Swinburne's case, the very genre of literature most sacred to the evangelical Christmas. Nonetheless, Swinburne did not reject Christmas altogether, nor did he shun the emotional outlet of Christmas reading. For three decades he celebrated an old-fashioned holiday with Theodore Watts-Dunton, who reported in 1908 that the poet spent part of Christmas day reading *Old Curiosity Shop* aloud to friends since, the reporter claims, "the poet is Dickensian to the core and believes that Christmas ought to be kept in the spirit of

Dickens."[46] It is indeed the social gospel of Dickens's holiday writing that Swinburne channels in his own contribution to Christmas poetry. Swinburne's call for a revised celebration of a reformed, brotherhood-of-man style Christmas would have resonated with many poets who likewise chose the spiritually open moment of Christmas to call for economic reforms. Religious poems that treated the needs of the destitute switched their focus from the ancient scriptures to contemporary images of destitution and poverty.

Of all the genres of printed text, Christmas verse cornered the market on overtly Christian expression. Likewise, the poetry written for and during December monopolized spiritual reflections on mutability. So much of prose and verse celebrated Christmas as the heightened moment of the year, it may seem initially surprising that there was also a body of poetry that commemorated a deep mournfulness associated with the holiday. Along with the celebration of home came Christmas's spiritual connection to the past as it served as a midwinter Memorial Day where the hearth rather than the cemetery was the site of honor. It is entirely fitting, therefore, that Wallace J. Brett's "Christmas Memories" mourned the lost loved ones:

> We miss their places, we miss their welcome,
> In the pure joy the season brings,
> We fancy we hear their far off voices,
> Mingling with rush of angel wings.[47]

Edith Nesbit used the mourned-for past in several Christmas poems. In "The City Clerk's Christmas" a lonely clerk leaves the office for the holiday vacation and begins remembering his true love, who he left behind when he came to the city. Through narrative deception, Nesbitt tricks the reader into thinking that the clerk is physically traveling back to his lover, but he and the reader are rudely awakened from his mental journey to the reality of Camden town and the inevitable Christmas bills awaiting him at home.[48] Elsewhere, for the adult observer, the holiday becomes the "ghost of a day from a lifetime of dreams" and the "most desolate day of our desolate year!"[49] This mournful element of the holiday appears in Dickens's Christmas novels as characters like Redlaw and Scrooge take stock of the past, but in those cases the past informs and enriches the present. Poetry of Christmas's mournful nature instead venerates the family circle even as it bows before its mutability.

Tennyson's *In Memoriam* is not a Christmas lyric, but it does contain Christmas poems. Vizetelly included an excerpt of Tennyson's cathartic Christmas bell ringing (section 106) in his notable anthology of Christmas verse. The poet structures the larger poem around three Christmas seasons that follow the death of Tennyson's best friend, and the three holiday sections harness the familiar, elegiac feature of Christmas. Arthur Hallam died 15 September 1833, and the letter informing the Tennysons of his death arrived 1 October. The poet's immediate spate of elegies predated his decision to combine them into one larger work, and so section 30, or the first Christmas, was originally imagined as an individual elegy.[50] It is furthermore dated "Christmas Eve, 1833" in J.M. Heath's *Commonplace Book*. During that first, painful Christmas Eve, the mourning narrator all but wishes for death before the next Christmas, but when that Christmas rolls around, he is shocked with the quieting of grief: "can sorrow wane? / O grief, can grief be changed to less?" By the third Christmas the narrator's family has revised their holiday customs since the death of the father has seen them moved into a new home and driven them further from the old associations that kept Hallam with them during the holiday. This is a more sedate celebration: "We keep the day. With festal cheer, / With books and music" but no dancing or singing. The wound in the Christmas circle never fully heals. The absent friend haunts the rituals, but his nonpresence adds a bitter sweetness to the ritual that has meaning because he once joined the living in their celebrations.[51]

The Christmas scenes are different from the rest of *In Memoriam* because they show the narrator interacting with other live people rather than trying to force an encounter with Hallam or meditating on faith and doubt. There is nothing inherently Christian about the Tennysons' celebrations; the English ritual performance of Christmas has overshadowed any contemplation of the nativity. Even in company, however, the narrator naturally turns inward to evaluate his own feelings. He is best suited to the tearful first Christmas Eve at which time everyone else's feelings are on display. After that he has to hunt for the clues to their grief. The Christmas scenes find a fitting conclusion in the epilogue, in which the narrator must once again engage with the living and the cycle of human ritual celebration during the preparations for a wedding.

People might have been absent from the family hearth for reasons other than death. Not every celebrant had the opportunity to sit beside a true English fire, but this did not stop emigrated poets from recalling what they had left behind. Like the prose profiles so common in the periodicals, Christmas poetry often led to a contemplation of the English Christmas by an emigrated narrator. If anything, the poetic profile reached a greater sentimental pitch in its sharp, pithy images of holiday ritual. Both Letitia Elizabeth Landon and Rudyard Kipling focused on parallels of community in two gloomy poems commemorating Christmas in India from perspectives of imperialists separated by nearly half a century. Another trope of emigrant Christmas poetry was a wistfulness for the English Christmas of one's childhood. *The Times of India*'s Christmas Day 1878 issue expressed a similarly gloomy sentiment:

> Christmas in India has not a cheerful sound. In our great Indian cities, the society and "ways"—to use a comprehensive word—of English residents are entirely modeled on those of the old country, and the recurrence of the "festive season" chiefly serves to remind us that we are exiles.[52]

Landon's "Thoughts on Christmas-Day in India" appeared in *Zenana and Minor Poems* (1839). The poem sets up parallels between the Indian landscape and the remembered community of home. For the narrating male imperialist, the break with his home community and what he remembers (and idealizes) of the early nineteenth-century Christmas revels ages him and separates him forever from home.[53]

Kipling's "Christmas in India" appeared in the Christmas 1886 issue of *The Pioneer* and reflects the desires of his Anglo-Indian audience. Coming forty-seven years after Landon's, Kipling's piece brings a willingness to acknowledge the indigenous community and deals frankly with themes only tacitly suggested in Landon's poem. It also revises Landon's reminisces of an eighteenth-century-style Christmas with the small family gatherings more common to the Victorian celebration. Kipling's narrator resents Englishmen at home who celebrate the holiday with a brief nod to the servants of imperialism only to "forget us till another year be gone!"[54] As he thinks of home, the imperialist is called back by the "grim Stepmother of our kind," India. By the end of the poem, he forlornly submits: "With the fruitless years behind us and the hopeless years before us, / Let us honour, O my brothers, Christmas Day!"[55] Kipling's narrator, like Landon's, has lost his youthful mirth through imperialistic endeavors. Both poets' arguments suggest that Christmas and community keep one young, and when a person is removed from community rituals and subject to the demands of acting as an oppressing, imperialistic authority, they becomes heart-weary. They focus on the past, on communal scenes enjoyed before experience undermined their youthful idealism. Christmas offers them a chance to pause and compare a concrete moment in the past—one of fellowship and cheer—with their disappointing, lonely present.

Of all the genres, the poetry of Christmas opened the door to the spiritual searching expected of a liminal season. It was a season out of time, and print materials consistently attest to how poets took advantage of the time set apart to evaluate their own sorrows, as Tennyson does in *In Memoriam*, or home-longing, as so many voices do in the poetry of emigration. The season's liminality and heightened home expectations also drove artists to look outward to take stock of humanity's ethical evolution. Hymns and devotional poetry could be revisited each Christmas since their dependence on scripture conferred on them a timeless quality, but other contemplative Christmas poems affixed themselves firmly in their contemporary time. Victorian poets frequently titled their Christmas pieces for a specific year, as in the case of Aubrey De Vere's "Christmas Eve, 1859," George MacDonald's "A Christmas Carol for 1862," Alfred Austin's "Christmas, 1870," and Hardy's "Christmas: 1924." Like a holiday letter or a journal entry collecting the thoughts of the passing year, the Christmas poem could serve as a personal evaluation of contemporary events like the Italian Revolution, the 1862 troubles in Lancashire, or the First World War. The poems' very datedness was a challenge to readers to look to their present day or, in the case of collected works, the recent past, to interpret the evolution of society or empire during those momentous days around Christmas. This outward searching led to the prevalence of condition of England Christmas novels, but it also directed artists to use Christmas as a yardstick for England's global involvement.

Finally, I would be negligent to ignore the overwhelming body of Christmas verse that wholly neglects the spiritual in favor of the material. Verse about the cultural celebration may well be the most reprinted form of Christmas poetry. Carol antiquarian John C. Hotten explains that the Puritanical banning of all things Christmas and the subsequent worldliness of Charles II's court led to an enduring heritage of carols about festivity rather than religion.[56] That tradition, blended with the renewed interest in fashionably rustic Christmas customs, resulted in a steady stream of nineteenth-century verses about boar-laden tables and wassailing. When readers came upon such poems, which were so often titled simply "Old Christmas," they could ready themselves for lists of antiquated food prepared for the landed gentry and shared with the local peasants. Hervey relied on poems celebrating the feudal Christmas in the early chapters of his *The Book of Christmas*. There and elsewhere poems informed readers like nonfiction prose pieces historicizing Christmases past; moreover, they offered loving retellings of the elements that contributed to the construct of the traditional English Christmas. Such retellings contributed to the historicity of an especially Saxon, predominantly Stuart English national heritage that came out of the celebrated readings that described Christmases past.

Some of the carols contributed to the antiquated version of Christmas that played a role in the contemporary performance of the holiday. John Hotten's collection, for example, included an entire category devoted to "Carols in Praise of the Boar's Head," which were mostly fifteenth- and sixteenth-century poems that lovingly depicted that extinct scene of hospitality. Birket Foster, who illustrated *Christmas with the Poets*, sketched the retainer lifting the boar's head high as he paraded it behind the dancing jester.[57] Representations of the obsolete scene, both visual and poetic, helped to evolve the understanding of the Victorian family feast. One *Belgravia* poet satirized the prevalent, poetry-based nostalgia by retelling the failed attempt to revive "the old English mode *à la* Gilbert" at Moat Hall. Guests survived rather than enjoyed the traditional food ("huge shields of brawn, which to eat is detestable, / ... / And of course the boar's head, looking most indigestible") and gymnastic pastimes ("forfeits and romps very near put an end to us, / And left us for dead on the floor of Moat Hall"). Done in the form of the typical poem of serious antiquarian zeal, this representation of a "dyspeptic," "hideous" Christmas shows how the nature of the holiday's performance had changed. The narrator expresses a longing for the new, more delicate traditions of the well-regulated Victorian Christmas.[58]

For those more interested in contemplating the contemporary holiday, plenty of poems presented idealized versions. Many early-nineteenth-century poems offer proof of a hearth-loving, liminal Christmas performance long before Dickens and his prose-writing colleagues revitalized the holiday. Leigh Hunt, a poet who loved to chronicle the elements of Christmas performance, asked, "What, do they suppose that everything has been said that *can* be said about any one Christmas thing?" He followed his question with a list of sixty elemental parts of Christmas performance, noting that contemporary writers were far from exhausting such beguiling topics as mince-pie, mumming, wassail, charity, and a host of holiday images.[59]

Each holiday season poets revisited historic elements as well as church bells and the angelic multitude, and for this reason the poetry of the holiday feels more repetitive than the other genres. Like hymns sung to God, Christmas poems often addressed Christmas itself, a lesser god of the Victorian hearth: "A thousand voices welcome thee from every English home."[60] That many readers chose to welcome Christmas by reading the poetry of the season demonstrates the marketability of this especially Christian genre. A brief article-length anthology of Christmas poetry in the *Manchester Times* insisted that "Indeed, poetry seems as natural to the season as does kindly feeling," and the writer prophesied that Christmas poetry would live on for centuries.[61] In fact, the Christmas poetry Victorians loved so well does make appearances in the twenty-first-century celebration, but, as the recent evidence to which I now turn shows, this particular genre has lost much of the marketable clout it had during the nineteenth-century holiday.

Chapter 7

Modern Marketing of the Victorian Christmas

The *Punch* contributor who had thought that "every little author" was preparing a 5s. Christmas book in 1846 would have been overwhelmed by the greater flood of Christmas materials that inundated the market a few decades later when a variety of gift items were to be had for a range of prices.[1] An 1861 entry in Thackeray's "Roundabout Papers" exposed a writer's subsequent appreciation for the annual packaging of Christmas cheer:

> We have all admired the illustrated papers, and noted how boisterously jolly they become at Christmas time. What wassail bowls, robin-redbreasts, waits, snow landscapes, bursts of Christmas song! And then to think that these festivities are prepared months before—that these Christmas pieces are prophetic! How kind of artists and poets to devise the festivities beforehand, and serve them pat at the proper time![2]

Victorian Christmas texts were didactic as well as prophetic, since they shaped the way the nation came to construct its own identity through the lens of Christmas even as cultural needs spawned new Christmas sales niches. This identity formation was never very far removed from the material object of Christmas print material, the covers and illustrations of which came to dominate the book market in the weeks leading up to the holiday.

The public celebration of Christmas contributed to the conversation about the continually changing national narrative. Print materials of more recent decades offer insights into how the Victorian Christmas participates in postmodern perceptions of the holiday. Twentieth- and twenty-first-century authors and publishers have revived Victorian texts and customs in print, but they have also created texts that reveal the current cultural needs for celebrants. The afterlife of the many Victorian Christmases previously discussed continues to affect the literature of Christmas.

Before I move into a discussion of modern Christmas books, I would like to pause to point out the continual evolution of the identity-building factor of this holiday, an element of Christmas used today to sell much more than Victorian booksellers ever imagined. As in the nineteenthcentury, Christmas continues to be wrapped up in ideas of national identity, especially how and by whom it should be celebrated. Changing ethnic landscapes and cultural perspectives have updated the nostalgic terms so that it is now typically the "British" Christmas rather than the "English" Christmas that serves as a touchstone for national character. Articles in periodicals like the *Financial Times* and *Farmers Weekly* access the dominant narrative of the British Christmas with just brief lists of the holiday's elementals, often before quipping about how the actual Christmas experience veers from those expectations. Consumption remains at the dead center of this modern British Christmas, allowing one insecure producer, fearful of European Commission regulations, to claim that, "brandy butter is a vital ingredient of the British Christmas."[3] If anything, retailers have perfected the heightening of tradition to increase sales. Like their Victorian ancestors, British audiences read about ways their holiday rituals establish national identity. For example, a 1985 *Times* article followed *Punch*-ian principles by depicting the world map as a perfectly round plum pudding to show the route of the most traveled Christmas pudding, the one served up in the distant British embassy in Ulan Bator, Mongolia. The Christmas setting continually allows print materials to colonize the map through this emblematic food. The *Times* story recorded that the holiday season transformed the official Queens's Messengers, typically the carriers of classified paperwork, into "emissaries from paradise, deities who are miraculously armed with all the potions and magic needed to sustain the morale, the sprit, the indomitable Britishness of the group stranded in the cheerless waste."[4] Thus the work of reifying the national character of Christmas continued its lively work here and elsewhere in twentieth-century print.

More recently, during the 2007 Christmas season, British identity and the public celebration of Christmas made headlines yet again when Trevor Phillips, MP and head of the Commission of Equalities and Human Rights and Black British Labor politician pushed schools to continue nativity plays despite fears of offending Muslim students and parents. Some schools had taken the precaution of eliminating Bible-based plays from their schedule in a self-motivated effort to secularize or silence Christmas. As a result, British sheiks voiced support for Trevor Phillips's Christmas vision. They expressed concern that removing the nativity plays might add to the stereotype that non-Muslim Britons hold about Muslim Britons altering society. Immigration may be changing the face and the faith of the average Briton, but Phillips urged adults to expose children to this "very important, fundamental national celebration and tradition; otherwise they are robbing their children of really being part of what it is to be British."[5] Thus the performance of Christmas in the form of the nativity play quite literally signified a ritual of Britishness according to Christians and non-Christians alike. Likewise, seasonal print narratives of today continue to offer guides to the performance of Christmas, especially its elements of performance, many of which are tied to a continual recreation of the Victorian holiday.

Upon embarking on this study I had hoped to carry the study of Christmas print far from the well-trod field of Dickens. That has been impossible. Dickens's influence marks nineteenth-century Christmas books from the prevalent cover format to the criteria by which they were reviewed, and even the frame tale structure some periodical editors chose to adopt for special numbers. His tone dominates much of the middle-class Christmas stories, especially those with moral messages such as novels by Benjamin Farjeon and the non-ghost stories of Anthony Trollope and Mary Elizabeth Braddon. Despite what some late-nineteenth-century fans and overly reductive twenty-first-century critics have alleged, Dickens could never have claimed to have revived Christmas alone, as David Parker argues compellingly in *Christmas and Charles Dickens.* According to Parker, in the late nineteenth century "a generation of Dickens enthusiasts . . . with no personal memories of the early years of the century, dazzled by Dickens's achievements" invented the idea that Christmas had been dying out everywhere before his holiday endeavors.[6] Nonetheless, Dickens's slim 1840s volumes outshine other Victorian discourses on Christmas of the nineteenth, twentieth, and, so far, twenty-first centuries. Articles about books for Christmas written today still open with references to Dickens, and it is unlikely that the shadow he casts over the holiday market will ever fade. He has become a beloved element of the holiday performance.

The holiday rituals of consumerism the Victorians promulgated continue to affect modern celebrants, especially when it comes to the narratives offered for sale. Those newer genres to develop seasonal narratives, television and film, often make over Victorian fantasies rather than developing new narratives of their own. December television is dominated not only by holiday showings but, in Great Britain, by any work of Dickens, causing the *Northern Echo* to herald the start of "the Dickens Season" with the various showings of not just *A Christmas Carol* films, but also various adaptations of Dickens's novels.[7] Producers of nonseasonal Dickens novels clutch at the coattails of the ghostly little book and use it to gain admittance to this consumer season. Paul Davis has argued that there are two texts to *A Christmas Carol*, the one that went on sale in 1843, and the "culture-text," or "the Carol as it has been re-created in the century and a half since it first appeared." This second culture-text is constantly being revised with every stage and film adaptation of the novel, as well as each advertisement that reimagines what it means to be Scrooge: "It is not limited by its original formulation or by all its past versions. It is open to the yet unspoken potentialities of Christmas Carols Yet-to-Come."[8] Tom Leitch has written that "for many viewers, film adaptations of *A Christmas Carol* are likely to substitute for Dickens, to become Dickens, rather than serving as merely a rung on the Dickens ladder."[9] Similarly the myriads of adaptations of *A Christmas Carol* have come to stand in for the wealth of Victorian Christmases, to become the Victorian Christmas. Hopefully by now it has become clear that there was no single Victorian Christmas; rather, the constructed holiday evolved to meet changing commercial and identity-based needs. Nonetheless, modern *Carols* eschew the bifurcated ancestry of the Victorian Christmas in their renditions of the monumental, textual obelisk of the nineteenth-century Christmas.

This study has been one of print materials; so, rather than explore the multitudes of *Carol* adaptations in film, I wish to direct the consideration of the afterlife of the Victorian Christmas back to paper texts. Dozens of editions of *A Christmas Carol* are for sale today, and their covers compete for the attention of the holiday reader. Many show various *Carol* characters, often in the obligatory snowy backdrop, as illustrators count on the cultural familiarity of *Carol* scenes—the encounter with Marley seems to be a favorite—which has replaced the nineteenth-century acquaintance with the small, red cloth covered volumes. Others, like the Norilana Books 2006 edition cover, depict random Victorian-esque groups of children unassociated with Dickens's plot. The Norilana Books cover encases the scenes in Christmas ball ornaments that reflect a montage of snowy Victorian scenes back at the potential consumer, as if to suggest that the scenes are part of the consumer's reality. Such tactics permit the consumer to claim the supposed heritage of *A Christmas Carol* as her own. Furthermore, the predominance of audio versions of the novel attests to the continual commodification of the reading aloud of this particular text.

Many of the literary samples of what Dianne F. Sadoff and John Kucich might call "post-Victorian borrowings" related to Christmas come in the form of reimagined Christmas Carols.[10] Such texts include novels marketed to the Christian consumer, like *Bah Humbug, Mrs. Scrooge* (2006) and *Boo Humbug* (2007, number four of the Boo Series). Louis Bayard's *Mr. Timothy* (2003) narrates a pedophile ring and murder mystery the twenty-three-year-old Timothy Cratchit solves during the 1860 London Christmas season. Timothy's occasional visits to his Uncle Ebenezer's house, which is perpetually decorated for Christmas, briefly carry readers back into memorable scenes from Dickens's novel. Bayard's narrative otherwise argues that Dickens got his characters all wrong, or, rather, the characters promoted unlikely versions of themselves. Inside Timothy's consciousness, readers learn that he was not "as good as gold," but only a character in a plot his father narrated who temporarily assumed the assigned role and took up the lines his family expected. Now, physically healed but mourning the loss of his father, Timothy must create his own narrative to inhabit. This airing of false sentimentality within in the holiday classic casts a postmodern chill onto the heartwarming Dickensian narrative. The pedophile ring may be broken in time for Christmas, but Mr. Timothy must leave England for a voyage of exploration to pursue the his own self-discovery taking place outside his father's maudlin narrative.

In another reimagining of *Carol* characters, Gregory Maguire's *Lost* (2001) also solves a mystery: this time a descendant of the man who supposedly inspired Dickens to create Scrooge unearths her ancestor's link to an undead medieval Frenchwoman burned for an unknown crime. Like her haunted/possessed ancestor, Winifred Rudge becomes possessed by Gervasa, a tortured spirit who bears no resemblance to Dickens's three fanciful visitors. Here, too, a descendant of Scooge comes to deal with her painful past through her sleuthing, suggesting that the story of the *Carol* is a talisman waiting to initiate the individual's psychological healing of grief and trauma, the new, postmodern conversion.

Carol-lust has taken deep root across the Atlantic, allowing a *Chicago Tribune* writer to identify the *Carol* as "the focus of so much of our holiday OCD," since the story relocated the heart of Christmas from Bethlehem to "snowy Victorian London . . . Naturally we obsess on it every Christmas—for many of us by now, it is Christmas."[11] For others, Christmas serves as a conduit into a historicized past. Elements of the perceived nineteenth-century Christmas—the relatively small family gathering, the focus on children, the consumer-based experience, and the performance of food rituals—appeal to the modern celebrant, while others, like the Memorial Day factor, have faded away. Victoriana has made its larger resurgence only since the early 1980s, and it has marked the modern home in a yearlong interest in collectables. The desire to clothe a modern home in Victorian-esque knickknacks has much to do with the desire to escape the here and now,[12] and the twenty-first-century Victorian Christmas reenactments similarly serve as escaping a world of all-too-present global injustice and pain. New performances of the Victorian Christmas do not belittle the expression of desires they offer celebrants; Christine L. Krueger reminds Victorianists of the present time not to "dismiss the popularity of things Victorian as bad faith or rank nostalgia."[13] Consumers can enter the modern performance of the Victorian holiday by buying tickets to several events, including A Victorian Festival of Christmas at the historic dockyard in Portsmouth, a market complete with bonneted actors, group caroling, and chimney sweeps; the Bury St. Edmunds Christmas Fayre, which claims to replicate the Victorian Christmas shopping experience; and Warwick Castle's Victorian Christmas display, including Ebenezer's haunted tower. The Victorian Christmas takes on an after hours afterlife in London's A Dickens of a Christmas, a business operating only in December that charges £95 to £125 a head to host office Christmas parties in a Dickensian setting complete with an opium den, carolers, and an end-of-party disco. Perhaps one of the best good-faith performances of the Victorian Christmas happens in Texas. Houston inhabitant Anne Boyd becomes Queen Victoria, the "beacon" of Dickens on the Strand, an annual celebration of Dickens and Victoriana. As the queen, Boyd serves as an ambassador from the nineteenth century, sharing facts and answering questions about Victoria's era. Americans might naturally look for a queen at celebrations of English life and culture, since Renaissance Fairs typically place the figure of Queen Elizabeth I at the heart of the entertainment. Localized Christmas events like Dickens on the Strand have become more decorous, nineteenth-century versions of the Renaissance Fairs with carolers and carriage rides replacing the mud fights and jousts. The Texas event even received genetic endorsement in 2007 when Dickens's great-great-great-grandson attended and carried on his progenitor's readings of the holiday classic.[14]

Book buying at Christmas may not rate very high as a Victorian tradition at these elaborate, ticketed events, but it is one way that modern celebrants can reenact an element of nineteenth-century holiday custom. Like the sales of 150 years ago, most of the books on display for the holidays in twenty-first-century Britain have nothing to do with the Christmas performance beyond gift-giving rituals. Works of nonfiction typically top the charts in recent years, especially celebrity biographies and quirky informative selections like Lynne Truss's *Eats, Shoots & Leaves* (2003). Cookbooks have gained a prominent position in the gift-edition racks, and in 2007 *Nigella Express* published by Random House Group gained widespread attention as a best-selling Christmas book in Britain. However, best-seller status is often greatly impacted by the depth of the publisher's wallet rather than grassroots popularity. Publishers' dependence on Christmas book sales have led to a double commodification of book sales, a turn of events that Lewis Carroll with his distrust of booksellers would surely have lamented. W.H Smith sells publishers slots on the recommended reading list, a scheme that in 2006 cost publishers £200,000 per book for the four weeks before Christmas. Books that garner a spot on the list will almost certainly be bestsellers, but not every publisher can afford the price.[15] Waterstone's has a similar scheme with graded packages for book displays and special mentions during the Christmas season costing from £45,000 (a package limited to just six books nationwide, guaranteeing prominent displays and national advertising campaigns) to £500 for a mention in the bookseller's Gift Guide. The chairman of one independent publisher has complained that declining a bookseller's offer almost guarantees a book's failure: "If Smith's offer you one of these slots and you say no, their order doesn't go down from 1,000 copies to 500 copies. It goes down to 20 copies."[16]

The 2007 Christmas season saw many elements that escaped the Victorian booksellers' marketing plans. Exclusive, signed, and specially bound editions are a growing part of booksellers' holiday stock, and independent booksellers turn to such tactics as a means of attracting consumers away from internet purchases.[17] Not only the Internet, which has become a rising force in holiday book sales since 1999, but expanded grocery chains like Tesco secure large portions of holiday sales. Recent Christmases have seen booksellers discount books in the weeks leading up to Christmas only to spike prices in the final week of trading to ensure maximum holiday profits.[18] All this has an amazing impact on the annual reports of publishing houses since publishers live and die by Christmas profits. In 2007 the publisher Hachette Livre UK did not begin to "make good" until the Christmas season began in November, and it ended 2007 with 16.6 percent of the market share and a growth in profit of 5.1 percent. In the same year Profile failed to bring out a Christmas success, and profits fell by an abysmal 30.1 percent.[19]

In the United Kingdom, sales in December comprise a quarter of booksellers' yearly revenue, and sales in the month before Christmas are 50 percent higher than sales during other months.[20] Industry analyzing agencies like Nielsen BookScan chart the sales of individual titles for 90 percent of the UK book market, which allows industry analysts like Richard Knight to make precise calculations about how Britons buy book for Christmas. The fact is, September beats out February by a 40 percent increase in sales activity. Knight said in 1999 that "[a] week at Christmas is like a month at any part of the year for sales," and the number has been on the increase. By 2005 one week at Christmas equaled three times the sales of a mid-year week.[21] Publishers schedule their entire year to maximize pre-Christmas sales, and they sign books accordingly. Biographies, which often find their way onto Christmas best-seller lists, will sell 300 percent better if they appear in October rather than in the spring.[22] Comedian Peter Kay's autobiography was the leading Christmas book in 2006, and it sold a nonfiction record of 165,462 copies the week before Christmas and 747,908 between 5 October and 23 December.[23] In comparison, Dan Brown's fictional *The Da Vinci Code* won best-seller bragging rights in the 2004 British market by selling 106,000 books in the week before Christmas.[24]

While many other industries rely on the October through December season for up to half of all sales, the American book market shows remarkable evenness throughout the year. Albert N. Greco's detailed study of the American book industry at the turn of the twenty-first century shows a "flattening" of sales from 1998 to 2001, as sales of adult trade book came to be perfectly distributed throughout the four seasons. Unlike the Victorian publishers who ran great risks when December deadlines were not met—like Moxon, who took a loss when an edition of Tennyson overshot the December market—the twenty-first-century publisher "can feel confident releasing new titles in January or March," although they "avoid February because

John Grisham traditionally releases his new novel in that month." Nonetheless, many of the books marketed specifically as Christmas buys like *I'm Dreaming of a Chocolate Christmas* (2007) are published in October, some in September, well in advance of the holiday rush. American publishers must also be aware that books have lost their status as the preeminent Christmas gift. In 2001 only 15 percent of American adult trade books and 41 percent of children's books were purchased as gifts, and this percentage lumps Christmas presents with all other gifts.[25]

American sales figures may show a level fourth quarter, but publishers have recently rediscovered the marketability of new Christmas titles by well-known authors. The *Washington Post* reported an upsurge in Christmas books in 2002:

> Book purveyors are banging into each other like liquored-up elves, hoping to discover the next Dickens. They are hyping a handful of Christmas offerings from mega-selling authors—including "Skipping Christmas" by John Grisham, "The Christmas Train" by David Baldacci, "Visions of Sugar Plums: A Stephanie Plum Holiday Novel" by Janet Evanovich and "Esther's Gift: A Mitford Christmas Story" by Jan Karon—in hopes that they'll become longtime and lucrative Christmas traditions. . . . Jim Milliot of *Publishers Weekly* says of the trend, "This is brand new."

Of course, the production of holiday tales by established writers is anything but new. The twenty-first-century authors cashing in on the perennial Christmas market realize how lucrative the Christmas book can be; in 2002 John Grisham instructed his publishers to bring out his *Skipping Christmas* each year in hardcover. Additionally, Milliot promises that newly tinseled mega-authors "don't have to deal with critics."[26] As in the case of Dickens's seasonal books that initially received poor reviews, the concept of Christmas and the hardback format overrules the dictates of humbug reviewers. Twenty-first-century Christmas books appear in a variety of smaller sizes, though typically not as small as the Victorian variety. Sentiment continues its reign in Christmas reading expectations, although the cultural touchstones have shifted. In *The Christmas Shoes* (2001) Donna VanLiere narrates a busy lawyer's sudden appreciation of his family alongside the deaths of one young and one elderly mother at Christmastime. A survivor of foster care abuse reconnects with her addict father and long-lost sister in *Finding Noel* (2006). The novel *The Shepherd's Prayer* (2006) serves as a devotional meditation on the faith of the Bethlehem shepherds and the horrific slaughter of the innocents that followed Christ's birth. Reunions, both physical and emotional, continue to feature in Christmas books. Rather than present the reading lesson Marion offers in *The Battle of Life*, today's characters are more likely to blatantly instruct audiences in how to read Christmas consumerism. While Victorian Christmas book audiences expected to finish their buys in one reading, the modern variety structures the narrative to allow readers to work through the book over several readings, as frequent plot summaries at the start of chapters attest. Twenty-first-century Christmas books by Grisham, Karon, and Evanovich still compete with Dickens's Christmas books for sales, as demonstrated by Blackwell's exclusively bound 2007 edition of *A Christmas Carol* from Oxford University Press.[27]

Christmas has become a recognizable and frequent setting for subgenres of fiction, such as the murder mystery and the romance novel. Murders set during the holiday feature in Kasey Michaels's *High Heels and Holiday;* the near annual Christmas mystery by Mary Higgins Clark, including *The Christmas Thief* (2004), *He Sees You When You're Sleeping* (2001), *Deck the Halls* (2000); and a host of other mysteries. Regency-romance writer Stephanie Laurens's *The Promise in a Kiss* (2001) might allege the subtitle *A Christmas Novel*, but the claim has far less relevance than the seasonal Victorian subtitles of a century and a half earlier. Instead, these seasonal offerings, as the Victorians would have called them, resemble those by Charlotte Riddell and other authors Routledge commissioned to fill its Christmas annuals since they depict the occasional Christmas setting rather than the emotionally charged Christmas scene. The telltale elements of the modern subgenres assert themselves and silence any attempt at a revised set of Christmas values; murder and lovemaking take precedence during the holiday as they do in their respective genres the rest of the year. For example, Anne Perry's Christmas murder *A Christmas Guest* (2005) depicts the sleuthing of a crotchety Victorian grandmother while the family of the murdered woman gathers for the Christmas festivities. The sleuth alternates her pointed questions with benign inquiries about the family's holiday traditions, and the occasional setting description sounds much like a Leigh Hunt Christmas rant listing each of the required elements of the performance.[28] While romance and murder mystery offer the largest list of festive narratives in the modern Christmas market (save for reprints of *A Christmas Carol*), the heightened experience of Christmas is abandoned for the mundane criteria of the respective genres. In the competitive and prolific worlds of modern prose subgenres, the claim to a Christmas title, cover, or subtitle gains authors a seasonal niche, a slight advantage over the rest of the crowd during the fourth quarter gift-buying season. The marketing technique casts a double net, appealing to readers devoted to mysteries while also drawing on consumers looking for a Christmas read.

While Dickens dominates the Victorian category of the modern holiday marketplace, he is not entirely alone. Not quite entirely alone. In keeping with the much-adored Victorian Christmas booksellers' tables, many books today recollect and repackage the Victorian Christmas—with various levels of accuracy—for the modern reader. Such books imitate Hervey's and other historians' attempts to historicize Christmas afresh using poems and narrated rituals, only now the focus has been reoriented away from the Victorians' beloved Stuarts to the nineteenth century itself. One such book, *A Victorian Christmas* (1990), vaguely outlines traditions and notes that "Our love of nostalgia at this particular time of year transports us naturally to the reign of Queen Victoria."[29] Of course, there is nothing "natural" about being transported to the nineteenth century rather than the twelfth or sixteenth centuries. One could, perhaps, rule out the seventeenth century, during which the Puritans temporarily cancelled Christmas. In the same way that Hervey's dreams of a stable hierarchy sent him to the Stuart Christmas, late-twentieth-century celebrants embarked on a path to the Victorian holiday predetermined by their hopes for respectable, orderly, simpler Christmases, an ironic goal when one realizes all of the additional preparations required of a real homemade middle-class feast circa 1850.

Many books for sale today suggest that Victorian Christmas print did its job too well. The Christmas how-to book is the other genre clambering for the holiday shopper's attention. Like nineteenth-century *Punch* readers, modern celebrants can take a break from holiday shopping to peruse alternative narratives that eschew the chaos of Christmas consumerism. Instead of devotional poetry, Christian readers may turn to *The Adventure of Christmas: Helping Children Find Jesus in our Holiday Traditions* (2004), *A Simple Christmas: A Faith- Filled Guide to a Meaningful and Stress-free Christmas* (2006), as well as *Gifts from the Heart: Simple Ways to Make Your Family's Christmas More Meaningful* (2007) and other volumes that instruct celebrants in how to avoid seasonal materialism. Grisham's *Skipping*

Christmas impishly toys with the idea of doing just that and has the main characters, Americans, taking pride in their "decision to forgo, at least for a year, the mindless materialism of our culture."[30] Today's Christmas-keeper has to choose between competing narratives: those that emphasize consumption—commercial advertising, song lyrics, class-based accumulation expectations—and the narratives of simplification that one hears from pulpits, television Christmases, and the books and magazine articles that supposedly guide the consumer to a simpler narrative of Christmas.

Other texts capitalize on the wealth of literature and documentation about the nineteenth-century Christmas this study investigated. Despite its publisher, *The Oxford Book of Christmas Poems* is designed for pleasure reading rather than scholarship, and the inscription in the copy at hand shows that anthologies of Christmas verse still make good Christmas gifts. In the 1990s Sutton Publishing of Stroud created a series of books for the amateur historian and the Victoria & Albert consumer rather than the scholar; this series was intended to capitalize on the literary nostalgia for the holiday: *Thomas Hardy's Christmas, Jane Austen's Christmas: The Festive Season in Georgian England, The Brontës' Christmas, A Shropshire Christmas*, (as well as the non-Victorian *Christmas in Shakespeare's England*). This series excerpts Christmas scenes, poems, and diary entries by the authors and their families in an attractive, illustrated, coffee table book-like format, commodifying the authors' experience of the holiday.

All of which forces me to reconsider the genre in which this study of the Victorian Christmas belongs. I have purposefully set out to avoid the table-book style Christmas historicizing that is so common in the many "histories" of Christmas that I have met along the way. Most studies offer generalities and adoring, uncritical descriptions of the elementals of the Victorian holiday. Even some of the best refrain from footnoting their sources, as if assuming the intended readership wants the glow of general information without corroboration. And the amount of nineteenth-century literature in this seasonal category is overwhelming. When confronted with the monumental glut of seasonal literature written and purchased by Victorians, it becomes a challenge to remain empathetic to the emotional reaction of first audiences. Much of this literature is at worst mawkish and empty but at best surprisingly touching. In the reading experience of print materials intended to educate readers in the Christmas performance and the books produced for the gift exchange market, multiple voices clearly assert themselves, defying the idea of any single, iconic Victorian Christmas. Only by reestablishing the cacophony of contemporary nineteenth-century Christmas print can we analyze the ways in which the sometimes clashing, sometimes harmonious voices contributed to the cultural hope contained within the secular Christmas.

Notes

Introduction

1. "Flood of Christmas Books," *Punch* 11 (1846): 210.
2. Krishna Kumar, *The Making of English National Identity* (New York: Cambridge UP, 2003), 7.
3. "Christmas at Hereford," *Mirror* 20:583 (December 1833): 438.
4. R. Chambers, *The Book of Days: A Miscellany of Popular Antiquities in Connection with the Calendar, Including Anecdote, Biography, & History, Curiosities of Literature and Oddities of Human Life and Character*, vol. 2 (Edinburgh: W. & R. Chambers, 1873), 747.
5. "Christmas at the Crystal Palace," *Punch* 40 (January 1861): 8.
6. Peter J. Manning, "Wordsworth and the *Keepsake*," in *Literature in the Marketplace: Nineteenth-Century British Publishing and Reading Practices*, ed. John O. Jordan and Robert L. Patten (New York: Cambridge UP, 1995), 65.
7. "Christmas Presents," Advertisement, *Illustrated London News* (16 December 1843): 399.
8. Kim Newman, "You Better Watch Out: Christmas in Horror Film," in *Christmas at the Movies*, ed. Mark Connelly (New York: Tauris, 2000), 136.
9. Peter Haining, Introduction to *Charles Dickens' Christmas Ghost Stories* by Charles Dickens (New York: St. Martin, 1993), 10.
10. Mark Connelly, *Christmas: A Social History* (New York: Tauris, 1999), 2.

1 Books for Christmas, 1822–1860

1. Joseph Shaylor, *The Fascination of Books, with Other Papers on Books & Bookselling* (New York: Putnam, 1912), 39–40.
2. Harry E. Hootman "British Literary Annuals and Giftbooks: 1823–1861," Diss. University of South Carolina, 2004, 1; Peter J. Manning, "Wordsworth in the *Keepsake*," in *Literature in the Marketplace*, ed. Jordan and Patten, 45.
3. Kathryn Ledbetter, "Lucrative Requests: British Authors and Gift Book Editors," *Bibliographical Society of America, Papers* 88 (1994): 214.
4. Alexis Weedon, *Victorian Publishing* (Aldershot: Ashgate, 2003), 19.

5. Caroline Anne Bowles Southey to Robert Southey, 3 April 1828, *The Correspondence of Robert Southey with Caroline Bowles*, ed. Edward Dowden (Dublin: Hodges, Figgis, 1881), 388, http://solomon.bwld.alexanderstreet.com.
6. Richard Altick, *The English Common Reader: A Social History of the Mass Reading Public 1800–1900* (Chicago: U of Chicago P, 1957), 362.
7. Shaylor, *The Fascination of Books*, 48.
8. Valerie Sanders, ed., *Record of Girlhood: An Anthology of Nineteenth-Century Women's Childhoods* (Aldershot: Ashgate, 2000), 97.
9. Thomas K. Hervey, *The Book of Christmas* (Ware: Wordsworth, 2000), 24.
10. Richard M. Dorson, *The British Folklorists* (Chicago: U of Chicago P, 1968), 17.
11. "New Year's Eve and New Year's Day," *Leigh Hunt's London Journal* 40 (31 December 1834): 314.
12. David Parker, *Christmas and Charles Dickens* (New York: AMS P, 2005), x, 78–90, 108.
13. "Ancient Christmas," *Mirror* 22:639 (December 1833): 420.
14. Hervey, *The Book of Christmas*, 21.
15. Julian Wolfreys, *Being English* (Albany: State U of New York P, 1994), 5–6.
16. Hervey, *The Book of Christmas*, 66; Julia Thomas, *Pictorial Victorians* (Athens: Ohio UP, 2004), 13.
17. David Bland, *The Illustration of Books* (London: Faber and Faber, 1951), 16.
18. Robert Burden, Introduction to *Landscape and Englishness* (New York: Rodopi, 2006), 17.
19. Peter Mandler, *The English National Character* (New Haven: Yale UP, 2006), 41.
20. Ibid., 3.
21. Ibid., 2.
22. Walter Benjamin, *Illuminations* (New York: Harcourt Brace & World, 1968), 265.
23. Hervey, *The Book of Christmas*, 43.
24. Ibid., 169–71.
25. B.E. Maidment, *Reading Popular Prints 1790–1870* (New York: Manchester UP, 1996), 80.
26. John Buchanan-Brown, *The Book Illustrations of George Cruikshank* (London: David & Charles, 1980), 47.
27. Hervey, *The Book of Christmas*, 148.
28. Ibid., 72.
29. Ibid., 120.
30. Henry G. Bohn, "Biographical Notice" in *Seymour's Humorous Sketches* (London: Henry G. Bohn, 1872), vi.

    Wordsworth Editions in association with the Folklore Society published a 2000 edition of *The Book of Christmas*. Unfortunately,

Steve Roud's introduction to this edition, as well as the frontispiece, misdate the first publication of Hervey's text at 1888. My research has dated the first edition to 26 December 1835, a period that makes a huge difference given the sources Hervey accesses (which are all eighteenth- and early nineteenth-century) and the stage of development of the "new" Christmas. Publication dating practices often saw late-year volumes postdated.

31. Hervey, *The Book of Christmas*, 30, 139.
32. Ibid., 38.
33. John Sutherland, *Victorian Fiction: Writers, Publishers, Readers* (New York: Palgrave Macmillan, 2006), 159.
34. Lorraine Janzen Kooistra, "Poetry in the Victorian Marketplace: The Illustrated Princess as a Christmas Gift Book," *Victorian Poetry* 45 (Spring 2007), http://proquest.umi.com.
35. Simon Eliot, "Some Trends in British Book Production, 1800–1919," in *Literature in the Marketplace*, ed. Jordan and Patten, 34.
36. There is, of course, an entirely different category of print material that is also termed "Christmas books." Privately printed, artistic salutation booklets were traded like valuable Christmas cards. Collectors like Walter Klinefelter and Jock Elliot have amassed collections and published catalogues of these small-run titles. The salutation booklets seem to have had a heyday in the early decades of the twentieth century. I do not include salutation "Christmas books" in the category of Victorian Christmas books I examine.
37. William M. Thackeray, "A Grumble about the Christmas-Books," *Fraser's Magazine* 35 (January 1847): 111.
38. Annie Russell Marble, "Christmas Books of the Past," *Critic* (December 1899): 1127.
39. Thackeray, "A Grumble about the Christmas Books," 117.
40. "Decorated Christmas-Books for 1848," *Times* (25 December 1847): 3.
41. "Christmas Books," *Dublin University Magazine* (January 1847): 134.
42. Cutting inside the Emory University Library first edition of this title.
43. "A Gossip about the Christmas Books," 40.
44. Kathleen Tillotson, *Novels of the Eighteen-Forties* (Oxford: Clarendon, 1954), 24.
45. Robert Tracy, "'A Whimsical Kind of Masque': The Christmas Books and Victorian Spectacle," *Dickens Studies Annual* 27 (1988): 113.
46. Charles Dickens, *The Christmas Books*, vol. 1, ed. Michael Slater (Harmondsworth: Penguin, 1971), xxix.
47. Charles Dickens to Miss Burdett Coutts, 1 December 1845, *The Letters of Charles Dickens*, vol. 4, ed. Kathleen Tillotson (Oxford: Clarendon, 1977), 443.
48. Charles Dickens to John Forster, 26–29 October, 1846, *The Letters of Charles Dickens*, vol. 4, ed. Tillotson, 648.

49. Tracy, "'A Whimsical Kind of Masque,'" 113; H.M. Daleski, "Seasonal Offerings: Some Recurrent Features of the *Christmas Books*," *Dickens Studies Annual* 27 (1998): 107.
50. Philip Collins, *Charles Dickens: The Critical Heritage* (London: Taylor & Francis, 2003), 145.
51. Sarah A. Solberg, "'Text Dropped into the Woodcuts': Dickens's Christmas Books" *Dickens Studies Annual* 8 (1980): 115, 110.
52. Golby and Purdue, *The Making of the Modern Christmas*, 45.
53. Robert L. Patten, *Charles Dickens and His Publishers* (Oxford: Clarendon, 1978), 146–49, 153, 167.
54. Ruth F. Glancy, Introduction to *Christmas Books* by Charles Dickens (New York: Oxford UP, 1988), xv.
55. Patten, *Charles Dickens and His Publishers*, 187. Thackeray's Christmas book sales would eventually improve. His 1850 *The Kickleburys on the Rhine* quickly sold out of its original run of 3,000 and went into a second edition almost immediately. Margaret Smith, ed. *The Letters of Charlotte Bronte*, vol. 2 (Oxford: Clarendon, 2000), 471, http://www.nlx.com.
56. Review of *The Haunted Man and the Ghost's Bargain, Macphail's Edinburgh Ecclesiastical Journal* (January 1849), 423–432 in *Charles Dickens: The Critical Heritage*, ed. Collins, 179.
57. Wilkie Collins, *Sharpe's London Magazine* 8 (January 1849): 188 in *Charles Dickens: The Critical Heritage*, ed. Collins, 145.
58. Charles Dickens to Rev. David Macrae, 1861, *The Letters of Charles Dickens*, vol. 9, ed. Graham Storey (Oxford: Clarendon, 1997), 556.
59. Charles Dickens to the Earl of Carlisle, 2 January 1849, *The Letters of Charles Dickens*, vol. 5, ed. Graham Storey and K.J. Fielding (Oxford: Clarendon, 1981), 466.
60. William Dean Howells, *Criticism and Fiction* (New York: Harper, 1891), http://lion.chadwyck.com.
61. Andrew H. Miller, *Novels behind Glass: Commodity Culture and Victorian Narrative* (New York: Cambridge, 1995), 6.
62. Ibid., 7.
63. "The Kickleburys on the Rhine," *Times* (3 January 1851): 3.
64. William M. Thackeray, "An Essay on Thunder and Small Beer," in *The Christmas Books of Mr. M. A. Titmarsh* (New York: Harper, 1899), 166–67.
65. Marble, "Christmas Books of the Past," 1127.
66. Richard Kelly, Introduction to *A Christmas Carol*, by Charles Dickens (Peterborough: Broadview, 2003), 16.
67. "The Winds and the Waves: A Legend for Christmas," Advertisement, *Times* (24 November 1848): 2.
68. Mary Poovey, *Making a Social Body: British Cultural Formation, 1830–1864* (Chicago: U of Chicago P, 1995), 133.
69. J.A.R. Pimlott, *The Englishman's Christmas: A Social History* (Hassocks: Harvester, 1978), 85.

70. J.M. Golby and A.W. Purdue, *The Making of the Modern Christmas* (London: Batsford, 1986), 49–51.
71. S.A. Muresianu, *The History of the Victorian Christmas Book*, Diss., Harvard University, 1981 (New York: Garland, 1987), 12.
72. Elizabeth Gaskell, "*The Moorland Cottage*," in *The Moorland Cottage and Other Stories*, ed. Suzanne Lewis (New York: Oxford UP, 1995), 61.
73. Jeffrey Cass, "'The Scraps, Patches, and Rags of Daily Life': Gaskell's Oriental Other and the Conversation of Cranford," *Papers on Language and Literature* 35:2 (Fall 1999): 429–30.
74. Carol Lesjak, "Authenticity and the Geography of Empire: Reading Gaskell with Emecheta," *Studies in the Literary Imagination* 35:2 (Fall 2002): 135.
75. See Ramona Lumpkin's "(Re)Visions of Virtue: Elizabeth Gaskell's *Moorland Cottage* and George Eliot's *The Mill on the Floss*," *Studies in the Novel* 23:4 (Winter 1991): 432–442. Lumpkin traces Eliot's obligation to Gaskell's narrative, themes, and characters.
76. Letitia Elizabeth Landon, "Christmas in the Olden Time, 1650," in *Fisher's Drawing-Room Scrap Book* (London: Fisher, Son and Jackson, 1836), 48.
77. The story to which Maggie refers can be found in volume two of *Evenings at Home; or, the Juvenile Budget Opened. Consisting of a Variety of Miscellaneous Pieces, for the Instruction and Amusement of Young Persons* by John Aikin and Anna Laetitia Barbauld. The six-volume text was published between 1792 and 1796. Editions of the volume continued to be published throughout the nineteenth century.
78. Gaskell, *The Moorland Cottage*, 61.
79. Ibid., 90.
80. Ibid., 92.

2 How Victorians Read Christmas

1. Charles Dickens, *A Christmas Carol* (London: Chapman & Hall, 1843), 51.
2. Harry Stone, "*A Christmas Carol*: Giving Nursery Tales a Higher Form," in *The Haunted Mind: The Supernatural in Victorian Literature*, ed. Elton E. Smith and Robert Haas (London: Scarecrow, 1999), 16.
3. Jennifer Hayward, *Consuming Pleasures: Active Audiences and Serial Fictions from Dickens to Soap Opera* (Lexington: UP of Kentucky, 1997), 34.
4. Richard Altick, *Writers, Readers, and Occasions* (Columbia: Ohio State UP, 1989), 116–17.
5. Charles Dickens, *The Letters of Charles Dickens*, vol. 4, ed. Tillotson, n95.

6. Jonathan Rose, "Rereading the English Common Reader: A Preface to a History of Audiences," *Journal of the History of Ideas* 53 (January–March 1992): 49–51.
7. Norman Holland, "Re-Covering 'The Purloined Letter': Reading as a Personal Transaction," in *The Reader in the Text: Essays on Audience and Interpretation*, ed. Susan R. Suleiman and Inge Crosman (Princeton: Princeton UP, 1980), 364.
8. Jonathan Cullers, "Prolegomena to a Theory of Reading," in *The Reader in the Text*, ed. Suleiman and Crosman, 53.
9. Chambers, *The Book of Days*, 743. Edmund S. Roscoe, "Christmas in Scotland," *Belgravia* 10 (January 1870): 319.
10. Pimlott, *The Englishman's Christmas*, 359.
11. William Donaldson, *Popular Literature in Victorian Scotland: Language, Fiction and the Press* (Aberdeen: Aberdeen UP, 1986), 32.
12. Charles Dickens to the Reverend David Macrae, December 1861, *The Letters of Charles Dickens*, vol. 9, ed. Storey, 557.
13. Charles Dickens, *The Battle of Life: A Love Story* (London: Bradbury & Evans, 1846) 43.
14. Pimlott, *The Englishman's Christmas*, 93.
15. David Barrett, "Eleanor Farjeon," in *Dictionary of Literary Biography, Volume 160: British Children's Writers, 1914–1960*, ed. Donald R. Hettinga and Gary D. Schmidt (A Bruccoli Clark Layman Book The Gale Group, 1996), 88–101. http://galenet.galegroup.com.
16. Michelle Persell, "Dickensian Disciple: Anglo-Jewish Identity in the Christmas Tales of Benjamin Farjeon," *Philological Quarterly* 73 (Fall 1994): 461.
17. Ibid., 466.
18. Ibid., 461.
19. Benjamin Farjeon, *Bread-and-Cheese and Kisses* (New York: Harper, 1873), 10.
20. "Suggestions about Gift-Books" *Fraser's Magazine* (18 February 1852): 143.
21. Michael Wheeler, *English Fiction of the Victorian Period 1830–1890* (New York: Longman, 1985), 4.
22. "The 'Music in the Hall,'" *Illustrated London News* (23 December 1843): 416; "Christmas in Lodgings," *Household Words* 2:39 (21 December 1850): 295–298.
23. Hayward, *Consuming Pleasures*, 33–34.
24. Pimlott, *The Englishman's Christmas*, 90, 94.
25. Thackeray, "A Grumble about the Christmas-Books," 118.
26. "Christmas Tactics," *Howitt's Journal* 2:54 (25 December 1847) 414.
27. Hans Robert Jauss, "Literary History as a Challenge to Literary Theory," *New Literary History* 2 (1970), 18–19.
28. Benjamin Farjeon, *Golden Grain* (New York: Harper, 1874), 9.
29. Betty Jane Breyer, Introduction to *Anthony Trollope: The Complete Short Stories*, vol. 1 (Fort Worth: Texas Christian UP, 1979), vi.

30. Charles Dickens, *A Christmas Carol*, 9.
31. Vincent Newey, *The Scriptures of Charles Dickens: Novels of Ideology, Novels of Self* (Burlington: Ashgate, 2004), 49.
32. Suzanne Lewis, Introduction to *The Moorland Cottage and Other Stories* by Elizabeth Gaskell (New York: Oxford UP, 1995), xiv.
33. Richard Walsh, "Why We Wept for Little Nell: Character and Emotional Involvement," *Narrative* 5 (October 1997): 312.
34. Pimlott, *The Englishman's Christmas*, 88.
35. Charles Dickens to Catherine Dickens, 2 December 1844, *The Letters of Charles Dickens*, vol. 4, ed. Tillotson, 234.
36. Charles Dickens, *The Letters of Charles Dickens*, vol. 4, ed. Tillotson, 656n.
37. William M. Thackeray, *The Letters and Private Papers of William Makepeace Thackeray*, vol. 2, ed. Gordon N. Ray (Cambridge: Harvard UP, 1945), 469.
38. Thackeray, "A Grumble about the Christmas-Books," 114.
39. "The Kickleburys On the Rhine," *Times* (3 January 1851): 3.
40. William M. Thackeray, "Christmas Books—No. I," *Morning Chronicle* (24 December 1845) in *Contributions to the Morning Chronicle*, ed. Gordon N. Ray (Urbana: U of Illinois P, 1955), 87–88.
41. Harold J. Laski to Judge Holmes, August 1926, *Holmes-Laski Letters*, vol. 2 (Cambridge: Harvard UP, 1953), 868, http://www.nlx.com.
42. Thackeray, "A Grumble about the Christmas-Books," 126.
43. Thackeray, "Christmas Books—No. I," 88.
44. "A Gossip about the Christmas Books," *Fraser's Magazine* 43(January 1851): 45.
45. Cecil Lang, ed. *The Letters of Matthew Arnold*, vol. 1 (Charlottesville: U of Virginia P, 1996), 181.
46. Lewis, Introduction, ix.
47. Robert Louis Stevenson to Mrs. Sitwell, September 1874, *The Letters of Robert Louis Stevenson*, vol. 2, ed. Sidney Colvin (New York: Scribner, 1911), 178.
48. Gesa Stedman, *Stemming the Torrent: Expression and Control in the Victorian Discourses on Emotion, 1830–1872* (Burlington: Ashgate, 2002), 2.
49. Ibid., 51.
50. K.J. Fielding, "Two Sketches by Maclise: The Dickens Children and the *Chimes* Reading," *Dickens Studies* 2 (January 1966): 11.
51. Daniel Maclise to Catherine Dickens, 8 December 1844, *The Letters of Charles Dickens*, vol. 4, ed. Tillotson, 234–235n.
52. Fielding, "Two Sketches by Maclise," 15.
53. Malcolm Andrews, *Charles Dickens and His Performing Selves: Dickens and the Public Readings* (New York: Oxford UP, 2006), 238, 94.

54. Philip Collins, *Charles Dickens: The Public Readings* (Oxford: Clarendon, 1975), xix–xxvii.
55. Collins, *Charles Dickens*, 465.
56. Collins, *Charles Dickens*, 127, 4, 75, 77, 380, 400.
57. Charles Dickens to Miss Burdett Coutts, 6 November 1848, in *The Letters of Charles Dickens*, vol. 5, ed. Storey and Fielding, 435.
58. Charles Dickens to John Forster, 20 September 1846, *The Letters of Charles Dickens*, vol. 4, ed. Tillotson, 623. *The Haunted Man*, Dickens's last Christmas book, was put aside for a year due to the author's busy writing schedule; he was working on *Dombey and Son*. Thus, no Dickens Christmas book appeared for the 1847 season.
59. Charles Dickens, *The Haunted Man and the Ghost's Bargain* (New York: Nichols, 1914), 188.
60. Alan Shelson, "*The Moorland Cottage*: Elizabeth Gaskell and Myles Birket Foster," *The Gaskell Society Journal* 2 (1998): 43.
61. "A Gossip about the Christmas Books," 42.
62. Lumpkin, "(Re)Visions of Virtue," 432.
63. Robert L. Selig, *Elizabeth Gaskell: A Reference Guide* (Boston: Hall, 1977), 10.
64. Richard Altick, *Victorian People and Ideas* (New York: Norton, 1973), 192.
65. Kate Flint, *The Woman Reader, 1837–1914* (Oxford: Clarendon, 1993), 14, 11.
66. Robert Darnton, "First Steps toward a History of Reading," in *Reception Study: From Literary Theory to Cultural Studies*, ed. James L. Machor and Philip Goldstein (New York: Routlege, 2001), 167.
67. Pimlott, *The Englishman's Christmas*, 88.
68. Darnton, "First Steps toward a History of Reading," 169.
69. Stewart Garret, *Dear Reader: The Conscripted Audience in Nineteenth-Century British Fiction* (Baltimore: Johns Hopkins), 32.
70. Andrew Bennet, Introduction to *Readers and Reading*, ed. Andrew Bennet (New York: Longman, 1995), 5.
71. Garret, *Dear Reader*, 18.
72. Flint, *The Woman Reader*, 256.
73. Dickens, *The Battle of Life*, 76–77, 80.
74. Ibid., 41, 43.
75. Lyn Pykett, *Charles Dickens* (New York: Palgrave, 2002), 96.
76. Dickens, *The Haunted Man*, 152.
77. Shelston, "*The Moorland Cottage*," 46.
78. Thackeray, *The Rose and the Ring* in *The Christmas Books of Mr. M. A. Titmarsh*, 215.
79. "Christmas Eve at the Moated Grange," *Punch* 99 (27 December 1890): 306.
80. "January—Fireside Stories," *Belgravia* (January 1867): 290.

3 HOW MR. PUNCH STOLE CHRISTMAS: THE EVOLUTION OF THE HOLIDAY IN PERIODICALS

1. "A Christmas Carol," *Punch* 81 (26 December 1885): 304, 305.
2. "The Spirit of Christmas Present," *Punch* 105 (30 December 1893): 307.
3. H.F., "British Problems of the Day," *New York Times* (8 October 1893): http://nytimes.com.
4. *Punch*, vol. 1, Advertisement, *Punch* 1 (17 July 1841): ii.
5. Richard Altick, *Punch: The Lively Youth of a London Institution, 1841–1851* (Columbus: Ohio State UP, 1997), 156.
6. "Almanack for 1844," *Mirror* 1:1 (January 1844): 7.
7. "*The Protestant Almanack*, for 1841," *Mirror of Literature, Amusement, and Instruction*, 36:1033 (November 1840): 332.
8. "Almanacs," *All the Year Round* 6:140 (December 1861): 318.
9. Margaret Beetham, "Toward a Theory of the Periodical as a Publishing Genre," in *Investigating Victorian Journalism*, ed. Laurel Brake, Aled Jones, and Lionel Madden (London: Macmillan, 1990), 23.
10. Preface in *Punch* 5 (1843): iv.
11. Harry Stone, *The Night Side of Dickens: Cannibalism, Passion, Necessity* (Columbus: Ohio State UP, 1994), 27.
12. Richard M. Kelley, *Douglas Jerrold* (New York: Twayne, 1973), 79.
13. Thackeray's kinswoman Blanche Warre Cornish chronicled her negative reaction to Doyle's gory images: "[Doyle's] illustrations of Mr. Thackeray's Rebecca Rowena [*sic*] alas! put us off from Scott, and I have no defense of parody in the general plea for humour in the schoolroom and in the first peep into life." *Some Family Letters of W. M. Thackeray Together with Recollections by His Kinswoman Banche Warre Cornish* (New York: Houghton Miflin, 1911), 40.
14. Altick, *Punch*, 118.
15. Thackeray's Christmas books are postdated to the year following the Christmas season in which they appeared.
16. Thackeray, *Mrs. Perkins' Ball* in *The Christmas Books of Mr. M. A. Titmarsh*, 13, 15, 19.
17. "How to Make a Constitutional Plum Pudding," *Punch* 15 (1848): 267.
18. "John Bull Guards His Pudding," *Punch* 37 (31 December 1859): 267. Parliament had authorized the official organization of the Volunteer Rifle Corp on 12 May 1859. Tennyson's "Riflemen Form!" poem was a resulting, patriotic reaction to French aggression, as was this cartoon, "Old England Forever."
19. "John Bull Guards His Pudding," *Punch* 37 (31 December 1859): 266.
20. "Greedy Boy," *Punch* 88 (10 January 1885): 18–19. Angra Pequena, now part of Namibia, was transferred to the German

Empire in 1884. Surrounding islands had been annexed to Great Britain in 1867. In November 1884 Germany proclaimed a protectorate over northeastern New Guinea, and three days later Britain did the same to southeastern New Guinea.

21. "Too Civil By Half!" *Punch* 23 (20 November 1852): 226.
22. "Keep Up Your Spirits," *Punch* 71 (23 December 1876): 276.
23. "Christmas Waits" *Punch* 17 (1849): 250.
24. Simon Houfe, *John Leech and the Victorian Scene* (Woodbridge: Baron, 1984), 54.
25. "Christmas Up His Own Tree!" *Punch* 67 (26 December 1874): 271.
26. "A Quarrel with Christmas," *Punch* 37 (31 December 1859): 266; "If This Should Meet His Eye," *Punch* 35 (25 December 1858): 253.
27. "A Really New Christmas Number," *Punch* 73 (22 December 1877): 280.
28. Beetham, "Toward a Theory of the Periodical as a Publishing Genre," 29.
29. Anthony Trollope, "Christmas Day at Kirkby Cottage," in *The Complete Short Stories*, vol. 1 (Fort Worth: Texas Christian UP, 1979), 65–96.
30. "Christmas Books for Men of Business," *Punch* 12 (1847): 21.
31. Altick has surmised that Jerrold was responsible for Mr. Chokepear, and he points out the friendship and mutual politics of Jerrold and Dickens as a link between the two men's Christmas reform rhetoric. Altick, *Punch*, 189.
32. "Preface," *Punch* 17 (1849): iii.
33. Altick, *Punch*, 186.
34. "Christmas in the Workhouse," *Punch* 32 (January 1857): 1.
35. "The 'Milk' of Poor Law 'Kindness,'" *Punch* 4 (January 1843): 46. Sally Ledger has identified this piece as the work of Douglas Jerrold.
36. Thomas Hood, "The Pauper's Christmas Carol," *Punch* 5 (1843): 269.
37. As the feasting paupers become a spectacle for the well-dressed guardians and their wives, one daring man, John, pushes his pudding aside as the story of his wife's last Christmas bursts out of him. One year ago John's wife was starving, but their parish offered no outdoor relief, and, rather than be separated by going to the poorhouse, the couple decided to weather the hungry Christmas Eve together. In her death-throes the wife begged for food, but the poorhouse refused it to her distraught husband when John went begging. She had died by the time he returned home. John cannot help writhing at the contrast between the refusal to offer outdoor relief to honest people and the relative plenty provided for the indoor paupers' Christmas feast. Thus Sims explores the empty performance of Christmas charity.
38. "Christmas-Day in the Workhouses," *Times* (26 December 1849): 5.

39. "Christmas-Day in the Workhouses," *Times* (27 December 1851): 7; "Christmas Day Under the London Poor Laws," *Times* (26 December 1870): 4.
40. Eliza Cook, "Christmas Song of the Poor Man," *The Poetical Works* (London: Frederick Warne, 1870), ll. 85–88, http://lion.chadwyck.com.
41. "The Consumption of Mince Pies," *Punch* 34 (January 1858): 13.
42. "The Song of the Festive Season," *Punch* 50 (13 January 1866): 20; "The Compliments of the Seasons," *Punch* 50 (20 January 1866): 26.
43. "Choosing Christmas Toys," *Punch* 103 (24 December 1892): 299.
44. "The Shops at Christmas," *Punch* 17 (1849): 250.
45. "Fiction of the Season," *Punch* 97 (26 December 1889): 303.
46. "A Philosopher's Christmas," *Punch* 57 (1 January 1869): 264.
47. "Christmas on View in 1988," *Punch* 96 (5 January 1889): 9.
48. "A Christmas Dinner," *Punch* 36 (1 January 1859): 2.
49. "Seasonable Folk-Lore," *Punch* 73 (29 December 1877): 292.
50. George Augustus Sala, "Miserable Christmas," *Belgravia* (January 1872), 341; "Christmas in Canada," *Belgravia* 10 (January 1870): 361–64.
51. "Christmas in Egypt," *Home Friend* (3 December 1855): 504.
52. "Christmas in India," *Fraser's Magazine* 9:50 (February 1874): 150.
53. "The 'Music in the Hall,'" *Illustrated London News* (23 December 1843): 416.
54. "Christmas in the Frozen Regions," *Household Words* 2:39 (December 1850): 306.
55. "Christmas in the Navy," *Household Words* 2:39 (December 1850): 300.
56. "What the Moon saw in India (at Christmas)," *London Society* 65:385 (January 1894): 51.

4 Ghost Stories at Christmas

1. Maurice Davies. "A Night in a Ghost-Chamber" *Belgravia* (January 1873): 377.
2. Ibid., 378.
3. John. O. Jordan and Robert L. Patten, Introduction to *Literature in the Marketplace*, ed. Jordan and Patten, 12–13.
4. E.J. Clery, *The Rise of Supernatural Fiction 1762–1899* (New York: Cambridge UP, 1995), 2–5.
5. Parker, *Christmas and Charles Dickens*, 105.
6. Washington Irving, *The Sketch Book of Geoffrey Crayon, Gent. History, Tales and Sketches* (New York: Library of America, 1983), 957.
7. Hervey. *The Book of Christmas*, 147.
8. Parker, *Christmas and Charles Dickens*, 106.
9. "Christmas Books and Book-Makers," *Graphic* 1:4 (25 December 1869), 87.
10. Harry Stone, "*A Christmas Carol*," in *The Haunted Mind*, ed. Smith and Haas, 12.

11. "Christmas Books and Book-Makers," 87.
12. E.F. Bleiler, Introduction to *Five Victorian Ghost Novels* (New York: Dover, 1971), v.
13. "The Latest Thing in Ghosts," *Once a Week* 6:134 (January 1862): 103.
14. Srdjan Smajic, "The Trouble with Ghost-Seeing: Vision, Ideology, and Genre in the Victorian Ghost Story," *ELH* 70:4 (Winter 2003), http://lion.chadwyck.com.
15. Amice Lee, *Laurels and Rosemary: The Life of William and Mary Howitt* (London: Oxford UP, 1955), 224.
16. Terry Castle, "Phantasmagoria: Spectral Technology and the Metaphorics of Modern Reverie," *Critical Inquiry* 15:1 (Autumn 1988): 38–42; Haining, Introduction to *Charles Dickens' Christmas Ghost Stories*, 19.
17. Albert Smith, "A Winter's Night with My Old Books; Chiefly Concerning Ghosts and Prodigies," *Bentley's Miscellany* 25 (January 1849): 91.
18. Ibid., 91.
19. Altick, *The English Common Reader*, 5.
20. A.T., "Lyrics of the Months: January," *Belgravia* 1 (January 1867): 290.
21. The last Christmas number of *All the Year Round* appeared in 1867.
22. T., "A Story-Telling Party," *Once a Week* 1:26 (December 1859): 148–535.
23. John Sheehan, "A Ghostly Night at Ballyslaughter," *Temple Bar* 31 (January 1871): 227–36.
24. "Old Hooker's Ghost; or, Christmas Gambols at Huntingfield Hall," *Bentley's Miscellany* 58 (1865): 637–52.
25. "Aunt Sarah's Ghost," *Bentley's Miscellany*, 11 (1842): 294.
26. Vanessa D. Dickerson, *Victorian Ghosts in the Noontide: Women Writers and the Supernatural* (Columbia: U of Missouri P, 1996), 40. A decade before the Christmas number Dickens was so well-read on the topic of spiritualism that he was able to write an informed critique of Crowe's famous *The Night Side of Nature: or, Ghosts and Ghost-Seers* (1847). Dickens spent Christmas 1847 reading this, her more famous work in preparation for his review "Ghost and Ghost-Seers" in *The Examiner*. Peter Haining, *Charles Dickens' Ghost Stories* by Charles Dickens (New York: St. Martin, 1993), 248.
27. Charles Dickens to William Howitt, 31 October 1859, *The Letters of Charles Dickens*, vol. 9, ed. Storey, 146.
28. Charles Dickens, "The Mortals in the House," in *The Haunted House* (New York: The Modern Library, 2004), 4.
29. Charles Dickens, "The Ghost in Master B.'s Room" in *The Haunted House* (New York: The Modern Library, 2004), 81. The debate between Dickens and Howitt continued in print beyond

the Christmas number, and it is clear that Howitt wanted to link the penning of ghosts with the preoccupation with spiritualism. Howitt names Dickens as a contemporary author who "has played with spiritualism as a cat with a mouse; it has a wonderful fascination for him. All his literary life through he has been introducing the marvelous and the ghostly into his novels, and has of late years, in his periodicals, been alternately attacking spiritualism, and giving you most accredited instances of it." Dickens would review this volume in *All the Year Round*. William Howitt, *The History of the Supernatural in All Ages and Nations, and in All Churches*, vol. 2 (London: Longman, Green, Longman, Roberts & Green, 1863), 413. For a fuller investigation of Dickens's and Howitt's debate see Louise Henson, "'In the Natural Course of Physical Things': Ghost and Science in Charles Dickens's *All the Year Round*," in *Culture and Science in the Nineteenth-Century Media*, ed. Louise Henson (Burlington: Ashgate, 2004), 113–123.

30. Davies, "A Night in a Ghost-Chamber," 379.
31. Smajic, "The Trouble with Ghost-Seeing."
32. Altick, *The English Common Reader*, 359.
33. Ouida, "Holly Wreaths and Rose Chains; or, How We Spent Christmas at Deerhurst," *Bentley's Miscellany* 46 (1859): 628.
34. As with several of these ghost stories, the heir apparent invites a friend home for the Christmas holidays only to see that friend woo and marry a daughter of the house. The narrator relates an aristocratic haunting associated with the family: two members of a love triangle return to haunt the house on Christmas Eve, the night the lover killed his beloved's chosen suitor and then committed suicide. The primary plot in this short story, however, follows the heir, Sydney Vivian, as he stifles his love for a coquette, Cecil, only to reveal his passionate secret as he departs for the Crimean War. Sydney, injured at the infantry charge of Balaklava, returns a year later, also on Christmas Eve, to the now contrite Cecil, who had been berating herself and comparing her history to that of the haunting spirit. The story involves three significant Christmas Eves: the night of the ancient murder and suicide, the night Sydney declares his love and leaves for the Crimea, and the night of Syndey's homecoming, when he finds his love returned. In this case the embedded ghost narrative serves as a mirror in which Cecil chooses to read her own sins.
35. Solvieg C. Robinson, "Editing *Belgravia*: M.E. Braddon's Defense of 'Light Literature,'" *Victorian Periodicals Review* 28:2 (Summer 1995): 110.
36. Barbara Onslow, "Sensationalizing Science: Braddon's Marketing of Science in *Belgravia*" *Victorian Periodicals Review*, 35:2 (Summer 2002): 162.

37. Ada Buisson, "The Ghost's Summons," *Belgravia* 4 (January 1868): 358–63.
38. "Seeing a Ghost," *Argosy* 24 (December 1877): 490.
39. Jennifer Uglow, Introduction to *Victorian Ghost Stories by Noted Women Writers*, ed. Richard Dalby (New York: Barnes & Noble, 1988), xi.
40. Charles Dickens, *A House to Let* (London: Hesperus Classics, 2004), 7–8.
41. Charles Ollier, "The Haunted Manor-house of Paddington, a Tale for November," *Bentley's Miscellany*, 10 (1841): 524.
42. Charlotte Riddell, "The Old House in Vauxhall Walk," in *Victorian Ghost Stories by Noted Women Writers*, ed. Dalby, 135–49.
43. Uglow, Introduction to *Victorian Ghost Stories by Noted Women Writers*, xvii.
44. Patricia Thomas Srebrnick, "Mrs. Riddell and the Reviewers: A Case Study in Victorian Popular Fiction," *Women's Studies* 23:1 (1994): 70, 71–72, 74–75.
45. Charlotte Riddell, "*Uninhabited House*," in *Five Victorian Ghost Novels*, ed. Bleiler, 52.
46. Ibid., 98.
47. Ibid., 20.
48. Smith, "A Winter's Night with My Old Books," 91.
49. "Outline of the History of Gas Lighting" *Mirror of Literature, Amusement, and Instruction* 10.290 (29 December 1827) http://www.gutenberg.org/ebooks/11404.
50. Christopher J. Castaneda, *Invisible Fuel: Manufactured and Natural Gas in America, 1800–2000* (New York: Twayne, 1999), 9.
51. Graeme J.N. Gooday, "'I Will Never Have the Electric Light in My House': Alice Gordon and the Gendered Periodical Representation of a Contentious New Technology," in *Culture and Science in the Nineteenth-Century Media*, ed. Henson, 174–78.
52. "The Danger from Gas," *Times* (14 June 1861): 5.
53. John Ruskin, *The Works of John Ruskin: Sesame and Lilies* (Sunnyside: George Allen, 1883), 1:91–92.
54. Thad Logan, *The Victorian Parlour* (New York: Cambridge UP, 2001), 182, 196.
55. Dickens, *The Battle of Life*, 108.
56. Riddell, *Uninhabited House*, 16.
57. Lara Baker Whelan, "Between Worlds: Class Identity and Suburban Ghost Stories, 1850 to 1880," *Mosaic* 35 (March 2002), http://lion.chadwyck.com.
58. Riddell, *Uninhabited House*, 11–12.
59. Ibid., 111–12.
60. Whelan, "Between Worlds."
61. Riddell, *Uninhabited House*, 41–42.
62. Ibid., 40, 41.

5 THE EXPANSION OF CHRISTMAS CONSUMERISM: GIFTS AND COMMODITIES

1. "Our Christmas Budget," *London Journal* 70:1820 (December 1879): 412.
2. "Decorated Christmas-Books for 1848," *Times* (25 December 1848): 3.
3. "Christmas Books" *Times* (December 13, 1864): 10.
4. "A Gossip about the Christmas Books," 38.
5. Shaylor, *The Fascination of Books*, 55.
6. "Decorated Christmas-Books for 1848," 3; "Christmas Gift Books," *Times* (24 December 1860): 10; "Christmas Books," *Times* (28 December 1861): 8.
7. "Christmas Books," *Times* (8 December 1884): 18.
8. "Christmas Books," *Times* (2 December 1884): 4.
9. John Buchanan-Brown, *Early Victorian Illustrated Books: Britain, France and Germany 1820–1860* (New Castle: Oak Knoll, 2005), 135.
10. Kooistra, "Poetry in the Victorian Marketplace."
11. "Christmas in the Metropolis," *Chambers's Edinburgh Journal* 469 (December 1852): 410; Redgap, *The Faces in the Fire* (London: Willoughby, n.d.), 125.
12. "Christmas Books," *Times* (24 December 1866): 6.
13. Thackeray. "Christmas Books—No. I," 87.
14. Chambers, *The Book of Days*, 715.
15. "Christmas Books," *Times* (13 December 1881): 3; "Christmas Books," *Times*, (13 December 1864): 10.
16. "Suggestion about Gift-Books," *Fraser's Magazine* 45 (18 February 1852): 141.
17. "A Gossip about the Christmas Books," 37.
18. "Christmas Books," *Times* (20 November1883): 4.
19. Buchanan-Brown, *Early Victorian Illustrated Books*, 135.
20. Breyer, *Anthony Trollope*, iv.
21. Anne Lundin, *Victorian Horizons* (Lanham: Scarecrow, 2001), 28.
22. Thackeray, "A Grumble about the Christmas-Books," 111.
23. William M. Thackeray, "Roundabout Papers—No. X.: Round about the Christmas Tree," *Cornhill Magazine* 31 (February 1861): 253.
24. "Christmas Story-Books and Illustrated Books for Presents," *Critic* 23:594 (November 1861): 520.
25. "Christmas Books," *Times* (13 December 1864): 10.
26. "Christmas Books," *Times* (20 November 1883): 4.
27. Daniel Miller, Introduction to *Unwrapping Christmas*, ed. Daniel Miller (Oxford: Clarendon, 1993), 19.
28. Kooistra, "Poetry in the Victorian Marketplace."
29. Mark Osteen, Introduction to *The Question of the Gift: Essays across Disciplines* (New York: Routledge, 2002), 2.

30. Paul Goldman, *Victorian Illustrated Books 1850–1870: The Heyday of Wood-engraving* (London: Trustees of the British Museum, 1994), 72.
31. G. Salmon, "What Boys Read," *Fortnightly Review* NS39 (1886): 248.
32. "Our Wheel of Fortune," *Punch* 89 (19 December 1885): 290. Sambourne illustrated this piece, and the accompanying poem praises Sambourne's illustration in Kingsley's Christmas book, *Water Babies.* "Mr. Punch Concedes Home Rule to the Only True Home-Rulers at Christmas-Time," *Punch* 89 (December 1885): 303.
33. Peter Hunt, *An Introduction to Children's Literature* (New York: Oxford UP, 1994), 30.
34. Lundin, *Victorian Horizons*, 46.
35. "New Books," *London Society* (December 1874): 556.
36. "New Books Received," *London Society* 27 (January 1875): 95.
37. "Christmas Books," *Punch* 133 (1907): 422.
38. Juliana Ewing to Randolph Caldecott, 17 November 1880, *Yours Pictorially: Illustrated Letters of Randolph Caldecott*, ed. Michael Hutchins (New York: Frederick Warne, 1976), 81.
39. Lundin, *Victorian Horizons*, 38.
40. "The Royal Birthday Book," *Punch* 81 (17 December 1881): 279.
41. M.V. Hughes, *A London Family 1870–1900* (Oxford: Oxford UP, 1991), 51–52.
42. Ibid., 140.
43. Sybil Lubbock, *The Child in the Crystal* (London: Jonathan Cape, 1939), 53.
44. "Christmas Books," *Times* (23 December 1870): 10.
45. Ironically, this particular manuscript was regifted in an act of generosity when, in 1948, American collectors pooled resources to buy the slim notebook and present it to the British Museum.
46. "Some Christmas Books," *Punch* 71 (6 January 1877): 297.
47. C.L. Dodgson to Alexander Macmillan, 17 December 1871, *Lewis Carroll and the House of Macmillan*, ed. Morton N. Cohen and Anita Gandolfo (New York: Cambridge UP, 1987), 97.
48. Alexander Macmillan to C.L. Dodgson, 6 November, 1871, *Lewis Carroll and the House of Macmillan*, ed. Cohen and Gandolfo, n98.
49. Alexander Macmillan to C.L. Dodgson, 5 January 1876, *Lewis Carroll and the House of Macmillan*, ed. Cohen and Gandolfo, n116.
50. John Feather, *A History of British Publishing* (New York: Routledge, 2006), 102.
51. Ibid., 227–28.
52. Cohen and Gandolfo, eds., *Lewis Carroll and the House of Macmillan*, 25–26.
53. C.L. Dodgson to Alexander Macmillan, 4 February 1877, *Lewis Carroll and the House of Macmillan*, ed. Cohen and Gandolfo, 134.

54. Cohen and Gandolfo, eds., *Lewis Carroll and the House of Macmillan*, 360.
55. Goldman, *Victorian Illustrated Books*, 45, 46.
56. "The Christian Knowledge Society," *Popular Science Review* 5:17 (January 1881): 168.
57. "Christmas Books," *Academy* 10 (16 December 1876): 583.
58. W.K. Lowther Clarke, *The History of the S.P.C.K.* (London: SPCK, 1959), 184.
59. Margaret Nancy Cutt, *Ministering Angels: A Study of Nineteenth-Century Evangelical Writing for Children* (Wormley: Five Owls, 1979), 155.
60. *The Letters of Anthony Trollope*, ed. Bradford Allen Booth (New York: Oxford UP, 1951), 430–31. *Past Masters* Pennsylvania State University, York Library, 25 November 2007.
61. "Ewing, Juliana Horatia," *Academy* 27 (23 May 1885), 366.
62. Louisa Molesworth, "Juliana Horatia Ewing," *Contemporary Review* 49 (1886): 676.
63. Christabel Maxwell, *Mrs Gatty and Mrs Ewing* (London: Constable, 1949), 190.
64. Randolph Caldecott to Juliana Ewing, 22 January 1884, *Yours Pictorially*, ed. Hutchins, 108.
65. Maxwell, *Mrs Gatty and Mrs Ewing*, 215, 233.
66. Juliana Ewing, *The Peace Egg and a Christmas Mumming Play* (London: SPCK, 1887), Digital Library, 27 November 2007, http://digital.library.upen.edu.
67. Parker, *Christmas and Charles Dickens*, 100–1.
68. Peter Millington, "Mrs Ewing and the Textual Origin of the St Kitts Mummies' Play," *Folklore* 107 (1996), 81, 77.
69. Alex Helm, *The English Mummers' Play* (Woodbridge: Boydell & Brewer, 1980), 57; Millington, "Mrs Ewing and the Textual Origin of the St Kitts Mummies' Play," 81.
70. "The Peace Egg," *Notes and Queries* 5.4:104 (25 December 1875), 511.
71. Ewing, *The Peace Egg and a Christmas Mumming Play.*
72. Ibid.
73. Millington, "Mrs. Ewing and the Textual Origin of the St. Kitts Mummies' Play," 83, 87.
74. Helm, *The English Mummers' Play*, 8.
75. Helm, *The English Mummers' Play*, 57, 62–63.
76. Jim Davis, "Boxing Day," in *The Performing Century: Nineteenth-Century Theatre's History*, ed. Tracy C. Davis and Peter Holland (New York: Palgrave Macmillan, 2007), 13; Thackeray, "Roudabout Papers—X.," 252.
77. A.E. Wilson, *Pantomime Pageant: A Procession of Harlequins, Clowns, Comedians, Principle Boys, Pantomime-Writers, Producers and Playgoers* (London: Stanley Paul, n.d.), 53.

78. Gillian Russell, "Private Theatricals," in *The Cambridge Companion to British Theatre, 1730–1830*, ed. Jane Moody and Daniel O'Quinn (Cambridge: Cambridge UP, 2007), 192; Katherine Newey, "Home Plays for Ladies: Women's Work in Home Theatricals," *Nineteenth Century Theatre* 26 (Winter 1998): 97.
79. "Books for Christmas Amusement," *Times* (15 December 1860): 12; Hughes, *A London Family*, 140.
80. Mary Elizabeth Braddon, *The Christmas Hirelings* (Hastings: Sensation, 2001), 15, 16.
81. "The Christmas Number," *Speaker* 6 (December 1892): 764.
82. "St. Sylvester's Eve," *Dublin University Magazine* 41 (January 1853): 116.
83. Cohen and Gandolfo, *Lewis Carroll and the House of Macmillan*, n98.

6 The Poetry of Christmas

1. "Old Christmas" *Bentley's Miscellany* 28 (1850): 600.
2. "Christmas Books" *Examiner* (21 December 1861): 806.
3. "Christmas Books," *Times* (24 December 1866): 6.
4. Lee Erickson, "The Market," in *A Companion to Victorian Poetry*, ed. Richard Cronin, Alison Chapman, and Antony H. Harrison (Malden: Blackwell, 2002), 350, 348.
5. Kooistra, "Poetry in the Victorian Marketplace."
6. Ibid.
7. George Buday, *The Christmas Card* (London: Rockliff, 1954, 1992), 2–3, 43, 72, 59, 201.
8. Buday, *The Christmas Card*, 252–61.
9. Ibid., xxiii, 187.
10. Altick, *Victorian People and Ideas*, 166, 167.
11. Hannah More, "A Christmas Hymn," in *The Works of Hannah More* (London: Cadell, 1830), ll. 1–2, http://lion.chadwyck.com.
12. John Castillo, "Merry Christmas as Kept in England," in *The Bard of the Dales* (Stokesley: Pratt, 1858), http://lion.chadwyck.com.
13. Edmund Gosse, *Father and Son* (London: Penguin, 1989), 111–12.
14. G.B. Tennyson, *Victorian Devotional Poetry: The Tractarian Mode* (Cambridge: Harvard UP, 1981), 4, 6.
15. Rodney Stenning Edgecombe, *Two Poets of the Oxford Movement: John Keble and John Henry Newman* (Madison: Fairleigh Dickinson UP, 1996), 36.
16. Ibid., 61.
17. Ibid., 59.
18. John Keble, "Christmas Eve: Vespers," *The Christmas Year, Lyra Innocentium and Other Poems* (New York: Oxford UP, 1914), ll. 21–24.
19. Luke 2:1–15.

20. Daniel Walker Howe, "Victorian Culture in America," in *Victorian America*, ed. Daniel Walker Howe (Philadelphia: U of Pennsylvania P, 1976), 3.
21. Ellen Thorneycroft Fowler, "A Carol for Old Christmas Day," *Wesleyan-Methodist Magazine* 14 (January 1890): 52.
22. J.R. Watson, "Hymns," in *A Companion to Victorian Poetry*, ed. Cronin, Chapman, and Harrison, 136, 151.
23. Bishop Heber, "Hymn for Christmas Day," *Saturday Magazine* 1:30 (December 1832): 239.
24. John C. Hotten, *A Garland of Christmas Carols, Ancient and Modern* (London: John Camden Hotten, 1861), 57.
25. J.M. Neal, "Toll! Toll! Because There Ends," *The Condensed Vocal Parts to the Carols for Christmastide* (London: Novello, 1854), http://lion.chadwyck.com.
26. Kenneth W. Osbeck, *Amazing Grace: 366 Inspiring Hymn Stories for Daily Devotions* (Grand Rapids: Kregel, 1990), Libronix Digital Library System.
27. Altick, *Victorian People and Ideas*, 204.
28. Linda H. Peterson, "Rereading 'Christmas-Eve,' Rereading Browning," *Victorian Poetry* 26:4 (Winter 1988): 365, 364.
29. Robert Browning, "Christmas Eve," *The Poetical Works* (London: Smith, Elder, 1888–1894), l. 144, http://lion.chadwyck.com.
30. Browning, "Christmas Eve," ll. 516–522.
31. Ibid., ll. 1324–25.
32. Altick, *Victorian People and Ideas*, 220, 221.
33. Stefan Hawlin, *The Complete Critical Guide to Robert Browning* (New York: Routledge, 2002), 89.
34. Erickson, "The Market," 347.
35. "W.H. Mallock," in *Dictionary of Literary Biography, Volume 18: Victorian Novelists After 1885*, ed. Ira B. Nadel and William E. Fredeman (Gale, 1983), 164–167, http://galenet.galegroup.com.
36. William H. Mallock, "Christmas Thoughts, by a Modern Thinker," in *Broadview Anthology of Poetry and Poetic Theory*, ed. Thomas J. Collins and Vivienne J. Rundle (Peterborough: Broadview, 1999), 1102, ll. 55, 67–68.
37. Michael Millgate, *Thomas Hardy, A Biography Revisited* (New York: Oxford UP, 1982), 530.
38. Gayle Holste, "Hardy's Christmas in the Elgin Room," *The Explicator* 59 (Summer 2001): 187–189, http://lion.chadwyck.com.
39. Margot K. Louis, "Gods and Mysteries: The Revival of Paganism and the Remaking of Mythography through the Nineteenth Century," *Victorian Studies* (Spring 2005), http://lion.chadwyck.com.
40. Augustus Swinburne, "Christmas Antiphones," *Songs Before Sunrise* (London: Ellis, 1871), ll. 11, 216.
41. Margot K. Louis, *Swinburne and His Gods: The Roots and Growth of an Agnostic Poet* (Buffalo: McGill-Queen's UP, 1990), 9, 63.

42. Swinburne, "Christmas Antiphones," ll. 196–200.
43. Ibid., ll. 296–300.
44. Louis, *Swinburne and His Gods*, 63.
45. Louis, "Gods and Mysteries."
46. "Swinburne's Christmas: Spends It with Watts-Dunton and Declares Against Woman Suffrage," *New York Times* (27 December 1908): C2.
47. Wallace J. Brett, "Christmas Memories," *Lloyd's London Magazine* 7:3 (December 1879): 161.
48. Edith Nesbit, "The Clerk's Christmas Dream," *Leaves of Life* (London: Longmans, Green, 1888), http://lion.chadwyck.com.
49. Edith Nesbit, "Christmas," *Lays and Legends* (London: Longmans, Green, 1886), http://lion.chadwyck.com.
50. Michael Mason, "The Timing of *In Memoriam*," in *Studies in Tennyson*, ed. Hallam Tennyson (London: Macmillan, 1981), 159.
51. Charles Tennyson, "*In Memoriam*," in *In Memoriam*, ed. Robert H. Ross (New York: Norton, 1973), 104; Eleanor B. Mattes, "Chronology of *In Memoriam*," in *In Memoriam*, ed. Ross, 139; Alfred Tennyson, *In Memoriam*, ed. Ross, 78: 15–16; 107: 21–22.
52. Connelly, *Christmas: A Social History*, 105.
53. Elizabeth Letitia Landon, "Thoughts on Christmas-Day in India," *The Zenana and Minor Poems* (London: Fisher, 1839), http://lion.chadwyck.com.
54. Rudyard Kipling, "Christmas in India," *Selected Poetry* (New York: Penguin, 1992). http://lion.chadwyck.com.
55. Kipling, "Christmas in India," ll. 39–40.
56. Hotten, *A Garland of Christmas Carols*, xv.
57. Henry Vizetelly, ed. *Christmas with the Poets*, 2nd ed. (London: Bogue, 1852), 17.
58. William Sawyer, "Christmas in the Olden Time," *Belgravia* 4 (January 1868): 357–58.
59. Leigh Hunt, "Christmas," *The Oxford Book of Christmas Poems* (New York: Oxford UP, 1984), 138.
60. "'The Music in the Hall,'" *Illustrated London News* (23 December 1843): 416.
61. "The Poetry of Christmas," *Manchester Times* (24 December 1875): 412.

7 Modern Marketing of the Victorian Christmas

1. "Flood of Christmas Books," *Punch* 11 (1846): 210.
2. Thackeray, "Roundabout Papers—No. X.," 251–52.
3. "The Last Christmas for 'Brandy Butter'?" *Grocer* 221:7381 (14 November 1998): 24.
4. "Have Pudding Will Travel," *Times* (24 December 1985): 6.

5. Rob Gifford, "U. K. Muslims Support Keeping Christ in Christmas," *Morning Edition* National Public Radio (19 December 2007).
6. Parker, *Christmas and Charles Dickens*, 15.
7. Steve Pratt, "What the Dickens! . . . Is Going on as Victorian Drama Dominates TV," *Northern Echo* (20 December 2007): 28, http://proquest.umi.com.
8. Paul Davis, *The Lives and Times of Ebenezer Scrooge* (New Haven: Yale UP, 1990), 4, 239. For more information on the plentiful adaptations of the *Carol*, see Paul Davis's exhaustive work or Fred Guida's encyclopedic *A Christmas Carol and Its Adaptations: A Critical Examination of Dickens's Story and Its Productions on Screen and Television* (Jefferson, NC: McFarland, 2000).
9. Tom Leitch, *Film Adaptation and its Discontents* (Baltimore: Johns Hopkins, 2007), 70.
10. Dianne F. Sadoff and John Kucich, Introduction to *Victorian Afterlife: Postmodern Culture Rewrites the Nineteenth Century* (Minneapolis: U of Minnesota P, 2000), xvi.
11. Tony Adler, "How 'Carol' Helped Make Christmas," *Chicago Tribune* (7 December 2007): 4.
12. Miriam Bailin, "The New Victorians," in *Function of Victorian Culture at the Present Time*, ed. Christine L. Krueger (Athens: Ohio UP, 2002), 39, 38.
13. Christine L. Krueger, Introduction to *Function of Victorian Culture*, ed. Krueger, xiii.
14. Lana Berkowitz, "Dickens on the Strand, It's Good to be the Queen," *Houston Chronicle* (30 November 2007): 1.
15. Robert Winnett and Holly Watt, "£50,000 to Get a Book on Recommended List," *Sunday Times* (28 May 2006), www.timesonline.co.uk.
16. Ben Hoyle and Sarah Clarke, "The Hidden Price of a Christmas Bestseller," *Times* (18 June 2007), www.timesonline.co.uk.
17. Victoria Arnstein, "Wrapping Up Exclusives," *Bookseller* (24 October 2007), thebookseller.com.
18. Graeme Neille, "Booksellers Push Up Christmas Prices," *Bookseller* (18 December 2007), thebookseller.com.
19. Alison Flood, Liz Bury, Joel Rickett, and Philip Stone, "Hachette Steals the Show," *Bookseller* (24 January 2008), thebookseller.com.
20. "Who's Got the X Factor?" *Times* (10 September 2005), timesonline.co.uk.
21. "Second Helpings for Delia Fans," BBC News (23 December 1999) news.bbc.co.uk; Damien Witworth, "Read On If You've Scanned any Good Books Lately," *Times* (28 December 2005), timesonline.co.uk.
22. "London's Great Flood," *Publishing Trends* (February 2003), publishingtrends.com.

23. Giles Elliott, "Record Christmas as Kay Hits Number One," *Bookseller* (2 January 2007), thebookseller.com.
24. Jack Malvern, "Da Vinci Thriller Cracks the Book Bestseller Code," *Times* (24 December 2004), timesonline.co.uk.
25. Albert N. Greco, *The Book Publishing Industry*, 2nd ed. (London: Lawrence Erblaum, 2005), 210, 215, 219.
26. Linton Weeks, "Move Over, Scrooge: Publishers Hope for New Holiday Classic," *Washington Post* (30 November 2002): C1.
27. Arnstein, "Wrapping Up Exclusives."
28. Anne Perry, *A Christmas Guest* (New York: Ballantine, 2005).
29. Evelyn Beilenson, ed. *A Victorian Christmas* (White Plains: Peter Pauper, 1990), 5.
30. John Grisham, *Skipping Christmas* (New York: Doubleday, 2001), 54.

Works Cited

Nineteenth-Century Sources

"Almanack for 1844." *Mirror* 1:1 (January 1844): 7.
"Almanacs." *All the Year Round* 6:140 (December 1861): 318.
"Ancient Christmas." *Mirror* 22:639 (December 1833): 420.
"Aunt Sarah's Ghost." *Bentley's Miscellany* 11 (1842): 294–300.
Bohn, Henry G. "Biographical Notice." In *Seymour's Humorous Sketches.* London: Henry G. Bohn, 1872.
"Books for Christmas Amusement." *Times* (15 December 1860): 12.
Booth, Bradford Allen, ed. *The Letters of Anthony Trollope.* New York: Oxford UP, 1951. http://nlx.com accessed on 3 February 2009.
Braddon, Mary Elizabeth. *The Christmas Hirelings.* Hastings: Sensation, 2001.
Brett, Wallace J. "Christmas Memories." *Lloyd's London Magazine* 7:3 (December 1879): 161.
Browning, Robert. "Christmas Eve." In *The Poetical Works.* London: Smith, Elder, 1888–1894. http://lion.chadwyck.com accessed on 3 February 2009.
Buisson, Ada. "The Ghost's Summons." *Begravia* 4 (January 1868): 358–63.
Castillo, John. "Merry Christmas as Kept in England." *The Bard of the Dales.* Stokesley: Pratt, 1858.
Chambers, R. *The Book of Days: A Miscellany of Popular Antiquities in Connection with the Calendar, including Anecdote, Biography, & History, Curiosities of Literature and Oddities of Human Life and Character.* Vol. 2. Edinburgh: W. & R. Chambers, 1873.
"Choosing Christmas Toys." *Punch* 103 (1892): 299.
"Christmas at Hereford." *Mirror* 20:583 (December 1833): 438.
"Christmas at the Crystal Palace." *Punch* 40 (January 1861): 8.
"Christmas Books and Book-Makers." *Graphic* 1:4 (25 December 1869): 87.
"Christmas Books and Book-Makers." *Graphic* 1:4 (25 December 1869): 87–88.
"Christmas Books for Men of Business." *Punch* 12 (1847): 21.
"Christmas Books." *Academy* 10 (16 December 1876): 583.
"Christmas Books." *Dublin University Magazine* (January 1847): 134.
"Christmas Books." *Examiner* (21 December 1861): 806.
"Christmas Books." *Punch* 133 (1907): 422.

"Christmas Books." *Times* (13 December 1864): 10.
"Christmas Books." *Times* (13 December 1881): 3.
"Christmas Books." *Times* (2 December 1884): 4.
"Christmas Books." *Times* (20 November1883): 4.
"Christmas Books." *Times* (23 December 1870): 10.
"Christmas Books." *Times* (24 December 1866): 6.
"Christmas Books." *Times* (25 December 1847): 3.
"Christmas Books." *Times* (28 December 1861): 8.
"Christmas Books." *Times* (8 December 1884): 18.
"A Christmas Carol." *Punch* 81 (26 December 1885): 304–5.
"Christmas Day Under the London Poor Laws." *Times* (26 December 1870): 4.
"A Christmas Dinner." *Punch* 36 (1859): 2.
"Christmas Eve at the Moated Grange." *Punch* 99 (27 December 1890): 306.
"Christmas Gift Books." *Times* (24 December 1860): 10.
"Christmas in Canada." *Belgravia* 10 (January 1870): 361–64.
"Christmas in Egypt." *Home Friend* 3 (3 December 1855): 504–11.
"A Christmas in India." *Fraser's Magazine* 9:50 (February 1874): 150–56.
"Christmas in Lodgings." *Household Words* 2:39 (21 December 1850): 295–298.
"Christmas in the Frozen Regions." *Household Words* 2:39 (December 1850): 306–9.
"Christmas in the Metropolis." *Chambers's Edinburgh Journal* 469 (December 1852): 410.
"Christmas in the Navy." *Household Words* 2:39 (December 1850): 298–300.
"Christmas in the Workhouse." *Punch* 32 (January 1857): 1.
"Christmas-Day in the Workhouses." *Times* (26 December 1849): 5.
"Christmas-Day in the Workhouses." *Times* (27 December 1851): 7.
"Christmas on View in 1988." *Punch* 96 (5 January 1889): 9.
"Christmas Presents." Advertisement. *Illustrated London News* (16 December 1843): 399.
"Christmas Story-books and Illustrated Books for Presents." *Critic* 23:594 (November 1861): 520–521.
"Christmas Tactics." *Howitt's Journal* 2:54 (25 December 1847): 414.
"Christmas Up His Own Tree!" *Punch* 67 (26 December 1874): 271.
"Christmas Waits." *Punch* 25 (1853): 268.
Cohen, Morton N., and Anita Gandolfo. *Lewis Carroll and the House of Macmillan*. New York: Cambridge UP, 1987.
Colvin, Sidney, ed. *The Letters of Robert Louis Stevenson*. Vol. 2. New York: Scribner, 1911.
Cook, Eliza. "Christmas Song of the Poor Man." In *The Poetical Works*. London: Frederick Warne, 1870.
———. "While the Christmas Log is Burning." In *The Poetical Works*. London: Frederick Warne, 1870.

Cornish, Blanche Warre. *Some Family Letters of W. M. Thackeray Together with Recollections by His Kinswoman Banche Warre Cornish*. New York: Houghton Miflin, 1911.
Davies, Maurice. "A Night in a Ghost-Chamber." *Belgravia* 9 (January 1873): 377–85.
"Decorated Christmas-Books for 1848." *Times* (25 December 1847): 3.
Dickens, Charles. *The Battle of Life: A Love Story*. London: Bradbury & Evans, 1846.
———. *The Christmas Books*. ed. Michael Slater. Vol. 1. Harmondsworth: Penguin, 1971.
———. *The Christmas Books*. ed. Ruth Glancy. New York: Oxford UP, 1988.
———. *A Christmas Carol*. London: Chapman & Hall, 1843.
———. *The Haunted House*. New York: The Modern Library, 2004.
———. *The Haunted Man and the Ghost's Bargain*. New York: Nichols, 1914.
———. *A House to Let*. London: Hesperus Classics, 2004.
———. *The Letters of Charles Dickens*. ed. Kathleen Tillotson, et al. 12 Vol. Oxford: Clarendon, 1965–2002.
Elrington, Stephen Nolan. "A Lyric for Christmas." Rev. of *Original Poems and Lyrics*. *Dublin University Magazine* (January 1853): 117.
"Ewing, Juliana Horatia." *Academy* 27 (23 May 1885): 366–67.
Ewing, Juliana. *The Peace Egg and a Christmas Mumming Play*. London: SPCK, 1887. Digital Library, 27 November 2007, http://digital.library.upenn.edu/women/ewing/peace/peace.html accessed on 3 February 2009.
F., H. "British Problems of the Day." *New York Times* (8 October 1893), http://nytimes.com accessed on 3 February 2009.
Farjeon, Benjamin. *Bread-and-Cheese and Kisses*. New York: Harper, 1873.
———. *Golden Grain*. New York: Harper, 1874.
"Fiction of the Season." *Punch* 97 (1889): 303.
"Flood of Christmas Books." *Punch* 11 (1846): 210.
Fowler, Ellen Thorneycroft. "A Carol for Old Christmas Day," *Wesleyan-Methodist Magazine* 14 (January 1890): 52.
Gaskell, Elizabeth. "*The Moorland Cottage*." In *The Moorland Cottage and Other Stories*, ed. Suzanne Lewis, 1–100. New York: Oxford UP, 1995.
"A Gossip about the Christmas Books." *Fraser's Magazine* 43 (January 1851): 37–46.
"Greedy Boy." *Punch* 88 (10 January 1885): 18–19.
Heber, Bishop. "Hymn for Christmas Day." *Saturday Magazine* 1:30 (December 1832): 239.
Hervey, Thomas. *The Book of Christmas*. Ware: Wordsworth, 2000.
Hood, Thomas. "The Pauper's Christmas Carol." *Punch* 5 (1843): 269.
Hotten, John C. *A Garland of Christmas Carols, Ancient and Modern*. London: John Camden Hotten, 1861.
"How to Make a Constitutional Plum Pudding." *Punch* 15 (1848): 267.

Howitt, William. *The History of the Supernatural in All Ages and Nations, and in All Churches.* Vol. 2. London: Longman, Green, Longman, Roberts & Green, 1863.

Hughes, M.V. *A London Family 1870–1900.* Oxford: Oxford UP, 1991.

Hunt, Leigh. "Christmas." *The Oxford Book of Christmas Poems*, 138. New York: Oxford UP, 1984.

Hutchins, Michael, ed. *Yours Pictorially: Illustrated Letters of Randolph Caldecott.* New York: Frederick Warne, 1976.

"If This Should Meet His Eye." *Punch* 35 (25 December 1858): 253.

Irving, Washington. *The Sketch Book of Geoffrey Crayon, Gent. History, Tales and Sketches.* New York: Library of America, 1983.

"January—Fireside Stories." *Belgravia* (January 1867): 290.

"John Bull Guards His Pudding." *Punch* 37 (31 December 1859): 266.

"John Bull Guards His Pudding." *Punch* 37 (31 December 1859): 267.

Keble, John. "Christmas Eve: Vespers." In *The Christian Year, Lyra Innocentium and Other Poems.* New York: Oxford UP, 1914.

"Keep Up Your Spirits." *Punch* 71 (23 December 1876): 276.

"The Kickleburys On the Rhine," *Times* (3 January 1851): 3.

Kipling, Rudyard. "Christmas in India." In *Selected Poetry.* New York: Penguin, 1992. http://lion.chadwyck.com accessed on 14 October 2003.

Landon, Letitia Elizabeth. "Christmas in the Olden Time, 1650." In *Fisher's Drawing-Room Scrap Book*, 48. London: Fisher, Son and Jackson, 1836.

———. "Thoughts on Christmas-Day in India." In *The Zenana and Minor Poems.* London: Fisher Sons &Co, 1839. http://lion.chadwyck.com accessed on 14 October 2003.

Lang, Cecil, ed. *The Letters of Matthew Arnold.* Vol. 1. Charlottesville: U of Virginia P, 1996.

Laski, Harold J., to Judge Holmes, August 1926, *Holmes-Laski Letters.* Vol. 2, 868. Cambridge: Harvard UP, 1953. http://www.nlx.com accessed on 9 February 2006.

Mallock, William H. "Christmas Thoughts, by a Modern Thinker." *Broadview Anthology of Poetry and Poetic Theory*, ed. Thomas J. Collins and Vivienne J. Rundle. Peterborough: Broadview, 1999.

Marble, Annie Russell. "Christmas Books of the Past." *Critic* (December 1899): 1122–32.

Molesworth, Louisa. "Juliana Horatia Ewing," *Contemporary Review* 49 (1886): 675–86.

More, Hannah. "A Christmas Hymn." In *The Poetical Works.* London: Cadell, 1830. http://lion.chadwyck.com accessed on 5 March 2008.

"Mr. Punch Concedes Home Rule to the Only True Home-Rulers at Christmas-Time." *Punch* 89 (December 1885): 303.

Neal, J.M. "Toll! Toll! Because There Ends." In *The Condensed Vocal Parts to the Carols for Christmastide.* London: Novello, 1854.

Nesbit, Edith. "Christmas." In *Lays and Legends.* London: Longmans, Green, 1886.

Nesbit, Edith. "The Clerk's Christmas Dream." In *Leaves of Life*. London: Longmans, Green, 1888.
"New Books Received." *London Society* 26 (December 1874): 555–58.
"New Books Received." *London Society* 27 (January 1875): 94–98.
"New Year's Eve and New Year's Day." *Leigh Hunt's London Journal* 40 (31 December 1834): 314.
"Old Christmas." *Belgravia* 28 (1850): 600.
"Old Hooker's Ghost; or, Christmas Gambols at Huntingfield Hall." *Bentley's Miscellany* 58 (1865): 637–52.
Ollier, Charles. "The Haunted Manor-house of Paddington, a Tale for November." *Bentley's Miscellany* 10 (1841): 519–24.
Ouida. "Holly Wreaths and Rose Chains; or, How We Spent Christmas at Deerhurst." *Bentley's Miscellany* 46 (1859): 623–50.
"Our Christmas Budget." *London Journal* 70: 1820 (December 1879): 412–13.
"Our Wheel of Fortune." *Punch* 89 (19 December 1885): 290.
"Outline of the History of Gas Lighting." *Mirror of Literature, Amusement, and Instruction* 10:290 (29 December 1827). http://www.gutenberg.org/files/13587/13587.txt accessed on 10 December 2007.
"A Philosopher's Christmas." *Punch* 57 (1 January 1869): 264.
Preface. *Punch* 5 (1843): iv.
Punch Vol. 1. Advertisement, *Punch* 1 (17 July 1841): ii.
"A Quarrel with Christmas." *Punch* 37 (31 December 1859): 266.
"A Really New Christmas Number." *Punch* 73 (22 December 1877): 280.
Redgap. *The Faces in the Fire*. London: Willoughby, n.d.
Riddell, Charlotte. "The Old House in Vauxhall Walk." In *Victorian Ghost Stories by Noted Women Writers*, ed. Richard Dalby, 135–49. New York: Barnes & Noble, 1988.
———. *The Uninhabited House*. In *Five Victorian Ghost Novels*, ed. E.F. Bleiler, 3–112. New York: Dover, 1971.
Roscoe, Edmund S. "Christmas in Scotland." *Belgravia* 10 (January 1870): 319.
Ruskin, John. *The Works of John Ruskin: Sesame and Lilies*. Vol. 1. Sunnyside: George Allen, 1883.
Sala, George Augustus. "Miserable Christmases." *Belgravia* 6 (January 1872): 341–49.
Salmon, G. "What Boys Read." *Fortnightly Review* NS39 (February 1886): 248–59.
Sanders, Valerie, ed. *Record of Girlhood: An Anthology of Nineteenth-Century Women's Childhoods*. Aldershot: Ashgate, 2000.
Sawyer, William. "Christmas in the Olden Time," *Belgravia* 4 (January 1868): 357–58.
"Seasonable Folk-Lore." *Punch* 73 (29 December 1877): 292.
"Seeing a Ghost." *Argosy* 24 (December 1877): 490–500.
Sheehan, John. "A Ghostly Night at Ballyslaughter." *Temple Bar* 31 (January 1871): 227–36.

Smith, Albert. "A Winter's Night with My Old Books; Chiefly Concerning Ghosts and Prodigies." *Bentley's Miscellany* 25 (January 1849): 91–101.

Smith, Margaret, ed. *The Letters of Charlotte Bronte*. Vol. 2. Oxford: Clarendon, 2000. http://www.nlx.com accessed on 8 November 2007.

"Some Christmas Books," *Punch* 71 (6 January 1877): 297.

Southey, Caroline Anne Bowles to Robert Southey. 3 April 1828. *The Correspondence of Robert Southey with Caroline Bowles*, ed. Edward Dowden, 388. Dublin: Hodges, Figgis, 1881. http://solomon.bwld.alexanderstreet.com accessed on 12 September 2005.

"St. Sylvester's Eve." *Dublin University Magazine* 41 (January 1853): 116.

"Suggestion about Gift-Books." *Fraser's Magazine* 45 (18 February 1852): 141–47.

Swinburne, Augustus. "Christmas Antiphones." In *Songs Before Sunrise*. London: Ellis, 1871.

T. "A Story-Telling Party." *Once a Week* 1:26 (December 1859): 148–535.

T., A. "Lyrics of the Months: January." *Belgravia* 1 (January 1867): 290.

Tennyson, Alfred. *In Memoriam*, ed. Robert H. Ross. New York: Norton, 1973.

Thackeray, William M. "Christmas Books—No. I." *Morning Chronicle* (24 December 1845). In *Contributions to the Morning Chronicle*. ed. Gordon N. Ray, 86–93. Urbana: U of Illinois P, 1955.

———. "An Essay on Thunder and Small Beer." In *The Christmas Books of Mr. M. A. Titmarsh*. New York: Harper, 1899.

———. "A Grumble about the Christmas-Books." *Fraser's Magazine* 35 (January 1847): 111–26.

———. *The Letters and Private Papers of William Makepeace Thackeray*, ed. Gordon N. Ray, Vol. 2. Cambridge: Harvard UP, 1945.

———. *Mrs. Perkins' Ball*. In *The Christmas Books of Mr. M. A. Titmarsh, Etc.* New York: Harper, 1899.

———. *The Rose and the Ring*. In *The Christmas Books of Mr. M. A. Titmarsh*. New York: Harper, 1899.

———. "Roundabout Papers—No. X.: Round about the Christmas Tree." *Cornhill Magazine* 31 (February 1861): 253.

"The 'Milk' of Poor Law 'Kindness.'" *Punch* 4 (January 1843): 46.

"The 'Music in the Hall.'" *Illustrated London News* (23 December 1843): 416.

"The Christian Knowledge Society." *Popular Science Review* 5:17 (January 1881): 168.

"The Compliments of the Seasons." *Punch* 50 (1866): 26.

"The Consumption of Mince Pies." *Punch* 34 (January 1858): 13.

"The Danger from Gas." *Times* (14 June 1861): 5.

"The Kickleburys on the Rhine." *Times* (3 January 1851): 3.

"The Latest Thing in Ghosts." *Once a Week* 6:134 (January 1862): 99–103.

"The Pauper's Christmas Carol." *Punch* 5 (1843): 269.

"The Peace Egg." *Notes and Queries* 5.4:104 (25 December 1875): 511.

"*The Protestant Almanack*, for 1841." Advertisement. Crisp, Liverpool: Baisley, London. *Mirror of Literature, Amusement, and Instruction*, 36:1033 (November 1840): 332.
"The Royal Birthday Book." *Punch* 81 (17 December 1881): 279.
"The Shops at Christmas." *Punch* 17 (1849): 250.
"The Song of the Festive Season." *Punch* 50 (1866): 20.
"The Spirit of Christmas Present." *Punch* 105 (30 December 1893): 307.
"The Winds and the Waves: A Legend for Christmas." Advertisement, *Times* (24 November 1848): 2.
"Too Civil By Half!" *Punch* 23 (1852): 226.
Trollope, Anthony. "Christmas Day at Kirkby Cottage." In *The Complete Short Stories*, Vol. 1, 65–96. Fort Worth: Texas Christian UP, 1979.
Vizetelly, Henry, ed. *Christmas with the Poets*. 2nd ed. London: Bogue, 1852.
"What the Moon saw in India (at Christmas)." *London Society* 65:385 (January 1894): 42–51.
Yonge, Charlotte M. *The Christmas Mummers*. London: Mozley, 1858.

SECONDARY SOURCES

Adler, Tony. "How 'Carol' Helped Make Christmas." *Chicago Tribune* (7 December 2007). http://proguest.umi.com accessed on 8 April 2009.
Allingham, Philip V. "Image, Allusion, Voice, Dialect, and Irony in Thomas Hardy's 'The Oxen' and the Poem's Original Publication Context." Victorian Web, 23 February 2008, http://www.victorianweb.org/authors/hardy/poems/pva141.html accessed on 9 March 2008.
Altick, Richard. *The English Common Reader: A Social History of the Mass Reading Public 1800–1900*. Chicago: U of Chicago P, 1957.
———. *Punch: The Lively Youth of a London Institution, 1841–1851*. Columbus: Ohio State UP, 1997.
———. *Victorian People and Ideas*. New York: Norton, 1973.
———. *Writers, Readers, and Occasions*. Columbia: Ohio State UP, 1989.
Andrews, Malcolm. *Charles Dickens and His Performing Selves: Dickens and the Public Readings*. New York: Oxford UP, 2006.
Arnstein, Victoria. "Wrapping Up Exclusives." *Bookseller.com* (24 October 2007).
Bailin, Miriam. "The New Victorians." In *Function of Victorian Culture at the Present Time*, ed. Christine L. Krueger, 37–46. Athens: Ohio UP, 2002.
Barrett, David. "Eleanor Farjeon." In *Dictionary of Literary Biography, Volume 160: British Children's Writers, 1914–1960*, ed. Donald R. Hettinga and Gary D. Schmidt, 88–101. Gale, 1996. http://galenet.galegroup.com accessed on 3 February 2009.
Beetham, Margaret. "Towards a Theory of the Periodical as a Publishing Genre." In *Investigating Victorian Journalism*, ed. Laurel Brake, Aled Jones, and Lionel Madden, 19–32. London: Macmillan, 1990.

Beilenson, Evelyn, ed. *A Victorian Christmas.* White Plains: Peter Pauper, 1990.

Benjamin, Walter. *Illuminations.* New York: Harcourt Brace & World, 1968.

Bennet, Andrew. Introduction to *Readers and Reading*, ed. Andrew Bennet. New York: Longman, 1995.

Berkowitz, Lana. "Dickens on the Strand, It's Good to be the Queen." *Houston Chronicle* (30 November 2007): 1.

Bland, David. *The Illustration of Books.* London: Faber and Faber, 1951.

Bleiler, E.F. Introduction to *Five Victorian Ghost Novels.* New York: Dover, 1971.

Breyer, Betty Jane, ed. *Anthony Trollope: The Complete Short Stories.* Vol. 1. Fort Worth: Texas Christian UP, 1979.

Buchanan-Brown, John. *The Book Illustrations of George Cruikshank.* London: David & Charles, 1980.

———. *Early Victorian Illustrated Books: Britain, France and Germany 1820–1860.* New Castle: Oak Knoll, 2005.

Burden, Robert. Introduction to *Landscape and Englishness.* New York: Rodopi, 2006.

Cass, Jeffrey. " 'The Scraps, Patches, and Rags of Daily Life': Gaskell's Oriental Other and the Conversation of Cranford." *Papers on Language and Literature* 35:2 (Fall 1999): 429–30.

Castaneda, Christopher J. *Invisible Fuel: Manufactured and Natural Gas in America, 1800–2000.* New York: Twayne, 1999.

Castle, Terry. "Phantasmagoria: Spectral Technology and the Metaphorics of Modern Reverie." *Critical Inquiry* 15:1 (Autumn 1988): 38–42.

Clarke, W.K. Lowther. *The History of the S.P.C.K.* London: SPCK, 1959.

Clery, E.J. *The Rise of Supernatural Fiction 1762–1899.* New York: Cambridge UP, 1995.

Collins, Philip. *Charles Dickens: The Critical Heritage.* London: Taylor & Francis, 2003.

———. *Charles Dickens: The Public Readings.* Oxford: Clarendon, 1975.

Connelly, Mark. *Christmas: A Social History.* New York: Tauris, 1999.

Cullers, Jonathan. "Prolegomena to a Theory of Reading." In *The Reader in the Text: Essays on Audience and Interpretation*, ed. Susan R. Suleiman and Inge Crosman, 46–66. Princeton: Princeton UP, 1980.

Cutt, Margaret Nancy. *Ministering Angels: A Study of Nineteenth-Century Evangelical Writing for Children.* Wormley: Five Owls, 1979.

Daleski, H.M. "Seasonal Offerings: Some Recurrent Features of the *Christmas Books.*" *Dickens Studies Annual* 27 (1998): 97–111.

Darnton, Robert. "First Steps toward a History of Reading." In *Reception Study: From Literary Theory to Cultural Studies*, ed. James L. Machor and Philip Goldstein, 160–79. New York: Routlege, 2001.

Davis, Jim. "Boxing Day." In *The Performing Century: Nineteenth-Century Theatre's History* ed. Tracy C. Davis and Peter Holland, 13. New York: Palgrave Macmillan, 2007.

Davis, Paul. *The Lives and Times of Ebenezer Scrooge*. New Haven, Yale UP, 1990.

Dickerson, Vanessa D. *Victorian Ghosts in the Noontide: Women Writers and the Supernatural*. Columbia: U of Missouri P, 1996.

Donaldson, William. *Popular Literature in Victorian Scotland: Language, Fiction and the Press*. Aberdeen: Aberdeen UP, 1986.

Dorson, Richard M. *The British Folklorists*. Chicago: U of Chicago P, 1968.

Edgecombe, Rodney Stenning. *Two Poets of the Oxford Movement: John Keble and John Henry Newman*. Madison: Fairleigh Dickinson UP, 1996.

Eliot, Simon. "Some Trends in British Book Production, 1800–1919." In *Literature in the Marketplace: Nineteenth-Century British Publishing and Reading Practices*, ed. John O. Jordan and Robert L. Patten, 19–43. New York: Cambridge UP, 1995.

Eliott, Giles. "Record Christmas as Kay hits Number One." *Bookseller* (2 January 2007), thebookseller.com accessed on 15 March 2008.

Erickson, Lee. "The Market." In *A Companion to Victorian Poetry*, ed. Richard Cronin, Alison Chapman, and Antony H. Harrison, 345–60. Malden: Blackwell, 2002.

Feather, John. *A History of British Publishing*. New York: Routledge, 2006.

Fielding, K.J. "Two Sketches by Maclise: The Dickens Children and the *Chimes* Reading." *Dickens Studies* 2 (January 1966): 7–17.

Flint, Kate. *The Woman Reader, 1837–1914*. Oxford: Clarendon, 1993.

Flood, Alison, Liz Bury, Joel Rickett, and Philip Stone. "Hachette Steals the Show." *Bookseller* (24 January 2008), thebookseller.com accessed on 15 March 2008.

Garret, Stewart. *Dear Reader: The Conscripted Audience in Nineteenth-Century British Fiction*. Baltimore: Johns Hopkins, 1996.

Gifford, Rob. "U. K. Muslims Support Keeping Christ in Christmas." *Morning Edition* National Public Radio (19 December 2007).

Glancy, Ruth F. Introduction to *Christmas Books* by Charles Dickens. New York: Oxford UP, 1988.

Golby, J.M. and A.W. Purdue. *The Making of the Modern Christmas*. London: Batsford, 1986.

Goldman, Paul. *Victorian Illustrated Books 1850–1870: The Heyday of Wood-Engraving*. London: Trustees of the British Museum, 1994.

Gooday, Graeme J.N. "'I Will Never Have the Electric Light in My House': Alice Gordon and the Gendered Periodical Representation of a Contentious New Technology." In *Culture and Science in the Nineteenth-Century Media*, ed. Louise Henson, 173–85. Burlington: Ashgate, 2004.

Gosse, Edmund. *Father and Son*. London: Penguin, 1989.

Greco, Albert N. *The Book Publishing Industry*, 2nd ed. London: Lawrence Erblaum, 2005.

Grisham, John. *Skipping Christmas*. New York: Doubleday, 2001.

Guida, Fred. *A Christmas Carol and Its Adaptations: A Critical Examination of Dickens's Story and Its Productions on Screen and Television*. Jefferson, NC: McFarland, 2000.

Haining, Peter. Introduction to *Charles Dickens' Christmas Ghost Stories* by Charles Dickens. New York: St. Martin's, 1993.

"Have Pudding Will Travel." *Times* (24 December 1985): 6.

Hawlin, Stefan. *The Complete Critical Guide to Robert Browning*. New York: Routledge, 2002.

Hayward, Jennifer. *Consuming Pleasures: Active Audiences and Serial Fictions from Dickens to Soap Opera*. Lexington: UP of Kentucky, 1997.

Helm, Alex. *The English Mummers' Play*. Woodbridge: Boydell & Brewer, 1980.

Henson, Louise. "'In the Natural Course of Physical Things': Ghost and Science in Charles Dickens's *All the Year Round*." In *Culture and Science in the Nineteenth-Century Media*, ed. Louise Henson, 113–123. Burlington: Ashgate, 2004.

Holland, Norman. "Re-Covering 'The Purloined Letter': Reading as a Personal Transaction." In *The Reader in the Text: Essays on Audience and Interpretation*, ed. Susan R. Suleiman and Inge Crosman, 350–70. Princeton: Princeton UP, 1980.

Holste, Gayle. "Hardy's Christmas in the Elgin Room." *The Explicator* 59 (Summer 2001): 187–189, http://lion.chadwyck.com.

Hootman, Harry E. "British Literary Annuals and Giftbooks: 1823–1861." Diss. University of South Carolina, 2004.

Houfe, Simon. *John Leech and the Victorian Scene*. Woodbridge: Baron, 1984.

Howe, Daniel Walker. "Victorian Culture in America." In *Victorian America*, ed. Daniel Walker Howe, 3–28. Philadelphia: U of Pennsylvania P, 1976.

Hoyle, Ben, and Sarah Clarke. "The Hidden Price of a Christmas Bestseller," *Times* (18 June 2007), timesonline.co.uk accessed on 30 March 2008.

Hunt, Peter. *An Introduction to Children's Literature*. New York: Oxford UP, 1994.

Jauss, Hans Robert. "Literary History as a Challenge to Literary Theory." *New Literary History* 2 (1970): 7–37.

Johnson, Jamie W. "The Changing Representation of the Art Public in *Punch* 1841–1896." *VPR* 35 (Fall 2002): 272–94.

Jordan, John. O. and Robert L. Patten. Introduction to *Literature in the Marketplace: Nineteenth-Century British Publishing and Reading Practices*, ed. John O. Jordan and Robert L. Patten, 1–18. New York: Cambridge UP, 1995.

Kelley, Richard M. *Douglas Jerrold*. New York: Twayne, 1973.

Kelly, Richard. Introduction to *A Christmas Carol*, by Charles Dickens. Peterborough: Broadview, 2003.

Kooistra, Lorraine Janzen. "Poetry in the Victorian Marketplace: The Illustrated Princess as a Christmas Gift Book." *Victorian Poetry* 45 (Spring 2007): 49–76, http://proquest.umi.com accessed on 29 January 2008.

Krueger, Christine L. Introduction to *Function of Victorian Culture at the Present Time*, ed. Christine L. Krueger. Athens: Ohio UP, 2002.

Kumar, Krishna. *The Making of English National Identity*. New York: Cambridge UP, 2003.

Ledbetter, Kathryn. "Lucrative Requests: British Authors and Gift Book Editors." *Bibliographical Society of America, Papers* 88 (June 1994): 207–16.

Lee, Amice. *Laurels and Rosemary: The Life of William and Mary Howitt*. London: Oxford UP, 1955.

Leitch, Tom. *Film Adaptation and its Discontents*. Baltimore: Johns Hopkins, 2007.

Lesjak, Carol. "Authenticity and the Geography of Empire: Reading Gaskell with Emecheta." *Studies in the Literary Imagination* 35.2 (Fall 2002): 123–46.

Lewis, Suzanne. Introduction to *The Moorland Cottage and Other Stories* by Elizabeth Gaskell. New York: Oxford UP, 1995.

Logan, Thad. *The Victorian Parlour*. New York: Cambridge UP, 2001.

"London's Great Flood." *Publishing Trends* (February 2003), publishingtrends.com accessed on 20 March 2008.

Louis, Margot K. "Gods and Mysteries: The Revival of Paganism and the Remaking of Mythography through the Nineteenth Century." *Victorian Studies* (Spring 2005): 329–261, http://lion.chadwyck.com accessed on 14 May 2008.

Louis, Margot K. *Swinburne and His Gods: The Roots and Growth of an Agnostic Poet*. Buffalo: McGill-Queen's UP, 1990.

Lubbock, Sybil. *The Child in the Crystal*. London: Jonathan Cape, 1939.

Luke 2:1–15.

Lumpkin, Ramona. "(Re)Visions of Virtue: Elizabeth Gaskell's *Moorland Cottage* and George Eliot's *The Mill on the Floss*." *Studies in the Novel* 23:4 (Winter 1991): 432–42.

Lundin, Anne. *Victorian Horizons*. Lanham: Scarecrow, 2001.

Lysaght, Patricia. *Food and Celebration from Fasting to Feasting*. Dublin: ZRC, 2002.

Maidment, B.E. *Reading Popular Prints 1790–1870*. New York: Manchester UP, 1996.

Malvern, Jack. "Da Vinci Thriller Cracks the Book Bestseller Code." *Times* (24 December 2004), timesonline.co.uk accessed on 16 March 2008.

Mandler, Peter. *The English National Character*. New Haven: Yale UP, 2006.

Manning, Peter J. "Wordsworth in the *Keepsake*." In *Literature in the Marketplace: Nineteenth-Century British Publishing and Reading Practices*, ed. John O. Jordan and Robert L. Patten, 44–73. New York: Cambridge UP, 1995.

Mattes, Eleanor B. "Chronology of *In Memoriam*." In *In Memoriam*, ed. Robert H. Ross. New York: Norton, 1973.

Mason, Michael. "The Timing of *In Memoriam*." In *Studies in Tennyson*, ed. Hallam Tennyson. London: Macmillan, 1981.

Maxwell, Christabel. *Mrs Gatty and Mrs Ewing*. London: Constable, 1949.

Miller, Andrew H. *Novels behind Glass: Commodity Culture and Victorian Narrative*. New York: Cambridge UP, 1995.

Miller, Daniel. Introduction to *Unwrapping Christmas*, ed. Daniel Miller. Oxford: Clarendon, 1993.

Millgate, Michael. *Thomas Hardy, A Biography Revisited*. New York: Oxford UP, 1982.

Millington, Peter. "Mrs Ewing and the Textual Origin of the St. Kitts Mummies' Play." *Folklore* 107 (1996): 77–89.

Muresianu, S.A. *The History of the Victorian Christmas Book*. Diss. Harvard University, 1981. New York: Garland, 1987.

Neille, Graeme. "Booksellers Push Up Christmas Prices." *Bookseller* (18 December 2007), thebookseller.com accessed on 19 July 2008.

Newey, Katherine. "Home Plays for Ladies: Women's Work in Home Theatricals." *Nineteenth Century Theatre*. 26 (Winter 1998): 93–112.

Newey, Vincent. *The Scriptures of Charles Dickens: Novels of Ideology, Novels of Self*. Burlington: Ashgate, 2004.

Newman, Kim. "You Better Watch Out: Christmas in Horror Film." In *Christmas at the Movies*, ed. Mark Connelly, 135–42. New York: Tauris, 2000.

Onslow, Barbara. "Sensationalizing Science: Braddon's Marketing of Science in *Belgravia*." *Victorian Periodicals Review* 35.2 (Summer 2002): 160–77.

Osbeck, Kenneth W. *Amazing Grace: 366 Inspiring Hymn Stories for Daily Devotions*. Grand Rapids: Kregel, 1990. Libronix Digital Library System.

Osteen, Mark. Introduction to *The Question of the Gift: Essays across Disciplines*. New York: Routledge, 2002.

Parker, David. *Christmas and Charles Dickens*. New York: AMS, 2005.

Patten, Robert L. *Charles Dickens and His Publishers*. Oxford: Clarendon, 1978.

Perry, Anne. *A Christmas Guest*. New York: Ballantine, 2005.

Persell, Michelle. "Dickensian Disciple: Anglo-Jewish Identity in the Christmas Tales of Benjamin Farjeon." *Philological Quarterly* 73 (Fall 1994): 451–68.

Peterson, Linda H. "Rereading 'Christmas-Eve,' Rereading Browning." *Victorian Poetry* 26:4 (Winter 1988): 363–80.

Pimlott, J.A.R. *The Englishman's Christmas: A Social History*. Hassocks: Harvester, 1978.

Poovey, Mary. *Making a Social Body: British Cultural Formation, 1830–1864*. Chicago: U of Chicago P, 1995.

Pratt, Steve. "What the Dickens!...Is Going on as Victorian Drama Dominates TV." *Northern Echo* (20 December 2007): 28, http://proquest.umi.com accessed on 20 June 2008.

Pykett, Lyn. *Charles Dickens*. New York: Palgrave, 2002.

Qualls, Barry V. "W.H. Mallock," in *Dictionary of Literary Biography, Volume 18: Victorian Novelists After 1885*. ed. Ira B. Nadel and William E. Fredeman 164–167, http://galenet.galegroup.com accessed on 7 April 2008.

Robinson, Solvieg C. "Editing *Belgravia*: M.E. Braddon's Defense of 'Light Literature.'" *Victorian Periodicals Review* 28:2 (Summer 1995): 109–22.

Rose, Jonathan. "Rereading the English Common Reader: A Preface to a History of Audiences." *Journal of the History of Ideas* 53 (January–March 1992): 47–70.

Russell, Gillian. "Private Theatricals." In *The Cambridge Companion to British Theatre, 1730–1830*. ed. Jane Moody and Daniel O'Quinn, 191–204. Cambridge: Cambridge UP, 2007.

Sadoff, Dianne F. and John Kucich. Introduction to *Victorian Afterlife: Postmodern Culture Rewrites the Nineteenth Century*. Minneapolis: U of Minnesota P, 2000.

"Second Helpings for Delia Fans." BBC News (23 December 1999), news.bbc.co.uk accessed on 3 March 2009.

Selig, Robert L. *Elizabeth Gaskell: A Reference Guide*. Boston: Hall, 1977.

Shaylor, Joseph. *The Fascination of Books, with Other Papers on Books & Bookselling*. New York: Putnam, 1912.

Shelson, Alan. "*The Moorland Cottage*: Elizabeth Gaskell and Myles Birket Foster." *The Gaskell Society Journal* 2 (1998): 41–58.

Smajic, Srdjan. "The Trouble with Ghost-Seeing: Vision, Ideology, and Genre in the Victorian Ghost Story." *ELH* 70 (Winter 2003): 1107–36.

Solberg, Sarah A. "'Text Dropped into the Woodcuts': Dickens's Christmas Books." *Dickens Studies Annual* 8 (1980): 103–18.

Srebrnik, Patricia Thomas. "Mrs. Riddell and the Reviewers: A Case Study in Victorian Popular Fiction." *Women's Studies* 23:1 (1994): 69–84, http://lion.chadwyck.com accessed on 12 December 2007.

Stedman, Gesa. *Stemming the Torrent: Expression and Control in the Victorian Discourses on Emotion, 1830–1872*. Burlington: Ashgate, 2002.

Stone, Harry. "*A Christmas Carol*: Giving Nursery Tales a Higher Form." In *The Haunted Mind: The Supernatural in Victorian Literature*, ed. Elton E. Smith and Robert Haas, 11–18. London: Scarecrow, 1999.

Sutherland, John. *Victorian Fiction: Writers, Publishers, Readers*. New York: Palgrave Macmillan, 2006.

Tennyson, Charles. "*In Memoriam*." In *In Memoriam*, ed. Robert H. Ross. New York: Norton, 1973.

Tennyson, G.B. *Victorian Devotional Poetry: The Tractarian Mode*. Cambridge: Harvard UP, 1981.

"The Last Christmas for 'Brandy Butter'?" *Grocer* 221:7381 (14 November 1998): 24.

Thomas, Julia. *Pictorial Victorians*. Athens: Ohio UP, 2004.

Tillotson, Kathleen. *Novels of the Eighteen-Forties*. Oxford: Clarendon, 1954.

Tracy, Robert. "'A Whimsical Kind of Masque': The Christmas Books and Victorian Spectacle." *Dickens Studies Annual* 27 (1988): 113–30.

Uglow, Jennifer. Introduction to *Victorian Ghost Stories by Noted Women Writers.* ed. Richard Dalby. New York: Barnes & Noble, 1988.

Walsh, Richard. "Why We Wept for Little Nell: Character and Emotional Involvement." *Narrative* 5 (October 1997): 306–21.

Watson, J.R. "Hymns." In *A Companion to Victorian Poetry.* ed. Richard Cronin, Alison Chapman, and Antony H. Harrison, 134–54. Malden: Blackwell, 2002.

Weedon, Alexis. *Victorian Publishing.* Aldershot: Ashgate, 2003.

Weeks, Linton. "Move Over, Scrooge: Publishers Hope for New Holiday Classic." *Washington Post* (30 November 2002): C1.

Wheeler, Michael. *English Fiction of the Victorian Period 1830–1890.* New York: Longman, 1985.

Whelan, Lara Baker. "Between Worlds: Class Identity and Suburban Ghost Stories, 1850 to 1880." *Mosaic* 35 (March 2002): 133–48.

Wilson, A.E. *Pantomime Pageant: A Procession of Harlequins, Clowns, Comedians, Principle Boys, Pantomime-Writers, Producers and Playgoers.* London: Stanley Paul, n.d..

Winnett, Robert, and Holly Watt. "£50,000 to Get a Book on Recommended List." *Sunday Times* (28 May 2006), www.timeonline.co.uk accessed on 12 July 2008.

Witworth, Damien. "Read On if You've Scanned any Good Books Lately." *Times* (28 December 2005), www.timesonline.co.uk accessed on 10 March 2008.

Wolfreys, Julian. *Being English.* Albany: State U of New York P, 1994.

Index